California

NORTHERN COASTAL REGION

GREAT INLAND VALLEY REGION

SOUTHERN CALIFORNIA REGION

Oroville

SACRAMENTO R.

Santa Rosa
St. Helena
Sonoma
Napa

Sacramento

Lodi

San Francisco
Livermore

Escalon
Modesto

Santa Clara

SAN JOAQUIN R.

Madera

Fresno

Hanford
Tulare

San Luis Obispo

Bakersfield

Santa Barbara

Ventura

San Bernardino

Los Angeles

Pacific Ocean

MAP BY palacios

GUIDE TO
California Wines

GUIDE TO
California Wines

BY JOHN MELVILLE

Introduction by Joseph Henry Jackson

DOUBLEDAY & COMPANY, INC.

Garden City, New York, 1955

TO WILLY

Library of Congress Catalog Card Number 55-7662

INTRODUCTION

$\mathcal{S}$INCE this is not intended to be a "literary" book about wine, but rather a practical and workable guide, perhaps the best way to suggest its exceptional usefulness is to quote a statistic or two.

These are brief and simple.

The annual distribution of all wines, American and foreign, in the United States, runs nowadays to something over a hundred and forty million gallons. Of these over 84 per cent are California wines. Of American wine only the United States consumes a hundred and thirty-four million gallons yearly. And of that total 88 per cent comes from California.

Clearly it is a good idea for the American who likes wine to know the basic facts about California wines, the table wines grown and made in the well-defined zones that best suit the shy-bearing grapes like the Pinot noir and Cabernet Sauvignon, the sweet dessert wines from the warmer inland valleys, where the sun develops more sugar, the sparkling wines made in several regions from the southern part of the state all the way to the north, in that famous vineyard where the grapes flourish among massive stumps of great redwoods long ago logged off. This *Guide,* the result of three years' work, is put together to help the American wine consumer discover and choose among the wines of California that best suit his palate.

It is an ancient maxim that, in any field, in order to get the right answers you must ask the right questions. Unhappily in this particular field most people ask the wrong ones.

The most frequent inquiry put to any Californian on this subject is, "Are California wines as good as European wines?" This, of course, has no real meaning. The only possible answer is, "Which California wines, and which European wines?" and if you make this reply the seeker for information, who does honestly want to be informed even though he has not phrased his query sensibly, is bound to think you either smug or rude or both. The next most common question is, "Which are the best California wines?" Again there is no real answer short of oversimplifying, on the one hand, or, on the other, telling far too much. In the one case you mislead; in the other you bore your inquiring friend and probably confuse him as well.

Yet there are sensible questions to be asked about California wines and there are sensible answers to them. In this *Guide* Mr. Melville asks and answers his own—the right ones. What wines of all types, including aperitif wines and brandies, are made in California? How are they grouped and classified? Of what grapes are they made and, roughly, how? What are the important winegrowing and wine-making regions of California? How do they differ, and what wines are best produced in each—in the sunny valleys of Napa, Sonoma, and Livermore, in the Santa Cruz Mountains area, or down in the southern portion of the state? And—as important as any—who makes them? It is this kind of thing that Mr. Melville covers in his *Guide,* and it is facts of this order that he provides. They are by no means as complicated as you may have thought.

California, as has been noted, produces something like 90 per cent of the wine made in the United States, wherefore the right answers are worth knowing. For that matter, when it comes to wine, California is its own best customer; its citizens consume some three gallons a year per capita against about one gallon a year per capita for the rest of the country.

One reason for this is that Californians, since they are closer to the source, know their wines. They know also that almost all California wine is soundly made and thoroughly potable. Moreover Californians recovered more rapidly than most from the violent infection that followed Repeal—what one writer on the subject has called, bitterly (and with some justice), Wine Hokum. Almost from the beginning Californians drank their own wines under their own labels and knew them for what they were as well as what they were not. They had always made wine; in his introductory chapter Mr. Melville sketches the story from the earliest days when the Mission Fathers brought their cuttings with them and planted their vineyards. A full century ago, when California was taken over from a defeated Mexico, the newly arriving farmers set out vineyards as naturally as they did orchards. In 1880, Robert Louis Stevenson, honeymooning high on the shoulder of Mt. St. Helena, came down into the lovely Napa Valley to visit the long-established winery of Jacob Schram and taste his wine, thereafter, in Davos and in Hyères, where he wrote his *Silverado Squatters,* recalling in tranquility the gentle delights of the Schramsberger that was his host's pride. Long before Prohibition, Californians were wine drinkers in the sense that Europeans are wine drinkers, regarding good wine as the pleasant, healthful accompaniment to good food that it is. And they had always taken the trouble to try their wines, compare them, and make up their own minds about what best suited their individual tastes, a process no more difficult than doing the same thing with anything else that is to be drunk or eaten. Very likely you have heard people say, "Yes, but it's so hard to remember all those names!" The ones who tell you this, though, seem to have little trouble recalling the labels of a dozen scotch whiskies, a like number of bourbons, four or five brands of rye, and the same number of gins. Half that much memory work will orient you beautifully among California wines, and the effort, as you will learn from Mr. Melville, is much less than you may have supposed.

There is always the matter of "better" and "best." A few general principles are involved here, and for those who do not know them already Mr. Melville makes them abundantly clear where the California wines are concerned. What it comes down to, actually, is what Woodrow Wilson, an excellent hand at a figure of speech, once called "the raw material of opinion." This, precisely, is what Mr. Melville provides in his book.

There are many signs that this *Guide to California Wines* is admirably timed. For one thing, American consumption of table wines last year was greater than in the days before Prohibition, and this consumption, instead of being concentrated as it once was among the foreign-born who were accustomed to wine with food and brought their liking with them, is now spread generally, among people of all sorts. For another, the battle to bring back California wines to the high place they held before Prohibition is being won on new fronts every year. If you know how and where to look, you may find California table wines whose excellence by any standard will surprise you.

With Mr. Melville's *Guide* for reference you will discover where to look, and how. As I have said, there is no Wine Hokum here, no precious wine jargon, merely the facts that will enable you to find your way around among the wines California produces. Excepting—and the exception is well worth noting—in the Appendix. Here, in one brief listing, the author steps for the first time out of his purely informative role. The section on *Outstanding California Wines* is based partly upon state- and county-fair awards in recent years, and partly upon the author's informed opinion, which is that of a man who possesses a sensitive palate trained on European wines, a pursuant of knowledge who, in the years he has worked on his book, has visited all of California's leading wineries and many of the lesser ones, always with an open mind—and indeed with an open mouth. I can conceive of this section alone being worth the price of the book several times over to many thousands of Americans who would honestly like to know how to choose among the great variety of good wines California has to offer.

JOSEPH HENRY JACKSON

Berkeley,
California

ACKNOWLEDGMENTS

THE FOLLOWING PERSONS have had the kindness to check either the whole or a major part of the section on California wine types, their many valuable suggestions having been gratefully received: Maynard A. Amerine, Professor of Enology, University of California; Louis A. Benoist, Almadén Vineyards, Los Gatos; Louis M. Martini and Louis P. Martini, St. Helena; Herman L. Wente, Wente Brothers, Livermore; Frank A. Whiteley, Wine Institute, San Francisco.

Thanks are due to James F. Guymon, Associate Professor of Enology, University of California, for information on California brandy and for background material on California fruit wines to Robert H. Gibson, Gibson Wine Company, Elk Grove and St. Helena.

The author's grateful thanks also to the winegrowers and executives for their co-operation regarding material on the winery which they head or with which they are prominently connected. Listed alphabetically by winery (or distillery) they are:

Dino Barengo, Acampo Winery and Distilleries,

Louis A. Benoist, Almadén Vineyards,

Margaret Shahenian, Alta Vineyards Company,

Ralph Bargetto, Bargetto's Santa Cruz Winery,

Marquis de Pins and Aldo Fabbrini, Beaulieu Vineyard Company,

Fred Abruzzini, Beringer Bros., Inc.,

Elise Black, Hollis M. Black Winery,

Leon L. Brendel, L. Brendel,

Philo Biane, Brookside Vineyard Company,

Frank H. Bartholomew, Buena Vista Vineyards,

Douglas Pringle, California Champagne Corporation,

J. Battista Cella, Cella Vineyards,

E. M. Cobb, California Growers Wineries,

Stanley Strud, California Wine Association,

Captain Joseph S. Concannon, Concannon Vineyard,

C. P. Kahmann, Cresta Blanca Wine Company,

A. B. Cribari, Cribari & Sons,

Edmund E. Accomazzo, Cucamonga Winery,

K. T. Anderson, East-Side Winery,

John B. Ellena, Ellena Brothers,

Walter C. Ficklin, Sr., Ficklin Vineyards,

Louis Foppiano, Foppiano Wine Company,

Siegfried Bechhold, Fountaingrove Vineyard,

Joe Franzia, Jr., Franzia Brothers Winery,

Michael Ahern, Freemark Abbey,

Ernest Gallo, E. & J. Gallo Winery,

F. W. Brenner, Garatti Winery,

L. J. Barden, Garrett & Company,

Robert H. Gibson, Gibson Wine Company,

John A. Parducci, Parducci & Sons,

W. D. Sanderson, Signature Vintners, Petri Wineries, and Mission Bell Wineries,

Frank I. Pirrone, Pirrone & Sons, Inc.,

F. E. Pocai, Pocai & Sons,

Martin Ray, Martin Ray, Inc.,

Walter Richert, Richert & Sons,

Paul Rhodes, Paul Rhodes Winery,

Colonel Albert H. Burton and James E. Woolsey, Roma Wine Company,

A. G. Frericks, St. George Winery,

Charles John Demateis, San Gabriel Vineyard Company,

Michael J. Filice, San Martin Vineyards Company,

Lewis Guerrieri, Santa Fe Vintage Company,

C. B. Meda, Santa Rosa Winery,

August Sebastiani, Sebastiani Winery,

Chauncey G. Bianchi and Leonard J. Berg, Solera Cellars,

J. Leland Stewart, Souverain Cellars,

F. M. Butler, Speas Company,

Frederick H. McCrae, Stony Hill Vineyards,

Lloyd A. Searing and Charles Altair, Valliant Vineyards,

Joseph S. Vercelli, Vercelli Brothers Wine Company,

John N. Verry, Nicholas G. Verry, Inc.,

Frederick E. Weibel, Jr., Weibel Champagne Vineyards,

Herman L. Wente, Wente Brothers,

L. K. Marshall, Wine Growers Guild,

Charles J. Pagani, Glen Ellen Winery and Distillery, Inc.,

W. A. Dunton, Jr., Golden State Winery,

James Pomeroy Howe, Gopher Gulch Ranch Wine Cellars,

Chaffee E. Hall, Hallcrest Vineyard,

John Daniel, Jr., Inglenook Vineyard Company,

F. H. Hawes, Italian Swiss Colony,

Leo V. Korbel, Korbel & Sons,

Hanns J. Kornell, Kornell Cellars,

Kenneth O. Dills, Charles Krug Winery,

Clovis T. Mirassou, Lone Hill Vineyards,

Ann Mayock, Los Amigos Vineyards,

Felix Mancuso, F. Mancuso Winery,

Louis M. Martini and Louis P. Martini, Louis M. Martini,

Elmo Martini, Martini Prati Wines, Inc.,

Alfred Fromm and Norman Fromm, Paul Masson Vineyards,

Mary Catherine Taylor, Mayacamas Vineyards,

Donald M. Ansel, Jr., Mendocino Grape Growers, Inc.,

Ed. A. Mirassou, Mirassou Vineyards,

Brother Timothy, Mont La Salle Vineyards (The Christian Brothers),

Paul Rossigneux, Napa and Sonoma Wine Company,

Reno Nonini, A. Nonini Winery,

Father James Ransford, S.J., Novitiate of Los Gatos,
Steve Forni, Pacific Coast Brands,
James L. Vai, Padre Vineyard Company,

Howard A. York, York Brothers,
Renald Mastrofini, Yosemite Winery Association,
George Zaninovich, George Zaninovich, Inc.

Some hundred wineries in all, large and small, were visited. The author wishes to thank the winegrowers, wine makers, chemists, and executives who so patiently answered the numerous questions put to them and who showed him around the wineries, the laboratories, and the vineyards. Wine growers are a hospitable race. A special word of appreciation to those who by their gracious hospitality made visits especially memorable. There are luncheons and dinners, washed down by some of California's great wines, which will always remain among the author's most cherished memories of the years he studied the California wine industry for the purpose of writing this book.

FOREWORD

$\mathcal{T}$HE GUIDE TO CALIFORNIA WINES is designed as a practical reference volume for the use of all those interested in the subject. It is addressed to the trade, the wholesaler, restaurateur, and retailer as well as to the public, the purchaser and consumer, the host and the hostess.

The author has aimed to present the wines of California in a comprehensive, accurate, and interesting manner in the hope that both public and trade can thereby the more easily know what to look for, what to choose, what to expect, to suggest, or to order. The subject is as fascinating as it is inexhaustible and comparatively little is available on it in book form.

California wines have their own and diversified charm. The best of them match in quality, flavor, and savor all but the finest estate-bottled wines of Europe and have the advantage of being very reasonable in price. Even the great wines of California are remarkably inexpensive.

California produces wines as different as the grapes from which they are derived and as the climate and soil vary according to region. The first part of the *Guide* is devoted to a discussion of all the various kinds of wines produced, grouped according to type. In each group the outstanding varietal types are capitalized. The second part tells about the more notable wineries producing directly for the public. In most cases a short history of the enterprise is given and the more important wines and brands listed. A special section is concerned with California brandy.

A list of California wines especially recommended on account of their outstanding character forms a separate Appendix.

The author hopes that the reader will derive as much satisfaction from consulting the *Guide* as he had pleasure in composing it.

Maps

Charts

CONTENTS

Part Two

CALIFORNIA VINES AND WINES

C ALIFORNIA WINES are produced from vines, imported from
Europe or from neighboring regions, and belonging to the famed
Vitis vinifera species of grapes, from which all Old World wines
have been made since civilization began.

The art of wine making was brought to California by the Spaniards. From Mexico winegrowing spread northward to Baja California and finally to what was then known as Alta California.
According to tradition Padre Junipero Serra, of Mission fame,
brought the first vines from Baja California and planted them at
Mission San Diego in or about 1769. The Franciscan Fathers planted
vines near the various Missions they established along their Camino
Real stretching northward to Sonoma. The oldest California winery
is to be found at Mission San Gabriel, where the famed Trinity
Vine, planted around 1775, flourished for over a century and a half.
It was from San Gabriel that settlers set forth one day to establish
the Pueblo, which was to become the city of Los Angeles.

The Mission Fathers planted what became known as the Mission
grape, popular for long and still used today, mainly in the production of dessert wines. They made wines mostly for religious and
medicinal purposes, but also for table use, some of which became
famous throughout the West as did their *aguardiente,* or brandy.

The first layman wine grower of record was Governor Pedro

Fages, who planted a vineyard along with his orchards in 1783, not far from his residence in Monterey, Alta California. Doña Marcelina Felix Domínguez, the first known woman wine grower of California, planted, in the early eighteen hundreds, at Montecito near Santa Barbara, a fabulous vine which was to bear, in good years, some four tons of grapes. Known as *La Vieja de la Parra Grande,* or "The Old Lady of the Grapevine," she was said to be 105 years old when she died in 1865.

For a time Los Angeles led the rest of California in winegrowing. There Joseph Chapman, an early immigrant, is conceded to have been the first viticulturist. He is far overshadowed in fame by Jean Louis Vignes, a native of the Bordeaux region in France and the possessor of a most appropriate name. By 1843 his celebrated Aliso Vineyard, in the heart of what is now downtown Los Angeles and named after a large sycamore which dominated the entrance to his property, covered over a hundred acres. Don Louis del Aliso, as he became known, was the first to import choice vines from Europe and to realize the great future of California wines, produced from these varieties. Many of his relatives followed him from France, including Pierre Sanssevain, who became a well-known grower in his own right.

In the northern region the first great winegrowing pioneer was General Mariano Guadalupe Vallejo. Born in Monterey of Castilian descent, he rose to prominence at an early age, becoming closely identified with the Mexican and early American history of California and especially with that of Sonoma, where he resided for many years. He was a great gentleman, farmer, soldier, and philosopher. He accepted the "manifest destiny" whereby Alta California, in its own interest and by the force of circumstances, was to become part of the United States. In June 1846 a company of Americans ran up the Bear Flag in the plaza of Sonoma and soon afterward the American Army raised the flag of the United States. Vallejo, in spite of a brief incarceration by the overly patriotic Bears, accepted the new regime. He continued to devote himself to his agricultural pursuits and to aid immigrant Yankees to settle in the newly opened region. He was the first non-missionary winegrower in the Sonoma

Valley and dominated the viticultural scene there for many years, until the advent of Haraszthy.

Colonel Agoston Haraszthy is often referred to as "the father of California's modern wine industry." It is greatly owing to his genius that a sound and lasting basis was created for the state's viticulture. It is a pleasing thought that the winegrowing estate near Sonoma, which Haraszthy called Buena Vista and made famous, is in operation today. It is there that some of the story of this colorful California winegrowing pioneer will be found.

California wineries have a long and proud tradition. Many of the better-known enterprises flourishing today were founded in the nineteenth century, some still being run by members of the founding family. Their listing by county and in approximate chronological order, according to the owners' claims, presents an intriguing historical and geographical picture.

In 1849, or earlier, the vineyards in San Benito County now known as Valliant Vineyards were started by Théophile Vaché. In Santa Clara, Almadén, Paul Masson, and Martin Ray are the successors to wine-making traditions begun in 1852. In the same county Mirassou Vineyards originated a year later, some four years earlier than Buena Vista in Sonoma. The early sixties saw the beginnings of Charles Krug in Napa and of Schramsberg. Dating back to the seventies are Padre in San Bernardino, Fountaingrove in Sonoma, Beringer Brothers in Napa, St. George in Fresno, Simi in Sonoma, and Inglenook in Napa.

In the eighties a galaxy of famous wineries was founded, including Italian Swiss Colony and Korbel in Sonoma, Mt. La Salle (The Christian Brothers) in Napa, Brookside Vineyard Company of Cucamonga, Cresta Blanca, Wente, and Concannon in Alameda, Italian Vineyards Company (I.V.C.) in San Bernardino (now owned by Garrett and Company with their own wine-making tradition dating back in the East to 1835), California Wine Association in San Francisco, Digardi in Contra Costa, Petri in San Joaquin, Ruby Hill in Alameda, the Novitiate of Los Gatos in Santa Clara, Los Amigos in Alameda, San Gabriel in Los Angeles, and Bisceglia Brothers in Fresno.

The nineties witnessed the foundings of Roma, now of Fresno, of San Martin in Santa Clara, and of the Napa and Sonoma Wine Company and of Foppiano, both of Sonoma. In 1900 the foundations were laid for Beaulieu in Napa.

Since then many other wineries, great and small, have risen to establish noteworthy wine-making traditions of their own.

Prohibition dealt a severe blow to American viticulture in general and that of California in particular. It was a senseless attack, as Prohibition has never led the way to moderation and encroaches deeply on man's freedom of judgment. A substantial part of California's vineyard acreage was maintained for the production of wines for sacramental and medicinal purposes and for supplying grapes to home wine makers, as allowed by the dry laws. Other vineyards were turned over to the cultivation of table grapes and to the manufacture of grape juice.

After Repeal the California wine industry was rebuilt on a sound basis with the State Department of Public Health and the federal government becoming joint guardians for the maintenance of standards as to the identity and labeling of wines.

California is responsible for roughly 90 per cent of the production of all domestic wines consumed in the United States. Aperitif and dessert wines constitute about 75 per cent of the total California wine production, the balance consisting mostly of table wines and of sparkling wines. Of the table wines approximately four fifths are red, including the rosés, and one fifth white.

The climate and soil of California are particularly well suited to the vines of the *Vitis vinifera* family. Beginning with the days of Jean Louis Vignes and of Agoston Haraszthy, practically every variety of these wines has been planted in California, many of them with great success. By the alchemy of local conditions they yield wines which often differ in character from those produced in their original environments. California wines, while often similar or identical in name to European types, should always be considered on their own merits, but comparisons, it seems, are often inevitable.

The same grapes also develop differently in the various regions and climates of California. Maturity is slow in cooler areas; grapes retain more acid and develop less sweetness, while dark grapes attain the maximum coloring matter in their skins. These regions are best suited for the production of dry table wines and of sparkling wines of quality. Under warmer conditions grapes develop less acid and a greater sugar content. These zones are better adapted to the production of dessert wines.

It is known exactly to which localities each grape variety is best suited or whether its cultivation should be avoided altogether. Such studies and recommendations are among the important functions of the Department of Viticulture and Enology of the University of California's College of Agriculture, which maintains an experiment station at Davis in Yolo County.

Full recognition must be given to a great line of university figures who have wisely guided California's viticulture and are seeking constant improvement. First of that line was the famed Dean Hilgard who was succeeded by Bioletti, or the great Bioletti, as he is often referred to. Both have long since passed on, to supervise, it may be hoped, the heavenly vineyards. Their places are ably taken today by such men, professors of viticulture or enology, as Winkler, Amerine, and Olmo, familiar figures to all members of the wine industry.

Winegrowing and wine production are important and fundamental parts of California's agriculture. There are many more farmer-growers than producers. The interests of both should be adequately protected. Wine making is also a business, subject to the hazards of weather and diseases, to fluctuating grape prices, and to high labor costs. It is at the same time an art, requiring the skill, patience, and devotion of experts.

Fine wines are produced from the better wine grapes, but the latter are often sparse yielders. Medium-grade wines are the product of the more heavily yielding vines of lesser quality. Inferior wines are not infrequently made with table grapes, or even using raisins and rejects. This is a deplorable practice, yielding wines of doubtful merit, even if sound in appearance, and educates part of the public to wines lacking in flavor and bouquet. It would be desirable that all wine grapes were legally classified as such and that any wine, produced from other than wine grapes, even in part, were to carry an indication of the fact on the label.

Wines produced from the finest grapes naturally will command a higher price. For such wines the name on the label of an outstanding winegrower is helpful as a guarantee of quality. If a sound standard-quality wine is sought at a lower price, then the name of a volume producer of a nationally distributed brand should be looked for. These wines are advertised widely and provide good value for the money.

California winegrowers often produce, bottle, and market wines of many different types, growing some grapes themselves and buying the rest from growers in the neighborhood or from other districts. It is customary for a large producer to market a variety of table wines as well as aperitif and dessert wines and often sparkling wines as well. One reason for this custom is that many different varieties of grapes flourish in the same vicinity; vines which are strangers or even rivals in Europe become friendly neighbors in California. Another, and very potent, reason is that it is much more profitable to market a large variety of wines than otherwise. Only a few California wineries produce wines only from grapes grown in their own vineyards. Most of them buy outside grapes as needed and many bottle wines they do not produce themselves in order to complete the selection of wines they want to market. It must be stressed in this connection that the fact that a wine is actually produced at a specific winery from home-grown grapes only can never be as important as the quality of the wine itself, backed by the reputation of the winery which either produces or markets it.

Two fairs are held yearly in California, to which many wine growers send their wines to compete for the Gold, Silver, Bronze, and Honorable Mention awards. The California State Fair is held at Sacramento around the beginning of September and the Los Angeles County Fair at Pomona during the latter part of the same month. Judgments at the State Fair represent the opinions of experts from the viticultural and wine-making points of view and tend to be more technical than those expressed at the Los Angeles

County Fair, which reflect more the tastes of the gourmet and connoisseur.

It was first planned to publish in this guide, as indication of
comparative merits, a complete listing of the awards to date won
by all wines at both fairs since 1949. Such a compilation, according
to both wine type and grower, did in fact form part of the research
done for this work. In some types a definite pattern can be observed
over the years of specific wines which consistently win awards at
either or at both fairs. In most cases, however, no clear picture
becomes apparent. Some growers, also, including producers of high-
quality wines, do not take part in the fairs at all. Award-winning
wines are not all available to the public, nor are they necessarily
identical to those sold in the trade. The fair awards are most valuable both as the result of the plural opinion of the judges and as
incentives to competition by the growers. At the same time they
do not constitute a complete picture of the comparative merits of
all the better and best wines of California. They are, naturally,
highly coveted prizes and great recommendations for the wines
concerned. Those interested can obtain copies of the wine awards
by applying direct to the fairs or to the Wine Institute.*

The wines of California fall in three great classifications: table
wines, sparkling wines, and aperitif and dessert wines. They will be
treated in that order, while a separate chapter is devoted to the
fruit wines.

*717 Market Street, San Francisco.

Part One

CALIFORNIA TABLE WINES

*I*N THIS GUIDE the table wines of California are classified according to color, red, white, or rosé, and according to whether they are *generic* or *varietal*.

By *generic* is meant a type of wine with a name, usually of European origin, which has become generic through long and popular usage. The best-known examples of these, among the table wines, are California claret, burgundy, and chianti in the reds; California sauterne, chablis, and rhine wine in the whites; California vin rosé in the pink or rosé wines.

By *varietal* is meant a wine, produced principally or exclusively from a particular variety of grape after which it is named. The most popular California varietal red table wines are Cabernet Sauvignon and Zinfandel; Pinot Noir and Gamay; Grignolino. In the white table-wine class they are California Semillon and Sauvignon Blanc; Chardonnay and Pinot Blanc; White Riesling, Traminer, Sylvaner, Grey Riesling and Riesling. In the California rosé group they are Grenache Rosé and Gamay Rosé.

In marketing a table wine with a generic name the producer either tries to approximate the European-wine type or he simply uses the name in response to the demand. The public insists on claret and burgundy, sauterne and chablis. The producers, to stay in business, must comply. In the less expensive brands there is sometimes remarkably little difference between various red or white types save the name of the wine on the label. Generic table wines, being usually the cheaper types to produce, are also the most in demand and there are many fine wines among them.

At the same time the trend toward California varietal table wines is increasing as the public becomes more particular as to quality and flavor. The laws are strict and a wine can—or should—be called after a grape only if 51 or more per cent of the wine is produced from that grape. A varietal wine, also, should possess the distinctive color, aroma and flavor of the dominant grape. These qualities should be easily recognizable, and not only by the experts. They should always be pleasing, representing the basic criteria of a fine wine. There is no point in producing a varietal wine just for the sake of a varietal name. Quality and character are essential. Less distinctive varietals had better be used in blending and bottled as generics.

Some very fine California wines are produced from a careful blending of choice grape varieties, each lending its own character to form that of the final product and with none predominating sufficiently to call the wine by a varietal name. Blends often result in better wines, as any wine maker can confirm. Blended wines of high quality, with *typical California* names, may well have a great future field of their own. There is a place for blends as well as for varietals, straight or otherwise. They each have their own merits.

Vintage years matter less in California than in France and Germany, where temperatures, affecting the grape harvest and the resulting wines, vary considerably. In California the sun distributes its favors more evenly and frequently so that successive vintages resemble each other closely, with an average variation estimated at 15 per cent. Even so, naturally, some years are more favorable than others, especially in the northern coastal districts.

Indication of a vintage on a California wine serves mostly to identify it and to give the consumer an idea of its age. Vintage charts would only be of real value if made up by each winery for the wines produced from grapes grown in its own vineyards, by type of wine and by vineyard. No such charts are available to date.

Some top-flight California winegrowers market vintage wines regularly; others prefer to blend the wines of various years to ensure continuity of character. If a vintage is mentioned on the label, the wine must, by law, have been produced for 100 per cent in the year indicated.

Which are the finest California table wines?

The answer involves three separate factors: the grapes from which the wines are made, the district of origin, and the reputation of the winegrower.

The best table wine grapes, that is, those imparting the right aroma, flavor, and color, yield the finest table wines. It is therefore useful to be familiar with these grapes, after which the finest varietal wines are named and which also contribute to the best of the generic types. Such varietals are treated in some detail in the text, the greatest of all being printed in capital letters.

The superior table wine grapes flourish the best, on account of climate and soil, in the northern coastal counties, where they like to grow and mature "the hard way." For that reason the finest of all California table wines are produced in that region, notably in the counties of *Napa* and *Sonoma,* the *Livermore Valley* in Alameda, and the counties of *Santa Clara* and *Santa Cruz.*

These are the so-called "appellations of origin" to look for on the label when desiring the highest-quality table wines. Any such appellation means, by law, that the wine has been produced from grapes grown and fermented for at least 75 per cent in the designated area.

Table wines of high quality are also produced in other northern sections, as in southern Alameda, San Benito, Contra Costa, and Solano counties. These wines are usually labeled as "California," the district of origin being less familiar to the public.

Separate mention must be made here of the fine table wines—notably those of red Italian types—produced in the Cucamonga district of San Bernardino County in Southern California. Many of these carry the *Cucamonga* appellation of origin on the label.

The inland valley region, home of many of the standard-quality table wines, also produces some finer ones. All wines of this vast region are labeled with the name of the state. Many of them are blended, for character and quality, with northern coastal county wines.

It is important to keep in mind that if the grapes do not originate in the same county or district where the winery is situated the resulting wines cannot be labeled with the appellation of origin. This explains why many wines produced or bottled by winegrowers in the best-known districts are nevertheless designated as "California" wines.

The ultimate guarantee of quality for a table or any other type of wine is the reputation of the winegrower or producer.

There are, finally, a number of small family wineries scattered throughout the state which produce good, sound, inexpensive "country" table wines which have a limited and local distribution. These are well worth while locating and tasting for those who have the interest and the leisure.

Information concerning the location of all California wineries, large and small, can be obtained from the Wine Institute in San Francisco or at its various branch offices.

The red, white, and rosé table wines of California, varietal and generic, are grouped in this guide according to over-all similarity in character. Each class is described in general terms and each varietal and generic type separately.

The normal use and service of each class of wine is indicated, as are suggestions for fullest enjoyment. By room temperature is meant the normal temperature of the room, around 65–75° Fahrenheit. By chilling is meant chilling in the refrigerator away from the freezing unit or from the deep freezer. Chilling a wine too long will kill its character. All table wines, red, white, and rosé, chilled or not, should be opened shortly before the meal to release their bouquet and flavor fully.

CHART OF THE MORE PROMINENT CALIFORNIA RED TABLE WINES

Varietals	Generics
California Claret Types	
CABERNET SAUVIGNON	Claret
Zinfandel	
California Burgundy Types	
PINOT NOIR	Burgundy
GAMAY BEAUJOLAIS	
GAMAY	
Red Pinot	
California Red Italian Wine Types	
Grignolino	Vino Rosso
Barbera	Chianti

II

CALIFORNIA RED TABLE WINES

THE RED TABLE WINES of California fall automatically in three great groups, those of the claret, burgundy, and red Italian wine types. Other groups are formed by the minor red table wines, by those of the muscat type which are not table wines in the usual sense of the term, and by the red specialty wines.

CALIFORNIA CLARET TYPES

The term "claret" was originally applied in England to the red table wines of the Bordeaux district in France, the name presumably being derived from their clarity of color.

Today claret, as a wine type, denotes any acceptable red table wine with preferably the same general character as Red Bordeaux. It should, on principle, be lighter in body than a red burgundy. The term is applied both to the wine as a type and to each wine of the type, from the indifferent to the best.

California clarets can be either varietal or generic. The latter is labeled "California Claret." Zinfandel is a popular varietal; Cabernet Sauvignon is by far the finest.

Use and Service—Most suitable with red meats and roasts and also with chicken and other fowl. Serve at room temperature. Do not chill unless, owing to the hot climate or other causes, the wine

has been stored in too warm a place. Even then chill only slightly.
Uncork the bottle an hour before the meal for full enjoyment.

Clarets are much used in cooking and make an excellent base for
red wine punches and cups.

VARIETALS

CABERNET SAUVIGNON (Ca-berr-nay′ So-vee-nyon′)

The Cabernet Sauvignon, to use its full and proper name, is the
premier claret grape of the world. It is mainly responsible for the
superb character and flavor of the celebrated château-bottled and
other clarets of France.

In California the Cabernet Sauvignon grape can yield, in the
northern coastal region, altogether superior wines which compete
very well with all but the very greatest château clarets of Bordeaux.
Napa, Santa Clara, Santa Cruz, and Sonoma counties produce the
finest, some of which are great wines anywhere under the sun.

The name of the wine is sometimes shortened to Cabernet, even
on the label. Some winegrowers bottle two qualities of the wine,
the better being called Cabernet Sauvignon and the lesser Cabernet.
It is, on the whole, advisable always to use the full name when re-
ferring to this wine, as there is also a Ruby Cabernet and other
Cabernet varieties which are less well known, and a wine labeled
simply "Cabernet" could conceivably be made from Cabernet grapes
other than the Sauvignon.

The finest California Cabernet Sauvignons are produced from
considerably more than the legally required minimum 51 per cent
of grapes of that name, as the wine will not stand much blending
without loss of character. The best have a deep ruby color, an ex-
pansive bouquet, and a remarkable flavor, easy to recognize and
appreciate. They are often slightly heavier in body than their French
prototypes. Like the latter, they possess, when young, a dryness and
aromatic pungency which smooth out to a rich mellowness with age.

There is a fairly wide range of California Cabernet Sauvignons,
depending on the location of the vineyard, the winegrower, and
the age. Some are lighter in body and color and should be con-

sumed when relatively young. Others are darker and heavier, mature considerably in the bottle, throwing off a deposit. The latter, which can also be purchased for laying-down purposes, should be decanted or poured carefully, the bottle resting in a wine basket or cradle.

When one desires the finest claret California can produce, Cabernet Sauvignon is the wine to purchase.

Zinfandel

The leading wine grape variety of California in acreage, production, and originality.

The experts disagree about its identity. It was at one time thought to be identical with the Hungarian Kadarka, but this has been disproved. Widely accepted is the theory that the vine was first imported to California by Colonel Agoston Haraszthy. The story is that he received a shipment of cuttings, presumably from Hungary, his native land, in February 1852 and could not decipher the name on the label attached to a certain bundle. It seemed to read Zinfandel* and that is what he named it. Eventually he planted some vines at his Buena Vista estate near Sonoma, where they flourished and made viticultural history.

Zinfandel varies considerably in quality and character, according to district and wine grower. It is, at best, a wine of peculiar charm, fruity, zestful, and aromatic with a raspberry flavor. It is essentially Californian and the only varietal table wine produced throughout the state. Most Zinfandels should be consumed young, as they will lose their zest and fruitiness with age. A few mature well and even ten-year-old Zinfandels can be satisfying in their mellowness.

Very fine Zinfandels come from the various counties of the northern coastal region. Those produced from gravelly soil, as in the Livermore Valley, remind one of a French red Graves. Other first-class Zinfandels hail from the Cucamonga district in Southern California and from San Luis Obispo County. The vine is also

*The Zierfandler, it may be noted, well known in Austria, especially around Gumpoldskirchen, and a member of the Veltliner family, is a *white* grape, yielding a rich and spicy white table wine of the Traminer type.

extensively cultivated in the inland valley region, where it yields a wine of greatly varying quality, the better ones coming from the cooler areas. The wine is also much used in blending and in the production of California port.

Ruby Cabernet

A new varietal in the red table wine field. Propagated by the Agricultural Experiment Station of the University of California, the vine is a hybrid of the Cabernet Sauvignon and of the Carignane from a cross made in 1936, which first fruited in the 1940 season. Purpose of the cross was to combine the outstanding character of the Cabernet Sauvignon with the productivity of the Carignane. It was the first attempt to combine high quality and yielding ability in the same variety.

The color of Ruby Cabernet is the same as that of its august parent, Cabernet Sauvignon. Its aroma and flavor, though similar, are less distinguished. On the other hand it matures more rapidly, becoming marketable sooner.

Ruby Cabernet rates as a claret of higher than average quality; it is still too soon to judge its future clearly. The wine, to be watched with interest, is produced as a varietal in Napa, Sonoma, Santa Clara, and other counties.

GENERIC

California Claret

The generic table wine labeled "California Claret" is dry, light to medium-dark red in color, and light to medium in body.

It can be made from any dark grape variety or from a blend, provided the wine is red, dry, and contains around 12 per cent alcohol. Its quality, therefore, depends strongly on the winegrower and the grapes used. Most producers bottle an inexpensive, standard-quality California claret.

CALIFORNIA RED BURGUNDY TYPES

Red Burgundy is always referred to simply as "Burgundy." It is the name used to describe the red table wines from Burgundy in France and those wines from other countries which possess the same over-all characteristics. They are usually fuller in body, and of a deeper red color than clarets.

There is a present tendency in the U.S.A. to call any generic red table wine burgundy. If this custom were to become general, "burgundy," in American wine parlance, would take the place once held by the term "claret."

California burgundies of the generic order are so labeled. The finest varietal is Pinot Noir. Very fine also are Gamay Beaujolais and Gamay. Some so-called Red Pinots have a charm of their own.

Use and Service—Traditionally served with turkey and other domestic fowl and with all wild fowl, venison, and game. Also with red meats and roasts.

Burgundy should be served at room temperature. Chill only, and then slightly, when the wine is much too warm. Uncork the bottle an hour before the meal.

Burgundies are very popular in cooking. As with all wines the better grades should always be used to obtain maximum flavor. So-called "Cooking Burgundy" should be avoided as flavorless and useless for the purpose.

Varietals

PINOT NOIR (Pee-nó Nwahr)

Pinot noir is the famous grape which yields the finest of the Red Burgundies of France and the "Blanc de noirs" wines from which most of the unblended French Champagnes are produced.

In California, where it is best suited to the cooler areas of the northern coastal counties, Pinot noir* produces what are by far

*Pinot Noir is the correct spelling for the *wine* and Pinot noir for the *grape* of the same name. This principle applies to all wines and vines where the second word is an *adjective*.

the finest wines of the red burgundy class in the country. They can be superb in aroma and flavor, harmonious, soft, smooth, and velvety. Some are darker in color and body than others, depending on the vineyard of origin. They vary much in quality, depending on the percentage of Pinot noir grapes in the wine.

Napa, Santa Clara, and Sonoma counties originate the best. Pinot noir, however, is a vine very difficult to cultivate and the wine itself as difficult to produce properly. The vine is only sparsely grown and is as sparse a yielder. Availability of the true Pinot Noir is therefore limited. The wine is bound to be expensive and there is many a so-called Pinot Noir which is in reality produced from dark Pinot grapes other than the true Pinot noir.

If the highest-quality California red burgundy is desired, Pinot Noir is the wine to purchase. It matures well and will sometimes throw off a deposit in the bottle. Such wines can also be acquired for laying-down purposes. They should be decanted or poured carefully from the bottle nestling in a wine cradle.

GAMAY BEAUJOLAIS (Ga-maý Bo-zho-laý) and GAMAY

The Gamay is the grape that made the Beaujolais wines of France famous and is responsible for their gay character and fruitiness. It was at one time outlawed in France as it threatened to displace the Pinot on account of its greater productivity, but yielded wines of less high quality and character. This, however, was in the fourteenth century. In Beaujolais and elsewhere today the Gamay is looked upon as a noble vine.

In California the Gamay produces a light-colored, lively and fruity wine with a delicate flavor, notably in Contra Costa and Santa Clara counties. It is labeled either as Gamay Beaujolais or as Gamay.

There are many varieties of the Gamay grape and vine. In Napa County a variety is grown which yields a wine similar in character to that of Gamay Beaujolais. This Napa wine is always labeled simply as Gamay.

It may be noted that Gamay, like Beaujolais in France, is often served at cellar temperature.

Red Pinot

A burgundy-type wine produced from dark Pinot grapes other than Pinot noir, such as Pinot St. George, Pinot Meunier, and Pinot Pernand. The best known are derived from the Pinot St. George grape and exert their own distinctive charm. They are soft, fruity, heavy-bodied, and fragrant at their best and some notably fine ones are produced in the Napa Valley.

It is important with wines of this name to ascertain the exact variety of grapes from which they have been produced and which should be indicated on the labeling.

Black Pinot

The term has been used as the translation of Pinot Noir to indicate that particular wine, but this leads to confusion. The modern tendency is to designate thereby a burgundy-type wine made from dark Pinot grapes other than Pinot noir. Some very good Black Pinot was produced at one time in Southern Alameda County from the Pinot Meunier grape.

Pinot Rouge

Another term used to indicate a red burgundy-type wine produced from dark grapes with a Pinot name other than Pinot noir.

GENERIC

California Burgundy

The generic table wine labeled "California Burgundy" is medium to deep red in color, dry, and full-bodied.

It is produced from a large number of grape varieties, the best of which include various Pinots, Gamays, Petite Sirah, Zinfandel and Refosco. California burgundy is often derived from the same grapes as claret, the lighter-bodied wines being labeled with the latter name and the heavier-bodied with the former.

Burgundy is the most popular of the California generic red table wines and most producers bottle an inexpensive standard-quality burgundy wine.

Note: So-called "Sweet Burgundy" is a contradiction in terms, as burgundy should always be dry. It is obvious that such a wine should never have been produced at all, or, at best, labeled "Sweet Red Table Wine."

CALIFORNIA RED ITALIAN WINE TYPES

Many of the California winegrowers are of Italian descent and numerous grape varieties have been imported from Italy, many of which have proved very successful in the California climate and soil. The Italian taste in wines has also been very influential, whether the varieties used were of Italian origin or not.

California red table wines of Italian type form a distinct group. They are usually full-bodied with a pronounced character which can be described as Italian, the particular flavor depending on the wine.

A popular generic wine of this group is California chianti. In recent years another generic type, a mellow red table wine, similar to that produced by so many Italian and other home wine makers, has won wide acceptance. For purposes of class identification this type of wine has been called "Vino Rosso" in the *Guide*.

The best-known varietal of this group is Grignolino; others are Barbera and Charbono.

Use and Service—Both California chianti and Vino Rosso are suitable with almost any meal, especially of the more informal kind. All red Italian table wine types, both varietal and generic, are especially suitable, naturally, with Italian dishes of any kind.

Serve at room temperature. Some, however, prefer their Grignolino or Vino Rosso slightly chilled, as chilling, especially of the Vino Rosso types, seems to bring out their flavor better.

VARIETALS

Grignolino

The grape is one of the many California varieties which are native to Piedmont in Italy, and produces a wine with an original and popular appeal.

California Grignolino is usually light or even orange red in color and is sometimes bottled as a natural rosé (see there). The best-known wines of this type hail from the Cucamonga district in Southern California, while other fine ones come from the northern region, notably Solano and Napa counties.

Barbera

Another native of Piedmont which has done very well in California. As a varietal type, it is a big, rugged, full-bodied, richly colored, robust wine with plenty of flavor and tang and needs some aging to reach its peak. Notable Barberas are produced in Napa and in Alameda.

Charbono

Also said to originate in Piedmont, this grape can produce a deep-colored, soft, and heavy-bodied wine, best known in the Napa Valley.

GENERICS

California Chianti

When Chianti is referred to as such, it is assumed to be red. In California it is usually marketed, as in Italy, in raffia- or straw-covered, bulb-shaped bottles.

In Tuscany, the home of Chianti, the wine is produced mainly from the Sangioveto grape. In California Chianti has become a type of wine, ruby red, fruity, rather full-bodied, medium tart, and with a pronounced and characteristic Italian flavor. It is produced from a number of grape varieties, usually blended to type.

The typical Chianti bottles are attractive also because of their decorative value and are much used as candleholders.

Vino Rosso

This type of wine, usually quite mellow and slightly sweet, is similar in character to the homemade red table wines produced by many throughout the country. The commercial wine, one of the least expensive of all types, has won wide acceptance. Many wine growers produce it, labeling it with various Italian names. The original edge of dryness in the wine is sometimes removed by the addition of a slight amount of port.

Vino Rosso comes in all sizes, from gallon containers to splits.

Barberone

A rough and rather coarse red table wine with plenty of body. Barberone literally means "Big Barbera," but is often a stranger to the grape of that name.

OTHER CALIFORNIA RED TABLE WINES

Grouped together here are the less well-known types of California red table wines, mostly dry. They include a number of secondary varietals and the generic types labeled simply "California Red Table Wine" or "California Red Wine."

The marketing of secondary varietals has generally been discouraged and with good reason. Varietals of no particular distinction, when not used for blending or for the production of dessert wines, had best be labeled under generic names.

Varietals

Carignane

The grape is primarily cultivated in California, as in Algeria and Southern France, on account of its great productivity. The wine, also spelled "Carignan," is usually only average in quality, although the best, from the cooler regions, can be sound and fruity. It is mostly used for bulk production, but has been varietally produced in Sonoma County and elsewhere. It is one of the parents of the Ruby Cabernet (see there).

Freisa

A fruity and often slightly effervescent wine of special charm from Piedmont, produced from the grape of the same name. Not often seen in California, where it is easily misspelled "Fresia," it may well have a future as a varietal type.

Mission

The famous vine, planted by the Mission Fathers and the first of the *Vitis vinifera* line in California. A vigorous grower, it is best suited for the production of dessert wines, notably Angelica, with which it has long been associated. Modern taste prefers other varieties to Mission for claret, but some has been produced as a varietal in Fresno County.

Mondeuse

Said to originate in Savoy, France, this vine is a good producer, but yields a wine of usually insufficient quality to bottle it as a varietal. It is mostly used for blending purposes.

Montonico

A tawny-colored newcomer from Calabria, Italy. Plans are to produce from it, in Santa Clara Valley, a table wine of some sweetness.

Mourestel

The grape is considered by some authorities to be related to the Carignane (see there). The wine, at its best, as has been produced in the Livermore Valley, can be soft, fruity, and pleasing.

Nebbiolo

Another native of Piedmont, where it yields a number of well-known and pleasing wines. The California varietal is only rarely seen.

Petite Sirah

The Petite Sirah of California, thought to be identical with the Duriff of Savoy in France, does extremely well in its adopted soil, where it is widely cultivated. It was once identified with the French Petite Sirah, which made Hermitage and other Rhône wines of France famous. The name is probably of Persian origin and a corruption of Shiraz.

Whatever its origin, the California Petite Sirah yields a wine of distinctive aroma and flavor. It is much used in California burgundy, although its character has little in common with the French wine of that name. It has occasionally been marketed as a varietal wine.

Refosco

This wine, nearly unknown in Italy, is used in California for blending in burgundy. It is famous for having been used by Hiram W. Crabb in his legendary "Black Burgundy," by which name the grape has also become known.

Tannat

Primarily used for blending purposes. A claret type, possessing a distinctive aroma and flavor and a full color and body. It has been bottled as a varietal in the Napa Valley.

Valdepeñas

This vine, introduced from Spain, ranks with the most vigorous and productive in California. In the cooler regions it yields clean, average-quality table wines, rarely seen as a varietal.

GENERIC

California Red Table Wine

A wine so labeled, with no further indication of type, is usually an inexpensive light red table wine of no pronounced character. Some wine growers bottle a standard-quality wine under this label, the best of which is dry and can be quite good. There are also medium-dry and sweet wines of this type.

CALIFORNIA RED MUSCAT TYPES

Although sometimes described as table wines on account of their low alcoholic content, of around 12 per cent, they are on the sweet side and for that reason grouped separately. They are better suited to service with the dessert or in the afternoon or evening like regular dessert wines. They should be chilled.

These wines, produced from muscat or similar-type grapes, all possess the typical muscat aroma and flavor to a greater or lesser extent, their exact muscat character depending on the variety.

VARIETALS

Malvasia (Red Malvasia)

A light red, semi-sweet wine derived from the Black Malvoisie grape and produced in Santa Cruz County.

Malvasia usually means the red wines of this variety, whether of the light sweet or of the dessert type. There are also California white Malvasias, properly called by their full name of Malvasia Bianca (see there).

Note: A dry light red table wine from the Black Malvoisie grape and called "California Malvoisie" was at one time produced in Alameda County.

Aleatico

The California Aleatico light wine is red, sweet, and spicy with the distinctive perfume and flavor of the grape by the same name. It is only rarely available as planting of the vine is very limited (see also Aleatico dessert wine).

GENERIC

California Light Red Muscat

Any light wine of around 12 per cent alcohol derived from dark muscat grapes without indication of variety. They are semi-sweet or sweet and sometimes labeled simply "California Light Sweet Red Wine."

RED SPECIALTY WINES

American Malaga

The name given to a type of sweet red wine of around 12 per cent alcohol produced mainly in the East and Midwest from the Concord grape, a *Vitis labrusca* variety, with its own typical aroma and flavor, yielding wines often described as "foxy," but quite popular in some areas.

The wine is a type of its own and has no similarity to Spanish Malaga or to California Malaga, a nearly extinct type of dessert wine (see there), nor is it named after the Malaga grape, a table variety.

American Malaga, from Concord and other grapes, has been produced in California, notably in Fresno County, to meet the competition of Eastern and Midwestern wines of this type. The wine is smooth and sweet with a grapy taste. It is kosher and is suitable for the sacramental rites of the Jewish religion. That produced in California is made exclusively from the juice of grapes as the state laws direct.

Wines of this type should be served cold, preferably in the afternoon or evening, and can also be used for flavoring desserts or as a dessert wine.

American Grape Wine

A wine so labeled, with no further indication of type, is a heavy-bodied sweet red wine of low alcohol content usually made from the Concord grape and with the Concord aroma and flavor. Some California growers bottle it, the wine being produced mostly from out-of-state grapes. It should be served cold.

California Red Grape Wine

A sweet red wine of low alcohol content made from any dark California *vinifera* grapes.

"Grape Wine" is here used in its restricted sense, as a type of sweet red wine. All wines made from grapes are, naturally, grape wines as distinct from fruit and berry wines. Occasionally other wines, such as those of the Vino Rosso type, also indicate on the label that they are grape wines in the general sense of the term.

CHART OF THE MORE PROMINENT
CALIFORNIA WHITE TABLE WINES

Varietals	Generics
California Sauterne Types	
SEMILLON	Sauterne
SAUVIGNON BLANC	Sweet Sauterne (incl. Haut Sauterne)
	Dry Sauterne
California White Burgundy Types	
CHARDONNAY (PINOT CHARDONNAY)	Chablis
PINOT BLANC	
Folle Blanche	
White Pinot	
California Rhine Wine Types	
WHITE RIESLING (JOHANNISBERGER)	Rhine Wine
TRAMINER (GEWURZTRAMINER)	
SYLVANER	
GREY RIESLING	
Riesling	

III

CALIFORNIA WHITE TABLE WINES

$\mathscr{T}$HE THREE most important groups are formed by the wines of the sauterne, white burgundy, and rhine wine types. Three lesser groups are constituted by the minor white table wines, by those of the white muscat types and by the white specialty wines.

CALIFORNIA SAUTERNE TYPES

Calfornia sauterne is usually spelled without the final "s" of French Sauternes. A few wine growers use the French spelling, but the general tendency is toward the shorter, Americanized form.

Sauterne is produced in California from a great variety of grapes, from the finest to the indifferent. The best are derived from Semillon and Sauvignon blanc grapes, while lesser varieties include Sauvignon vert, Palomino, or Golden Chasselas, and many others, including Thompson Seedless, essentially a raisin and table grape. If a truly fine sauterne is desired, the name of a well-known quality-wine grower is essential on the label.

California sauterne, the most popular of the generic white table wines, ranges from dry to very sweet in character, from straw to golden in color, while its bouquet and flavor depend on the grapes used for its production.

The three main generic types are, according to sugar content,

"California Sauterne" (medium dry or medium sweet), "California Dry Sauterne," and "California Sweet Sauterne." The term "California Haut Sauterne" is also used for the medium-sweet and sweet wines, and "Chateau" for the sweetest types. The exact degree of dryness or sweetness of any particular sauterne depends on the producer's judgment.

The two great varietals of the California sauterne family are Semillon, which is generally considered the finest, and its close rival Sauvignon Blanc.

Use and Service—California sauterne is an all-purpose white table wine, the dry and medium wines being most appropriate with all the lighter meats, plain fish, and seafood courses, and also with chicken and other fowl. Chill for about two hours. Sweet sauternes are most suitable with rich, creamed dishes of any kind and with sweet desserts. Chill for about three hours.

All fine wines of the sauterne order are popular in cooking, especially those with the most flavor. So-called "Cooking Sauterne" should be avoided as ineffectual. Sauternes make a good base for white wine punches and cups.

VARIETALS

SEMILLON (Sem-me-yon')

One of the finest white wine grapes of the world and responsible for most of the character of the famous château-bottled Sauternes of France.

Superior Semillon wines are produced in California in the northern coastal region and the grapes, as in France, can be made to yield a naturally sweet wine by allowing them to become overripe, causing a slight and desirable raisining.

Semillons, the finest of the California sauternes, are golden, medium- to full-bodied, full-flavored, and have a flowerlike bouquet. There are two main types, the more typical and slightly more expensive sweet Semillon and the Dry Semillon. Some Semillon is also available in the medium range.

Outstanding Semillons, both sweet and dry, with a special fullness of body, bouquet, and flavor, originate in the Livermore Valley of Alameda County, noted as the home of the finest sauterne-type wines of the state. Dry Semillons of high quality, and some sweet, are also produced in Santa Clara, Napa and Sonoma counties.

SAUVIGNON BLANC (So-vee-nyon' Blon)

The second most important varietal member of the sauterne family. It is the principal grape variety used in the production of the white Graves wines of France and is also important in that of French Sauternes. Known in France as Sauvignon, it is called Sauvignon blanc in California to distinguish it from the grape named Sauvignon vert, which is not comparable in any way in the quality and character of the wines it yields (see there).

In California the Sauvignon blanc produces high-quality wines with a distinctive aromatic character, fuller in body, and heavier than the Semillons. The finest hail from the Livermore Valley in Alameda County, while some excellent ones are also produced in the Santa Clara and Napa valleys.

Sauvignon Blanc ranges from dry to sweet with the dry types more typical and better known. The grapes flourish particularly well in gravelly soil and the resulting wines could be called the Graves type if it were not sounder to consider California wines on their own merits.

Sauvignon Vert

The origin of this vine is obscure. It is very productive and widely cultivated, being much used in California sauterne of average quality and in blending.

The varietal wine, bottled notably in Mendocino, Solano, and Napa counties, can be quite pleasing with its own dry character and slight muscat flavor.

Sauvignon vert, the grape, is also known as the Colombard, but should not be confused with the French Colombard from which the wine of that name is produced.

Generics

California Sweet Sauterne

The sweetest of the California generic sauternes, golden and full-bodied.

Some wine growers prefer to call their sweet sauterne "California Haut Sauterne," while others produce both wines, reserving the "Haut Sauterne" name for the medium-sweet type. It may be noted that this term, meaning literally "High Sauterne," is actually meaningless and should also not be pronounced as "Hot," which sounds peculiar, to say the least, but rather as "Oht." In France the term has no official recognition and is only tolerated. The grapes are not grown on higher ground, nor is the wine of higher quality. In California the term has come to mean a sauterne type, sweeter than that labeled simply as "Sauterne."

Some of the finest California sweet sauternes are produced from a blend of Semillon and Sauvignon blanc grapes with the sporadic addition of a little of the Muscadelle du Bordelais variety, this being the formula for the great château-bottled Sauternes of France. Such California sauternes are sometimes bottled under the "Chateau" appellation, followed by the name of the winegrower or of the winery.

California Sauterne

The medium-dry or medium-sweet type of sauterne, varying from straw to golden in color and from medium to full in body.

This wine, the most in demand of the generic white table types, varies exceedingly in quality, according to the producer and the grapes used.

California Dry Sauterne

The driest of the sauterne group and actually not so much a sauterne as a dry white table wine. As with all sauternes, the best are derived from Semillon or Sauvignon blanc grapes and these are of high quality. Others vary considerably, the cheaper kinds being often similar, and sometimes identical to California chablis.

CALIFORNIA WHITE BURGUNDY WINES

This group consists of those California wines which have the general character associated with white burgundy. They are usually marketed, like the red types, in the typical stout burgundy bottles.

The generic type of this group is known as "California Chablis." The finest varietal is Chardonnay or Pinot Chardonnay, followed closely in quality by the true Pinot Blanc. Folle Blanche is also a first-class varietal, while so-called "White Pinots" can have their own particular merits.

Use and Service—Excellent with all manner of fish and seafood, white meats, and fowl and traditionally the wines to serve with oysters and clams. Chill for about an hour. Good also for cooking, especially fish.

Varietals

CHARDONNAY or **PINOT CHARDONNAY** (Pee-nó Shardon-naý)

One of the greatest white wine grapes of all and celebrated for producing the finest white Burgundies of France as well as the "Blanc de blancs" wines used for French Champagne.

Some authorities consider the vine a variation of the Pinot noir, which it resembles in several respects, while others prefer to classify it as a separate variety. Hence the two names, both of which are current in California.

Chardonnay yields in the cooler wine-growing districts of California an eminently distinguished wine, golden, full-bodied and fragrant, flavorful and smooth, reminiscent of still champagne. The vine is a very sparse yielder and experts are agreed that only those should attempt to grow it who are prepared for great efforts in its cultivation and in the production of the wine itself, which will of necessity be one of the most expensive on the market. Alameda, Napa, and Santa Clara counties are its California homes.

When the finest California white burgundy is looked for, this is the wine to secure, bottled by an outstanding grower.

PINOT BLANC or PINOT BLANC VRAI (Pee-no' Blon Vray)

An outstanding white wine grape and second only to Chardonnay in the white burgundy class. In France it is famous for producing the finest Chablis.

In California the wine is sometimes called the true Pinot Blanc, or Pinot Blanc Vrai, to distinguish it from those derived from white grapes with a Pinot name other than Pinot blanc and Chardonnay (see White Pinot).

Pinot blanc yields in California an excellent white wine of the white burgundy type, of distinct aroma and flavor, smooth and dry, fresh and fruity. Alameda and Santa Clara are its main counties of origin; some also is grown in Sonoma and in Napa.

Pinot Blanc should never be used to denote wines produced from the Chenin blanc grape, wines that are properly called White Pinot (see there).

Folle Blanche (Fol Blonsh)

The grape is one of the principal varieties grown in the Charente district in France for the distillation of cognac. Transplanted to California, it has become a much better drinking wine than in its native soil.

Folle Blanche has a very high acid content, which makes it an excellent stock for the production of champagne. It is also used in the better grades of California chablis.

The wine is occasionally met with as a varietal type, notably from Napa Valley hillsides, and is tartly dry, fresh and fruity, and very clean both to nose and palate. It is a typical nice light luncheon wine.

White Pinot

The name of this wine has become generally identified in California with that made from the Chenin blanc or Pineau de la Loire grape. While not a "true" Pinot, it is famous in its own right in France for the white wines of Anjou and Touraine, of which the delightful Vouvray is probably the best known.

In California the Chenin blanc has done extremely well also, notably in Napa County, where it yields a very pleasing, dry, light, and fruity wine which has won wide acceptance under the name of White Pinot.

White Pinot is very occasionally used to denote wines made from the Pinot blanc grape, but this practice should be discontinued, as it only leads to unnecessary confusion.

GENERIC

California Chablis

The generic type of California white burgundy, called after the French wines of that name, from the Chablis region of France, northwest of Burgundy proper.

California chablis is pale, straw-colored, and dry, usually more delicate and lighter than sauterne and fruitier and less tart than rhine wine types. It is made from a large variety of grapes, the best of which include Chardonnay, Pinot blanc, Folle blanche, and French Colombard.

Most growers bottle a standard-quality California chablis; some especially fine ones are produced in the northern coastal counties. The cheaper ones are often not to be distinguished from dry sauterne and rhine wines.

CALIFORNIA RHINE WINE TYPES

These wines have in common that they are dry, pale green or pale golden, tart, and light. They are mostly derived from the same grapes as the German Rhine and Moselle or the French Alsatian wines or possess the same general characteristics. They are marketed in the tall and tapering amber or white bottles in which the German Rhine and Moselle wines are sold.

California rhine wine is the typical generic wine of this group, which includes a number of very fine varietals. The most important of these are White Riesling, also called Johannisberg(er) Riesling, Traminer, Sylvaner, Grey Riesling, and Riesling.

Use and Service—Traditional with fish, seafood, and the lighter white meats. Chill for about an hour.

It must be noted that in Germany, where very little red table wine is produced, Rhine and Moselle wines are served with most any course. This is a typical example of a more general use of table wines than the traditional, a practice which this *Guide* heartily recommends, considering it foolish to restrict the use of any type of wine unnecessarily.

Rhine wine types are also recommended for cooking, especially fish, and make an excellent base for punches and cups.

Varietals

WHITE RIESLING or JOHANNISBERG(ER) RIESLING
(Rees'-ling)

The premier rhine wine grape of the world, responsible for the great German Rhines and Moselles, as well as for many other wines of the same order in Alsace, Switzerland, California, and elsewhere.

In Europe the grape is usually referred to simply as Riesling. In California it is called White Riesling to distinguish it from other grapes with a Riesling name. Some California growers call the wine Johannisberg or Johannisberger Riesling after some of the finest of all Rhine wines, those produced by Prince Metternich at Schloss Johannisberg in the Rheingau district of Germany. This custom, also practiced in some parts of Switzerland, seems slightly presumptuous and in California the correct name of White Riesling would seem to do sufficient honor to one of the state's truly great wines, while trespassing on no foreign glory.

White Riesling is a most refreshing wine, with a pronounced fragrance of bouquet and a rich, satisfying flavor. Napa, Sonoma, Santa Clara, and Santa Cruz counties are best known for its production; some very fine ones have come from San Benito.

White Rieslings, like their cousins from the Rhine, vary between two extreme types, depending upon the vineyard location and the grower. There are the fresh and fragrant, pale green, delicate wines which should be consumed young. There are also the fuller-bodied, heavier, softer, fruitier, and darker golden wines, which are rich in sugar and improve with age in the bottle for a considerable time.

TRAMINER and GEWURZTRAMINER (Gewurts-tra-meé-ner)

Well known in Alsace, France, this white wine grape is known in California as the Red Traminer on account of the red flush on its skin when ripening. It is generally considered to be the finest rhine wine type grape after the White Riesling.

The wines are fragrant and distinctly aromatic with a spicy scent and flavor. They are produced in Napa, Santa Clara, and Sonoma counties.

Gewurtztraminer, also spelled Gewurz-Traminer and Gewurz Traminer, is obtained from selected strains of the Red Traminer grape. Famed in Alsace, Gewürtztraminer is probably the most scented and pungent wine of Europe. A limited qauntity is produced in the Napa Valley and the tendency is developing in California to label as such the more aromatic and spicy of the Traminer wines.

SYLVANER

This is the principal rhine wine type grown in California. It is known as the Sylvaner in Alsace and as the Franken Riesling in some parts of Germany. In California it is known under both names, but more correctly under that of Sylvaner.

The wines are of superior quality, fragrant, and fresh with a distinct and delicate aroma and flavor. It is bottled as a varietal in Napa, Santa Clara, and Sonoma counties. It is also used in the blending of the higher-quality California rhine wines and in the production of the better California Rieslings, under which name it is sometimes marketed (see there).

GREY RIESLING

The grape, actually the Chauché gris of France and not a true
Riesling, yields in California a white wine of the rhine type, soft and
pleasing, with a mild, spicy flavor. Its name is caused by the grey-
colored tinge which develops on the grapes as they approach ripeness.

Grey Riesling has attained a great popularity, especially in the last
years. The best known comes from the Livermore Valley, but it is
also bottled as a varietal in the Napa, Santa Clara, Cucamonga, and
other districts. Additional plantings and production are probable,
considering the great demand for this wine.

Riesling

California Riesling can be one of a number of varietals or a blend
of them. There are four California grapes with a well-known
Riesling name or connotation: White or Johannisberg(er) Riesling,
Sylvaner or Franken Riesling, Grey Riesling, and Emerald Riesling
(see those wines).

A wine labeled simply "California Riesling" must, by law, contain
at least 51 per cent of wine made from one or more of the Riesling
grapes listed above. This leaves a wide choice open to the producer.
The result is that California Riesling varies greatly in character and
quality, depending on the grapes used, the district of origin, and the
grower.

Note: Riesling is sometimes misspelled and mispronounced
"Reisling," presumably because of an erroneous impression that it
sounds more Germanic.

Emerald Riesling

A recent variety, propagated by the University of California at its
Agricultural Experiment Station at Davis, Yolo County. It is a
hybrid of the White Riesling and the Muscadelle of California, derived from seeds collected in 1935 which bore grapes in the 1939
season.

The wine has a clean, fresh, tart taste, is medium-bodied and rates as a table wine of above-average quality. Production as a varietal has been limited; some is available, notably in the Evergreen district of the Santa Clara Valley.

GENERICS

California Rhine Wine

The typical generic wine of this group. The wine so labeled is produced from a number of grapes and often from the same as those from which California chablis is derived, but blended in such a manner that a paler, drier, and tarter wine is obtained.

The best California rhine wines are the product of one or more of the Riesling grapes and then possess the aroma, character and flavor of the latter.

California Moselle

This term used to be popular to designate the generic California rhine wines and also to distinguish the softer, paler, and lighter-bodied wines of that class. Some is still produced, but the name is more familiar as describing sparkling white wines of the carbonated type.

California Hock

"Hock" is an abbreviation of Hochheimer, a German Rhine wine at one time very popular in Britain. It was pronounced as "Hocka-more" and became a class term to designate any wine of the Rhine type. The name is still used in California, but has almost disappeared.

OTHER CALIFORNIA WHITE TABLE WINES

The less well easily known white table wines, not classifiable in any particular group. Some are more readily available than others; a few varietals of this group have been discontinued altogether or are only very rarely bottled as such.

VARIETALS

French Colombard

A vigorous and highly productive vine, originally known in California as West's Prolific, at one time renamed Winkler* and later identified as the French Colombard. The wine should not be confused with the Sauvignon Vert (see there), produced from the grape of that name and also known as Colombard.

French Colombard has a high acid content which makes it useful for blending in California chablis and rhine-wine types. As a varietal, it is dry, light, tart, pale golden with a neutral flavor. It is produced in the inland valley region and in the northern coastal counties, notably Solano, Mendocino, and Napa.

Golden Chasselas

Known in the Napa Valley and adjacent districts as the Golden Chasselas and elsewhere in the state under its proper name, the grape is not a variety of Chasselas, but none other than the Palomino, celebrated for the production of Sherry in the Jerez district of Spain and elsewhere.

Palomino is a vigorous producer, unequaled for yielding the best California sherry (see there). It is not usually suitable for obtaining white table wines of quality, but has occasionally been bottled as a varietal. Presumably Schramsberger Golden Chasselas, praised by Robert Louis Stevenson in his *Silverado Squatters,* was made from this grape.

In spite of the similarity in name Golden Chasselas has no connection with the Chasselas doré (see Gutedel).

Green Hungarian

The vine is said to originate in Hungary, from where it was imported to California by way of Swabia in Germany. It yields a dry white wine which is mostly used for blending purposes, but has been

*After Dr. A. J. Winkler, Professor of Viticulture, University of California.

successfully produced as a varietal, especially in Napa and also in Sonoma.

Gutedel

A wine, produced from the Chasselas doré grape, the best known of many Chasselas varieties in California and also known as Sweet-water. It is the leading table grape of France, where it is little used for wine. In Germany the Gutedel wines are made from this variety, as are the Fendant wines of Switzerland. In California it is not usually flavorful enough for wines of quality.

Ugni Blanc (Oon-yeé Blon)

Also known as St. Emilion in the Charente region of France, where it is grown for the distillation of cognac, Ugni Blanc is the same as the Trebbiano of Tuscany in Italy, where it is well known especially for producing white Chianti. It has nothing in common, save the name, with the clarets of the St. Emilion district of Bordeaux.

California Ugni Blanc is mostly neutral in character and best suited for blending. It has occasionally been bottled as a varietal type.

Veltliner (Velt'-leener)

The Red Veltliner grape can produce a pleasing white wine, somewhat similar to Traminer. The grapes have a slight pink blush when ripe, which explains their name, although they produce only white juice. The varietal wine, called simply Veltliner, was produced at one time in the Santa Clara Valley.

GENERICS

California White Table Wine

A wine so labeled, with no further indication of type, is usually an inexpensive light white wine of no pronounced character. Some producers bottle a standard-quality wine under this name. It can vary from dry to sweet, according to brand.

Vino Bianco

The name given in this *Guide* to the mellow and slightly sweet type of wine, similar to the homemade product. It is the white counterpart of the popular Vino Rosso (see there) and is labeled with varying Italian names.

California White Chianti

This wine is marketed, like its much more popular red type, in raffia covered bottles. In Italy white Chianti is produced from Trebbiano and Malvasia bianca grapes. In California it is derived from various grapes; production is limited.

CALIFORNIA WHITE MUSCAT TYPES

These wines are grouped separately on account of their muscat character and because they are mostly too sweet for use as table wines, even if so classified, owing to their low alcohol content.

They are best suited to service as light dessert wines or in the afternoon or evening with cookies or cake. They should be chilled.

VARIETALS

Malvasia Bianca (White Malvasia)

The grape is a muscat-flavored variety of the Malvasia vines which originated in Greece and are widely grown in Southern France, Italy, Spain, and Madeira, and to some extent in California.

Although generally better suited to the production of sweet dessert wines (see there), the Malvasia bianca grape can yield a sweet light wine of delicate bouquet and flavor, produced notably in Alameda and Santa Clara counties.

The wine is variously labeled by its correct name of Malvasia Bianca and as California Malvasia without indication of color. They should not be confused with the red Malvasia wines of table and dessert type (see there).

Muscat Canelli or Muscat Frontignan

A light and delicate sweet wine from this grape has at times been produced under the name of Moscato Amabile. The dessert wine is better known and then usually is labeled Muscat Frontignan (see there).

Orange Muscat

A light sweet wine from the Orange Muscat variety, rich in muscat aroma and flavor.

GENERICS

California Light Muscat

Any light wine of around 12 per cent alcohol produced from white muscat grapes without indication of variety. They are often produced from the Muscat of Alexandria grape and both sweet and very sweet types are made. They are sometimes labeled simply "California Light Sweet Wine."

Moscato Amabile

A generic name for the light, sweet, and delicate wines produced from the Muscat Canelli or other white muscat grapes.

Dry Muscat or Moscato Secco

As the name indicates, this is a dry white wine from muscat grapes. It has a limited appeal as the wine is easily harsh and the muscat character, which needs sweetness to bring out the flavor, is not apparent. Some dry muscat, however, is quite palatable. It is sometimes marketed in rhine-wine type bottles.

WHITE SPECIALTY WINES

American May Wine

May wine is a rhine or moselle, in which leaves of the sweet-scented woodruff, or waldmeister, herb have been infused. It is very popular in Germany, where it is traditionally served from a bowl cold, with fresh fruit in season, especially strawberries, floating in the wine.

American May wine is commercially available, made from a light California white wine which has been sweetened and flavored with woodruff.

California Retsina Wine

The Greeks, who were the first Europeans to make wine, used pine barrels in which to store it, as that wood is native to the country. In this manner they became used to the pine flavor which the wood transmitted to the wine. Later they started adding resin, or the pitch of pine trees, to their wines in the processing stage. This custom has survived to this day.

Retsina wine is produced in California in Fresno County from California white wine and with resin imported from Greece. It is made from ripe white grapes, the juice being fermented without the pomace in closed fermenting tanks for a period varying from sixty to ninety days. The resin is added during the second week of fermentation.

Retsina contains about 13 per cent alcohol, is dry, and has a special tang, appealing particularly to those of Greek descent or origin. It should be served chilled.

California Grape Wine

In the restricted sense this is a sweet and heavy-bodied white wine of low alcohol content and with a rather grapy taste. It should be served cold.

Many other wines, both white and red, indicate on the label that they are grape wines in the more general sense of the term.

IV

CALIFORNIA ROSÉ TABLE WINES

CHART OF THE MORE PROMINENT CALIFORNIA ROSÉ (PINK) TABLE WINES

Varietals	Generics
GRENACHE ROSÉ	Vin Rosé (Rosé Wine)
GAMAY ROSÉ	or
Grignolino Rosé	Rosé
Pinot Noir Rosé (a rarity)	

CALIFORNIA ROSÉ or pink table wines are, in general, light, fruity, tart, crisp, and bright reddish pink in color. They have known a great surge of popularity in recent years.

The finest California rosé wines are made by letting the dark skins of the grapes remain long enough in the fermenting vats for the wine to obtain the proper pink color. A few dark grapes automatically yield a light-colored wine which is then sometimes bottled as a rosé. The cheaper rosés are made simply by blending red and white wine together to the desired color.

The best known varietals include Grenache, Gamay, and Grignolino, while even the precious true Pinot noir grape is used for the purpose. The generic rosé wines are labeled either as "Vin Rosé" (Pink Wine) or simply as "Rosé."

Use and Service—All rosés are popular as light luncheon or supper wines, with all simple and informal meals and on picnics. They are best when served very cold. Chill for about three hours.

A rosé also makes a fine cooling drink when served in a tall glass with ice.

VARIETALS

GRENACHE ROSÉ (Gre-nash′ Ro-zay′)

The Grenache is the grape responsible for the famous French Rosé wines from the Tavel region in the Rhône Valley.

In California the Grenache is best suited to the coolest regions of the northern coastal counties where it yields one of the most typical and best rosé wines of California. While generally dry, some semisweet Grenache Rosé is also produced.

GAMAY ROSÉ

Produced from one of the varieties of the Gamay grape, this is an excellent rosé table wine, hailing notably from the Napa Valley. It is also used in a number of generic rosés, bottled under special names thought up by the winegrower.

Grignolino Rosé

The Grignolino grape yields a light-colored red wine and with little effort, therefore, a rosé type of wine can be produced from it. This popular varietal is mostly identified with the Cucamonga district in San Bernardino County.

Cabernet Rosé

The Cabernet Sauvignon grape is used in a number of generic rosés. Plans are to produce it also as a varietal.

Pinot Noir Rosé

A rare and choice rosé table wine produced in the mountains of the Santa Clara Valley.

GENERIC

California Vin Rosé or Rosé

These wines are produced from a variety of grapes including those used for the varietal types and from a number of others such as Zinfandel, Mourestel, and Valdepeñas. They are often marketed under a special name. The lesser grades of generic rosés are simply blends of red and white wines.

While the more typical and best rosé wines are dry in character, quite a few are on the sweeter side, containing a slight amount of residual sugar. Some even are quite sweet.

CHART OF THE MORE PROMINENT CALIFORNIA SPARKLING WINES

Method of Production	Sparkling Wine Type	
Naturally fermented in the bottle (Champagne process)	Champagne *Brut*	really dry
	Extra Dry	medium dry
	Sec, or *Dry*	to
	Demi-Sec	rather sweet
	Sweet	quite sweet
or	Pink Champagne or Champagne Rosé	medium dry to sweet
Naturally fermented in glass-lined vats (Bulk [Charmat] process)	Red Champagne and Sparkling Burgundy	on the dry side on the sweet side
	Sparkling Muscat or Moscato Spumante	sweet

V

CALIFORNIA SPARKLING WINES

*T*HE HIGHEST-QUALITY California sparkling wines are produced according to the French champagne method, whereby the secondary fermentation takes place in the bottles in which the wines are sold. They include California champagnes from very dry to sweet, Red Champagne, Pink Champagne, Sparkling Burgundy, and Sparkling Muscat.

The same wine types are produced by the faster and less costly method whereby the secondary fermentation occurs in glass-lined vats, according to the so-called "Charmat" process, which is also of French origin. The law requires that champagne produced in this manner be designated as bulk process on the label.

In both methods indicated above the wines have been fermented naturally to obtain their sparkle. Wines where the sparkle has been induced by artificial means are known as Carbonated or as Effervescent wines and cannot be labeled as Sparkling.

All sparkling wines are expensive, a major element in the cost to the consumer being the very high federal excise tax, which is twenty times that on table wines, taxing in effect not so much the wine as the bubbles.

Use and Service—Sparkling wines, especially champagne, are the appropriate beverages for all festive occasions. Champagne is the wine par excellence at a formal dinner when a dry type is most suitable throughout the meal or a sweeter one with the dessert. Champagne is traditional for weddings, christenings, both of infants and of ships, anniversaries, New Year's Eve parties, dances and balls, and for all formal receptions.

A very dry champagne makes a first-class aperitif, while all types can be served at any time of day or night, with or without accompanying refreshments. It is the lightest and gayest of beverages and the easiest of all to assimilate.

Sparkling wines should be chilled but not served too cold, as often happens. Two or three hours in the refrigerator are sufficient, chilling the sweeter types longer than the drier. For a private supper party chilling champagne in a wine bucket with ice is an effective method; twenty minutes to half an hour is enough, twirling the bottle occasionally for even chilling as well as for effect.

CALIFORNIA CHAMPAGNE

The finest California champagnes come from the counties of Sonoma, Santa Clara, Alameda, and Napa in the northern coastal region. Good bottle-fermented champagnes, especially of the sweeter types, are also produced in the Cucamonga district of Southern California. Bulk-fermented champagnes of quality are made in both these regions as well as in the inland valley districts.

Pinot noir and Pinot Chardonnay, the grapes used to make the great champagnes of France, also yield the very best champagnes of California. Other grapes used for high-quality California champagnes are Pinot blanc, Semillon, Sauvignon blanc, White Riesling, Sylvaner, and Folle blanche. Lesser qualities are produced from Ugni blanc, French Colombard, Sauvignon vert, Green Hungarian, and many others. It is a great pity that only rarely the grape varieties from which California champagne has been produced are indicated on the label.

In California, as elsewhere, a so-called dosage or liqueuring is added to the finished wine before inserting the final cork. This dosage consists of brandy, wine, and sugar, the amount depending on the degree of sweetness the producer desires to give the champagne.

Now it is a peculiar fact that a great many people, in America as in Europe, like to order a dry or very dry champagne while they actually prefer the wine itself to be on the less dry side. This explains why a champagne labeled *"Extra Dry"* is only relatively so and one marked *"Sec,"* or *"Dry,"* is usually quite sweet. This system works out to the great satisfaction of all concerned.

The five designations most commonly used by California wine growers to indicate the dryness or sweetness of their champagnes are: *Brut, Extra Dry, Sec,* or *Dry, Demi-Sec* and *Sweet.* No official regulations exist for the labeling of these types, so they vary according to the individual producer. The designations themselves are the same as those used by the Champagne producers of France. The specifications for the judges at the California State and Los Angeles County fairs recognize only three types: *Brut, Demi-Sec,* and *Sweet.* Intermediate types are entered and judged in the most appropriate class.

California champagne should be straw-colored or pale golden, its body light to medium, and its bouquet fragrant. The finest of the bottle-fermented champagnes are always higher in quality and character than bulk-fermented brands; the latter, however, can be very good indeed and have the advantage of being less expensive.

California Brut Champagne

This type is the driest of all and the most difficult to produce properly, as the natural acidity, causing the typical "clean" sensation of champagne to the palate, is not compensated or masked by added sweetening. A good Brut Champagne should taste absolutely dry without being acid. It is the kind most highly prized by experts, connoisseurs, and gourmets.

California Extra Dry Champagne

A popular type, less dry than the *Brut* and really in a class by itself. It is the ideal compromise between the desire for a very dry labeling and a not so very dry wine; the perfect all-purpose champagne. It is sometimes labeled *"Extra-Sec."*

California Sec Champagne or Dry Champagne

Medium sweet—or medium dry, if one prefers to express it that way—and the type of champagne which appeals to the majority of people.

California Demi-Sec Champagne

Similar to the *Sec* or *Dry;* sweeter, if there is a difference.

California Sweet or Doux Champagne

The sweetest type of champagne; a dessert wine.

Champagne producers usually market a few of the types described above. California champagne, with no indication of type, is in the medium-dry or medium-sweet class.

California Pink Champagne or Champagne Rosé

A pink or rosé sparkling wine of the champagne order, either bottle-fermented or produced according to the Charmat-type process. Its color should be bright pink. The wine varies from medium dry to quite sweet and is favored especially by the ladies.

The name "Oeil de Perdrix" or "Partridge Eye" has been given to this type of champagne in California. In France the term refers to the pinkish tinge sometimes acquired by champagne and other white wines when made exclusively from dark grapes.

California Red Champagne or Champagne Rouge

The name is a relative newcomer to the champagne family. It was invented by winegrowers who felt that a top-quality, bottle-fermented, red sparkling wine should have a name other than "Sparkling Burgundy," as the regulations do not require the latter, as with champagne, to indicate on the label whether it is bottle-fermented or produced by bulk process.

In order to do its name justice, Red Champagne or Champagne

Rouge should be bottle-fermented and produced from a substantial percentage of Pinot noir grapes to give the wine the desired Pinot character and flavor, traditionally associated with all the better champagnes.

OTHER CALIFORNIA SPARKLING WINES

These sparkling wines can be either fermented in the bottle or in bulk, but the method of production does not have to be indicated, as with California champagne, on the label. When they are bottle-fermented, however, the fact is usually designated.

California Sparkling Burgundy

The most popular California sparkling wine after champagne. It is produced from a variety of grapes, of which Pinot noir, Carignane, Mondeuse, and Petite Sirah are among the favored.

The wine is blended to quality and does not usually possess the character of any particular grape variety. It is medium red in color, medium-bodied, and often on the sweet side.

California Sparkling Muscat or Moscato Spumante

Produced from one or more of the muscat grape varieties, of which the Muscat Canelli, or Frontignan, is especially desirable for the purpose.

Sparkling Muscat, or Muscatel, as it is also called, should always possess the distinctive muscat aroma and flavor. The wine is medium- to full-bodied and either sweet or very sweet.

For the Italian trade the wine is usually marketed as Moscato Spumante or Gran Spumante, after the well-known Asti Spumante and other *spumante,* or sparkling, wines of Italy.

California Sparkling Malvasia

A white varietal sparkling wine made from the Malvasia bianca grape with a delicate muscat character and sweet.

CALIFORNIA EFFERVESCENT WINES

Classified as such are all California wines with a sparkle but which cannot, by law, be labeled as "Sparkling" wines. The best known are the so-called "Carbonated" wines, where the sparkle is caused by artificial carbonation. While the best of these measure up favorably in quality and character with some of the naturally fermented sparkling wines, they will lose their sparkle more rapidly once the bottle has been opened.

California Carbonated Burgundy

The usual name for the red wine of this type.

California Carbonated Moselle

The usual name for the white wine of the group.

Crackling wines, the name sometimes given to those wines, both red and white, which have a light, natural sparkle, as do the *pétillant* wines of France and the *frizzante* of Italy, are not marketed in California at present on account of present high taxation, but may well have a great future before them.

CHART OF THE MORE PROMINENT CALIFORNIA APERITIF AND DESSERT WINES

Varietals	Generics	Aperitif or Dessert
PALOMINO	*California Sherry (regular and flor)* Pale Dry Sherry Cocktail Sherry (dry) Golden Sherry (medium) Cream Sherry (sweet)	aperitif aperitif aperitif dessert
Tinta Madeira	*California Port* Port Ruby Port Tawny Port White Port	dessert and aperitif dessert
Muscat Frontignan or Muscat Canelli	*California Muscat and Muscatel* Muscatel Black Muscat	dessert dessert
	California Angelica Angelica	dessert
Flame Tokay	*California Tokay* Tokay	dessert
	California Vermouth Dry Vermouth Light Dry Vermouth Sweet Vermouth	cocktail and aperitif

VI

CALIFORNIA APERITIF AND
DESSERT WINES

*T*HE WINES of this group constitute about three fourths of California's wine production. They are sometimes called "Sweet" wines and although most of them have a high sugar content, there are dry types among them as well and all the variations in between. In this *Guide* they are grouped together as "Aperitif and Dessert Wines" for the simple reason that they are all used either as aperitifs before the meal, or as so-called "dessert wines."

The term "aperitif" is used in preference to "appetizer," as the latter can also mean light, appetite-inducing foods. The expression "dessert wine" traditionally means that the wine in question is suitable with the dessert on account of its sweetness. In practice such wines are served even more frequently for light entertainment in the afternoon or evening. For this reason they are also called "occasional wines," "entertainment wines," and "refreshment wines."

It must be noted that some of the sweeter dessert wines are commonly consumed, both in the United States and abroad, as aperitifs, notably the ports, the sweeter sherries, and sweet vermouth. Customs vary according to national and individual taste. Both the traditional service of each type of wine will be indicated as well as its more general use.

Most aperitif and dessert wines contain about 20 per cent alcohol by volume. Some kinds, with a slightly lower percentage of around

18 per cent alcohol, are produced especially for sacramental purposes of the Roman Catholic and Protestant churches and for certain states with local restrictions. The latter are labeled with the word "Light" preceding the name of the wine, such as "Light Sherry" and "Light Port." Some growers advocate the marketing of such wines for the general public, requiring first a change in the present laws.

The appellation of origin and the varietal designation are not nearly as usual with the California aperitif and dessert wines as with the table types. Most of them are labeled simply as "California" wines and with the exception, in some brands, of the Palomino, from which all the finer sherries are derived, of the Tinta varieties used for some excellent ports, of the Muscat Frontignan, which yields outstanding muscats, and of a few minor instances, mention of varietal derivation is absent.

The answer to the question of which are the best California aperitif and dessert wines lies, therefore, mostly with the few growers or producers marketing the varietal types. High-quality wines are produced in the great inland valley region, in Southern California, and in the northern coastal region, often from inland valley grapes. Standard-quality wines form the bulk of production, with Fresno and Lodi the two most famous centers of the inland valley region.

The finest of the California aperitif and dessert wines—even if more correctly judged on their own merits—compare favorably with imported products of the same class and are then, like the California table and sparkling wines, better buys, as they are less costly.

The standard-quality wines are mostly good, sound, inexpensive wines which do not pretend to do anything more than to fulfill their own place in worthy fashion. The name of a producer of standing, nationally advertised, is a useful guide on the label.

The aperitif and dessert wines of California are grouped in the *Guide* according to their main classifications. The three most important ones, by far, are California Sherry, California Port, and California Muscat and Muscatel. Two minor groups are formed by California Angelica and Tokay. Vermouth is in a classification by itself.

CALIFORNIA SHERRY

The main characteristic of sherry, wherever it is produced, is its more or less pronounced nutty flavor, and it is to this end that the grower develops his basic wine. Most suitable for its production in California, as in its native Spain, is the Palomino grape, also known in some California winegrowing districts as the Golden Chasselas or Napa Golden Chasselas.

It is from the Palomino that all the finer California sherries are derived and the fact is then often indicated on the labeling. Other grape varieties for sherry production include the Mission, fermented off the skins, as it is a dark grape, and the prolific Thompson Seedless.

California sherries are produced by two entirely different methods. The regular sherries, as this *Guide* terms them, are the result of the heating or "baking" method, similar to that used for Madeira wines in the island of that name off the west coast of Africa. California *flor* sherries owe their special character to a process resembling that used in Spain for Spanish Sherries of the drier types. Some California sherries are the product of blending both types of wine.

Most California sherries are produced by the heating method. The basic wine is fermented to the desired degree of dryness, brandy being added to check the fermentation, as in all wines of the dessert type. It is then heated in oak or redwood containers for a number of months up to a year and at a temperature of about 120° Fahrenheit. This takes place either in a hot cellar or with the containing vats heated by coils and at times by the warmth of the sun. When the process is completed the wine is gradually cooled and then aged for the desired period of time. It is the oxidation which takes place during the heating of the wine which gives it the typical character associated with sherry.

In the *flor* process, which is more and more being adopted in California, a special kind of secondary fermentation is induced in the basic wine by a species of yeast, for long considered to be a strain of *Mycoderma vini,* but later identified as belonging to the genus of Saccharomyces. This yeast covers the wine, as it is stored in open vats, with a flowerlike crust—hence the term *flor* or flower —and imparts to the wine, by some mysterious alchemy of nature, the characteristic light, nutty tang of all fine sherry. When the wine is fully impregnated, it is brought up to the desired alcoholic strength and blended and aged by the so-called "Solera" system.

A number of California wineries have developed their own Solera systems, which vary considerably, resembling to a greater or lesser degree the method by which sherries are aged and blended in Spain. A Solera consists basically of an arrangement of communicating barrels or vats lying in superimposed rows, four or five tiers high. At periodic intervals the matured sherry is drawn from the bottom row of barrels to be bottled, this row then being replenished with wine from the row above and so on to the top range, which in turn is filled with new wine. In this manner the young wine mixes and ages with the older in one perpetual blend while the Solera itself has been started with aged wine in the first place. The finest California sherries, with a few exceptions, are produced by the *flor* and Solera systems.

California sherries, both regular and *flor,* come in three main types, dry, medium, and sweet. There is only one varietal, the Palomino, from which grape the better generics are also derived.

Varietal

Palomino Sherry

Produced principally or exclusively from the Palomino grape and can be either dry (Pale Dry or Cocktail), medium (Golden) or sweet (Cream). The finest are the *flor* Palominos, aged and blended by a Solera system.

Generics

California Pale Dry Sherry or Cocktail Sherry

The drier wines, varying from very dry and very pale to dry and light amber. Some producers bottle both a Pale Dry and a Cocktail Sherry, the former being then the paler of the two.

California Sherry or Golden Sherry

The medium-dry or medium-sweet types, golden amber in color. California Sherry, without further indication, falls in this class, as does Amber Sherry.

California Sweet Sherry or Cream Sherry

The sweeter and sweetest types, usually of a dark amber color.

Use and Service—Dry sherries are typical aperitifs, served before the meal. Many, however, prefer the medium types for that purpose, and some even the sweet wines. Dry sherry can be served at a formal lunch or dinner with the soup.

All sherries are useful as refreshment wines in the afternoon or evening; the sweet types are traditional with a sweet dessert or after dinner.

Sherry can be served either at room temperature or slightly chilled, stored for an hour in the refrigerator. It is much used in cooking, when the finer wines are preferable, with the most flavor. Sherry also makes an excellent base for flips and cobblers.

CALIFORNIA PORT

Port has been made in California at least since the days of the Gold Rush and is one of the most popular of all dessert wines. Conforming to the present tendency in the American taste, it is, on the whole, sweeter and deeper red in color than the red Port wines from Portugal.

VARIETALS AND GENERICS

California port is produced from many different grapes, only a few of which are used for the wine in its native Portugal. To this selected group belong the Tinta Madeira, Tinta Cão, Alvarelhão, and Touriga. Another is the Trousseau, which has been identified with the Portuguese Bastardo. This grape was once quite popular in California as a varietal, but is now generally considered to lack sufficient color for that purpose, owing to the current preference for darker wines. There are plans, however, to produce Trousseau Port in Contra Costa County.

The grapes most commonly used for California ports include the Carignane, Grenache, Mission, Petite Sirah, Valdepeñas, and Zinfandel, while the Alicante Bouschet, Alicante Ganzin, a crossbreed, Grand noir, and Salvador are useful for the color they contribute in blending.

California ports are generally sweet, rich, heavy-bodied, and fruity, but often rather neutral in flavor unless produced from the finer and more flavorful grape varieties. Older ports, and those where the better brandy has been used in their production, are naturally smoother and mellower.

The three generic names for the red wines of this group are California Port, California Ruby Port, and California Tawny Port. A few varietals have recently been produced, notably Tinta Madeira and Tinta Cão in Madera County. When blended with other grapes, with either or both of the Tinta varieties predominating, they are known as "Tinta Ports." Vintage Ports, matured partly in the bottle and derived from grapes harvested in one particular year, are available in Sonoma County and plans are to produce them also in Madera County. When matured in the bottle, port will throw a natural deposit, so these fine wines should be poured carefully or decanted before serving.

California White Port, a different wine entirely, is discussed with this group only on account of the name.

California Port and California Ruby Port

There is little difference, if any, between these two wines. Most of those, labeled simply as "Port," are ruby red and could equally well be marketed under the latter designation.

California Tawny Port

This can be a port wine which has been aged for some years in small oak casks and thereby acquired a russet or tawny shade. Such wines will be fully mature and soft and mellow.

It can also be a wine made from grapes such as the Trousseau, which naturally yield a wine of a tawny hue.

In the least expensive brands there is little or no difference between the tawny and other red port types.

California White Port

A light-straw-colored, medium-bodied, sweet dessert wine with neutral flavor. It is usually not as sweet as Angelica, which it otherwise often resembles. The wine is made both from white grapes, including the Thompson Seedless, and from dark varieties, such as the Grenache and Mission, fermented off the skins. Sometimes a decolorizing process is applied, as the typical coloring of the wine is very light.

Use and Service—Port, whatever its type, can be served at any time during the day or evening. In British countries it is traditional with the sweet, or dessert, always passing the bottle to the left.

In many countries, including the United States, the less sweet port wines are also popular as aperitifs. At the table it is the typical wine to serve at the end of dinner, with cheese, fruit, and nuts, as well as with the dessert.

Port is served at room temperature. It is much used in cooking, especially in ham dishes and in fruit and other desserts. It makes a good base for flips and cobblers, as well as for negusses and sangarees.

CALIFORNIA MUSCAT AND MUSCATEL

These are among the sweetest of the California dessert wines and the most in demand after sherry and port.

Muscat wines are of very ancient origin and were mentioned in literature more than 2000 years ago. They have always been great favorites and are produced in many parts of the world. The great center of California's muscat cultivation lies in the San Joaquin Valley, where the grapes attain their maximum sugar content, owing to the warm climate.

Standard-quality California muscat wines are usually called "Muscatel" while the finer wines are often labeled as "Muscat" or with the varietal designation. All possess the typical aroma and flavor of muscat grapes and are sweet, rich, and fruity.

Varietals include Muscat Frontignan or Muscat Canelli and Malvasia Bianca in the whites and Aleatico and Malvasia in the reds. Black Muscat (or Black Muscatel) and Red Muscat are names given to wines produced from dark muscat grapes.

Varietals (white)

Muscat Frontignan or Muscat Canelli

One of the finest California muscats, delicate, golden or russet amber in color, and very sweet, with a concentrated muscat perfume and flavor. It is produced notably in the Livermore, Napa, and Santa Clara valleys.

The French name is derived from the town of Frontignan in Southern France, well known for its muscat wines. The grape originated in Canelli, near Asti, in the Italian province of Piedmont, where it is famed for some of Italy's best muscat wines, both still and sparkling, including Asti Spumante.

In California the grape is best known under its Italian name of Muscat Canelli, or Muscat di Canelli, while the wine it yields is known under both its Italian name and the French appellation of Muscat Frontignan, or Muscat de Frontignan.

Malvasia Bianca (White Malvasia)

The dessert wine from the muscat-flavored grape of the same name. It must not be confused with the table wine of that name (see there) or with the red Malvasia wines of both table and dessert type (see there).

Malvasia Bianca is produced as a dessert wine in the Napa Valley.

VARIETALS (RED)

Aleatico

A soft, fruity, aromatic dessert wine, light red in color and sometimes called a red muscatel. It is not often met with, as plantings of the grape are limited. Some is produced in the Cucamonga district.

The grape has also been used to produce a table wine of the same name (see there).

Malvasia (Red Malvasia)

Another light red dessert wine produced notably in the Cucamonga district. Not to be confused with the white Malvasia dessert wine (see there) or the red and white Malvasia table wines (see there).

GENERICS

California Muscatel

This wine varies from light to dark amber and from sweet to very sweet. In order to achieve its full muscat character it should be made from a considerably higher percentage of muscat grapes than the required legal minimum of 51 per cent. For the purpose of this *Guide* the wine is generic in so far as the particular muscat variety from which it has been produced is not indicated.

The Muscat of Alexandria, pre-eminently a raisin grape, is the variety most generally used for producing the wine labeled "California Muscatel." The grape does extremely well in the San Joaquin Valley and in Southern California, particularly in the Escondido district in San Diego County. The more aromatic Orange Muscat yields higher quality muscatels, as do the delicate Muscat Canelli, or Frontignan, and the Malvasia bianca, the latter two being marketed under their varietal names (see there).

Black Muscat or **Black Muscatel**

The name given to high-quality red muscatels, derived from various grapes, depending on the grower. It is produced notably in Santa Clara County from Muscat Hamburg grapes and in Southern Alameda from a blend of Muscat Hamburg and Aleatico.

Use and Service—Muscats and muscatels are most appropriate when served in the afternoon and evening with cookies, cake, or sandwiches, or at dinner with a sweet dessert. The white types are also used in cooking, especially with ham, and make a refreshing drink when served in a tall glass with ice and a slice of lemon, the acidity of which perfectly counterbalances the sweetness of the wine.

CALIFORNIA ANGELICA

The wine, said to have been named after the city of Los Angeles, is the sweetest of the California dessert wines. It is light to dark amber in color, full-bodied, smooth, and fruity with no special varietal character. It fulfills the demand for a very sweet, liqueur-like wine and often resembles California White Port, though it is usually sweeter than the latter.

Angelica has been traditionally associated with the Mission grape, from which it has been made since the early days of California wine making. Other grapes used for its production include the Grenache, Palomino, or Golden Chasselas, and Thompson Seedless. The excessive sweetness is obtained by arresting the fermentation of the wine at an early stage by the addition of brandy, so that the grapes retain the maximum of their sugar content.

Use and Service—In the afternoon or evening for those who like an extremely sweet wine.

CALIFORNIA TOKAY

A medium-sweet dessert wine, amber pink in color and with a slight nutty flavor. It is often a blend of angelica, dry sherry to reduce the sweetness, and port to achieve the desired pink tinge. Production is relatively small and considerably less than that of any other of the better-known dessert wines.

California Tokay has nothing in common with the renowned Tokay, Tokaj, or Tokai wines of Hungary, which are naturally sweet wines of low alcoholic content, derived mainly from the Furmint grape.

Nor is the Flame Tokay necessarily used for the production of California Tokay. In Lodi, however, the center of a vast Flame Tokay cultivation, the wine is sometimes made varietally from that grape. Flame Tokay is one of California's leading table-grape varieties and has a special appeal on account of its brilliant light red color. A native of Algeria, its Arabic name is Ahmeur bou Ahmeur.

Use and Service—In the afternoon and evening with cookies, cake, or sandwiches.

CALIFORNIA VERMOUTH

Most American vermouths are made with California white wine as a base, while much of the flavoring material is imported. The basic wine is fortified and either infused and later filtered or simply has an extract added to it. It is then aged, sometimes in small chestnut barrels.

Vermouth is named after its most typical flavoring ingredient, wormwood, derived from the woody herb of that name, called *Wermuth* in German and *Artemisia absinthium* in Latin. For the production of vermouth only a mild form of the essential oil of this shrub is used, a much more potent form of which gave its name to the cordial known as Absinthe. Besides wormwood a host of other flavoring ingredients give vermouth its aromatic and pungent character, including the berries, roots, seeds, peel, gum, bark, flowers, leaves, dried fruit, and other parts of a number of herbs, plants, shrubs, and lichens. Exactly which substances are used depends on the producer and the brand.

There are two main kinds of California Vermouth, the dry and the sweet. Recently a very light and very dry type has won separate recognition.

California Dry Vermouth

Dry vermouth is also known as French vermouth, as it originated and became famous in France. California Dry Vermouth is pale golden or light amber in color and averages about 18 per cent alcohol by volume. It is made with a neutral white wine base of relatively high acid content which is fortified and blended, about half an ounce of herb mixture or extract equivalent being added per gallon of wine to obtain the desired character.

California Light Dry Vermouth

This very light and very dry type of vermouth was created because of the fashion to order an ever lighter and drier martini cocktail. Were this trend to develop to its logical conclusion, a vermouthless dry martini would be the final result or one with only a soupçon of one of the world's oldest wines, to the detriment of the vermouth producers. The latter therefore developed, and with success, a special type of extremely pale and extremely dry vermouth, light and dry enough to satisfy the most rigorous advocates of the driest and palest of dry martinis.

California Light Dry Vermouth has the same alcoholic content as the regular dry type. It is variously labeled as Extra Dry, Very Dry, Triple Dry, and as White Vermouth. Under this last name it must not be confused with the Vermouth Bianco of Italy, a *sweet* white vermouth not produced, so far, in California, to the *Guide's* best knowledge.

California Sweet Vermouth

Sweet vermouth is also known as Italian vermouth, as it originated in that country, where a number of world-famous brands are produced. It is reddish to dark amber in color, very aromatic and sweet, and contains on the average 16 per cent alcohol by volume.

Muscatel or angelica is used as base, to which from one to one and a half ounces of herbs are added per gallon to give the wine its typically rich and aromatic character. It is aged in the wood, preferably in oak, for only a short period of time to prevent loss of aroma through volatilization.

Use and Service—Dry vermouth is used in many cocktails, especially martinis and gibsons. It is also consumed straight as an aperitif and is mixed in Vermouth-Cassis. It makes a refreshing long drink with any of the sweet berry wines with ice, sparkling water and lemon.

Light dry vermouth makes the driest and palest martinis and gibsons.

Sweet vermouth is used in Manhattans and many other cocktails and makes a good aperitif when served neat, with or without a lemon rind.

Dry and sweet vermouth, half and half, constitute a popular aperitif served with ice in an old-fashioned glass. Both types, also, are used in cooking to give the dish an aromatic flavor, the sweet vermouth being quite popular in preparing chicken.

OTHER CALIFORNIA APERITIF AND DESSERT WINES

Grouped together here are the least known California wines of both kinds, some of which are recent innovations and others are obsolete.

California Aperitif Wines

Various herb-flavored wines have been marketed of the Dubonnet, Byrrh, St. Raphaël, and similar French aperitif types. They include both red and white wines, none of which, so far, has proved very successful. Other producers have tried to approximate the Campari type of Italian *aperitivo* with equal lack of success.

It is not improbable that eventually California will produce original aperitif wines of quality, based on special and new formulas, to fulfill the demand for good California wines of this type.

California Grenache (Dessert Wine)

A fruity varietal dessert wine from the Grenache grape, produced in Fresno and possibly elsewhere. Considering the great popularity of the rosé table wines, it is not surprising that Grenache dessert wines were also created. It is still too soon to judge whether they, too, will find wide and ready acceptance.

California Madeira

A dessert type of restricted importance, consisting of a blend of sherries or of sherry and angelica, in an effort to approximate the character of the Madeira wines from the island of that name.

California Malaga

An ill-defined type of California dessert wine of the sherry order and now obsolete. It has been supplanted, in name, by American Malaga (see there).

California Marsala

Another dessert type of minor importance, amber to brown in color, and the result of a sherry blend trying to approach the character of the Marsala wines from Sicily, so popular as aperitif and dessert wines and in cooking. An herb-flavored Marsala aperitif is also produced.

California Palomino

A varietal aperitif produced from the Palomino grape of around 17 per cent alcohol, making it ineligible to be labeled as California Sherry, as the latter requires a minimum content of 19.5 by volume.

American Grape (Dessert Wine)

Although most "grape wines" of the Concord type are of table-wine strength, some have also been produced of the dessert type, containing around 20 per cent alcohol by volume.

VII

CALIFORNIA FRUIT WINES

𝓕RUIT WINES are produced by fermentation from fruit other than grapes. Most fruit wines average about 12 per cent alcohol by volume, but a few types are also marketed at 20 per cent alcohol, the latter being produced by the addition of fruit brandy or spirits from the same kind of fruit from which the wine was made.

Berry wines are fruit wines derived from a number of berries, of which the blackberry, boysenberry, elderberry, loganberry, raspberry, red currant, and strawberry are the most popular. Fruit wines other than those made from berries include notably those produced from cherries and apples.

Fruit wines had been available in California to a limited extent when Robert H. Gibson, in the belief that an extensive market for berry and other fruit wines could be developed, entered this field on a large scale in the late nineteen forties. His venture met with success and he became the modern California pioneer in the field. Other wineries followed suit, either by added production or by purchasing fruit wines and marketing them under their own brands. The importance of fruit wines was acknowledged by the California fairs, where they are included in the yearly wine judgings.

There are no set rules used in the labeling of the origin of berry and other fruit wines. Wines produced from fruit grown in California can legally be designated on the label with the name of the state. Several fruit wineries, however, frequently do not use the word "California" in connection with their labels. Some use the term "American," notably for those wines produced from out-of-state fruit, and many labels refer only to the fruit itself without any designation of origin.

BERRY WINES

California has the largest berry production of any state in the country. All berry wines are highly flavored, fruity, and sweet, each with the typical character and taste of the particular berry from which it is derived.

Blackberry Wine

The blackberry, or bramble, is a native of the temperate regions and is particularly abundant on the Pacific coast, where it grows from British Columbia to Southern California.

There are over 600 named varieties of blackberries, of which the boysenberry is the best known for wine production (see there).

Blackberry wine is produced at both 12 and 20 per cent alcohol by volume.

Blackberry Wine of the Boysenberry Variety

Boysenberries constitute over three fourths of the cultivated blackberry varieties grown in the United States and about 90 per cent of those raised in California. The boysenberry is practically black when ripe, with a slight blue or purple tinge. The wine it yields is the most popular of all berry wines, possessing an especially fine aroma and flavor.

The name of the boysenberry has been the subject of much controversy. While it was generally recognized that it was a blackberry variety, the alcohol-tax authorities objected to the use of the blackberry name in conjunction with it. Robert H. Gibson, together with several California berry growers associations, entered into litigation to protect the standing of the boysenberry, considered the finest of the blackberry varieties. During this litigation the origin of the boysenberry was brought out.

About 1920 John Lubben, a saloon operator of Alameda, received some rootings of the shrub from an unidentified customer who ran a nursery, and Lubben planted them at his ranch near St. Helena in Napa County. The berry's superior qualities were soon recognized, becoming a favorite under the name of lubbenberry. One of Lubben's employees on the ranch was Rudolph Boysen, who later moved to Anaheim, near Los Angeles, taking a supply of young lubbenberry plants with him. In about 1933 Boysen showed the plants to Walter Knott, who sold produce from his ranch at a roadside near Buena Park. Knott realized the special qualities of the berry, raised it in large numbers, and renamed it boysenberry in honor of the man who brought him the first plants.

The court decided that while the tax official in question had the right to make the ruling—a right which Gibson and the berry growers had disputed—the ruling itself was an incorrect one. Rather than proceed with further litigation a compromise was reached with a new ruling of the Tax Bureau, affirming that it would be correct and permissible to call the wine "Blackberry Wine of the Boysenberry Variety." The nationwide publicity given to the case naturally proved of great value to the sales of berry wines in general and of that of the boysenberry varietal in particular.

Blackberry Wine of the Boysenberry Variety is produced both at 12 and at 20 per cent alcohol by volume.

Elderberry Wine

This wine is made from the umbrella-shaped purple berry clusters of the American, or sweet, elder, which grows in moist soil from Manitoba east to Nova Scotia and south to Texas and Florida.

Elderberry wine is purplish red in color and has the typical tangy flavor of the fruit. It is marketed at an alcoholic strength of 12 per cent.

Loganberry Wine

The loganberry is a vigorous plant with bright red, tart, and highly flavored berries. While belonging to the over-all class of bush berries, or Rubus, it is not a blackberry, although it has sometimes been called the logan blackberry. The view that it is hybrid of the wild blackberry of the Pacific coast and of the American red raspberry has also been disputed.

What is certain is that the loganberry was raised by Judge J. H. Logan from seed in his garden at Santa Cruz, California, in 1881 and was named after him. The loganberry is grown commercially in large quantities in the states of Oregon and Washington. Luther Burbank, the famed botanist of Santa Rosa, Sonoma County, originated a similar plant, called the Phenomenal.

Loganberry wine is brilliant red in color and has a pronounced fruity flavor of its own. It is produced at 12 per cent alcohol by volume.

Raspberry Wine

This wine is derived from the red raspberry and possesses the delicate aroma and flavor of that fruit. Its alcoholic strength is 12 per cent.

Red Currant Wine

Produced from the small tangy berries of the red currant shrub, from which the popular jelly of that name is also made. The wine is light red in color, less sweet than most other berry wines, and contains 12 per cent alcohol by volume.

Strawberry Wine

In California strawberries are raised notably in the Santa Clara Valley, where much of the wine derived from that fruit is also produced. Strawberry wine is delicately flavored and is marketed at an alcoholic strength of 12 per cent.

OTHER FRUIT WINES

Grouped together here are those fruit wines derived from fruit other than berries. Of these cherry wine and apple wine are the most popular. Pear wine, sometimes called perry, and peach wine have also been produced.

Apple Wine

California apple wine is made principally from the Gravenstein apple, which is especially well suited for the making of wine because of its fine flavor, high sugar content, and juiciness. It is grown largely in the vicinity of Santa Rosa and Sebastopol in Sonoma County.

Apple wine can also be designated as cider, although this term usually indicates the unfermented and non-alcoholic juice of apples.

Although some apple wine of low alcoholic strength has been produced, notably during the war, it is generally agreed that, to make a satisfactory quality which will remain stable after being bottled, it should be 20 per cent alcohol by volume.

Cherry Wine

Cherry wine has become increasingly popular during recent years. Most of the better cherry wine is made from the sour or pie-type cherry, which gives the wine a brilliant red color and a strong fruity flavor. It is marketed at 12 per cent alcohol by volume.

Use and Service of Fruit Wines—All fruit wines are at their best when chilled, to bring out the full character and flavor. They can be served in the afternoon or evening as refreshing and flavorful beverages, either straight or with ice and sparkling water.

Berry wines can also be used in a fruit wine highball with the addition of a slice of lemon or with dry vermouth. Red currant wine makes an excellent beverage when mixed with vodka, charged water, and cracked ice in a tall glass.

Fruit and berry wines can be used to flavor fruit salads, puddings, ice cream, and fruit sauces.

Part Two

VIII

NOTABLE WINERIES BY REGION
AND DISTRICT

*T*HERE ARE TWO accepted ways of classifying the wine-growing districts of California.

The first, as worked out by the viticultural scientists of the University of California, is of primary interest to the growers. The method is based on the adaptability of the different grape varieties to the climatic conditions of the various wine-growing localities of the state. These have been grouped, regardless of location, according to the average degrees of heat above 50° Fahrenheit from April 1 to October 31, and correspond to what can be termed the cool, moderately cool, intermediate, moderately hot, and hot climatic zones.

The type of soil, naturally, also influences the grape as to the character of the wine it will yield. It is generally agreed, however, that the vine actually draws much of its nourishment from the surrounding atmosphere, the leaves of all plants nourishing themselves by breathing in the air.

The second system is the geographical one, which makes it possible to progress from region to region and from district to district or county. This makes it easy to follow the various winegrowing districts on a map and is the method utilized by this *Guide* (see Wine Map of California and regional maps).

The geographical system is also preferable for the purpose of this

Guide, as many wineries obtain grapes, and sometimes wines, from vineyards located in more than one climatic zone, be it from their own vines or from other growers, and either from the same general area or from other districts. Growers in the inland valley often produce table wines from grapes grown in the coastal districts, or blend them with the valley wines, and coastal growers often make dessert and even table types from grapes grown in the inland valley areas.

Whether or not a wine has been wholly produced by the grower is indicated on the labeling. The term "produced and bottled" means that a minimum of 75 per cent of the wine has been produced, that is, fermented into wine, by the grower whose name appears on the label. "Made and bottled" means that at least 10 per cent of the wine has actually been produced and that the balance has received some cellar treatment by the grower on the label, although it may not necessarily have been produced in his winery. The difference between the two methods of production does not necessarily indicate a graduation in quality among the wines, although wineries are naturally the proudest of those wines which they themselves have wholly grown and produced. Wineries which only market the latter are sometimes described as having a chateau operation.

The term "bottled" on the label means that the wine has merely been purchased and bottled.

"Winegrower," or "grower," is used in the *Guide* to designate both the producer who makes wine only from his own grapes and the one who buys outside grapes, and possibly wines, to complete the selection he wishes to market. The term "vintner" is restricted to the producer who does not own vineyards, but who buys wines to blend and age them before marketing.

The more notable wineries of California are presented in the following pages by region and district. In each district they are arranged *alphabetically within the locality.* Selection has been governed by the quality, both of premium and sound standard wines produced. No prices are indicated, as they may vary slightly according to the part of the country where they are purchased and will presumably change over the years.

Only those wineries are included which produce and market directly for the public, with brands which are distributed nationally or on a more restricted basis. Winegrowers who have consistently won awards at either or both California fairs since 1950 are automatically included, with the exception only of those who have had to close their doors. Also included are prominent growers both of high and of sound standard quality wines who send their wines to the fairs only irregularly or not at all. Small, non-exhibiting wineries who produce wines of special merit are mentioned, including a few who only recently started operations.

A complete listing of all California and other American wineries is published in the "Annual Directory Issue" of the publication *Wines and Vines,** while a practical series of *Guide Maps* to all California wineries is available at the Wine Institute.*

The California wine-producing areas can be grouped geographically in three great regions, as follows:

The cool to moderately cool *northern coastal region,* where all the finest table wines are produced, the top-quality champagnes, and some notable dessert wines.

The hot *inland valley region,* the home especially of the dessert wines, but producing also table wines and bulk-fermented champagnes.

The warm *Southern California region,* where dessert wines, champagnes, and table wines of note are produced.

*717 Market Street, San Francisco.

IX

THE NORTHERN COASTAL REGION

*T*HIS REGION, sometimes referred to as that of the northern coastal counties, lies close to the coast north and south of San Francisco and takes in the winegrowing districts west of the coastal range of mountains. They are, from north to south:

The *Sonoma-Mendocino, Napa-Solano, Livermore-Contra Costa,* and the *Santa Clara-Santa Cruz and Central Coastal* districts, lying respectively northwest, northeast, southeast, and south of the Golden Gate. The city of San Francisco, where a number of wineries are located, is discussed as a separate area.

A. *SONOMA-MENDOCINO DISTRICT*

This district consists of the two counties which have given it their joint names. Sonoma County yields some high-quality table wines and champagnes which rate among the very finest of the state. It also produces vast quantities of standard-quality table wine, mostly red, as does Mendocino County.

Sonoma, with over fifty active bonded wineries, leads all other counties in that respect by a wide margin. Its wines can conveniently be grouped according to the three valleys where they are produced: the Sonoma, Santa Rosa, and Russian River valleys.

SONOMA COUNTY—SONOMA VALLEY

The appellation Sonoma Valley is restricted in the *Guide* to denote the valley proper. The name has often been loosely applied to a larger area, taking in the neighboring Santa Rosa Valley, but the latter is actually part of the Russian River basin and is therefore treated separately. Sonoma Valley is some eleven miles long and is named after Sonoma Creek, which empties in San Pablo Bay to the south.

Sonoma Valley is familiar to many as the Valley of the Moon, made famous in literature by Jack London, who wrote and died there, not far from the ruins of the once famous Kohler winery, destroyed by the great earthquake of 1906.

The Valley of the Moon, or of the Moons, as the Indians used to call it, does its name full justice, for, separated from the Napa Valley to the east by the Mayacamas Range, the moon, to those down below, seems to rise, not once, but many times among the succeeding mountain peaks.

Buena Vista Vineyards, Sonoma

It seems only suitable to begin the presentation of the wineries of California with Buena Vista, once the home of Haraszthy, the "father of modern California viticulture."

Agoston Haraszthy, a man of temperament and of many talents, came from a noble Hungarian family. Because of wanderlust or because he aided in plotting Magyar independence, he left his Hungarian domain and sailed for America. He first settled in Wisconsin, where he founded the town of Haraszthy, which was to become Sauk City. Known as the "Count," he later shed this title for the more democratic one of "Colonel."

In 1849 he came West, to San Diego, which he helped to develop and where he was elected the town's first sheriff. He later represented that county as state assemblyman and moved north to Sacramento. San Francisco, thriving with the Gold Rush, next attracted the colonel's energetic spirit and he became the official melter and refiner of the U. S. Mint. He landed in difficulties, accused of exceeding his legal limit of gold wastage, but was absolved by the court and his name completely cleared.

Haraszthy had been interested in viticulture ever since his early Hungarian days. In California he had planted vineyards near San Diego and in San Francisco near Mission Dolores as well as at Crystal Springs, in what is now San Mateo. He realized, from the example of Jean Louis Vignes at Los Angeles, that the better California wines were produced from European grape varieties and he himself had already imported many such vines, including, as has been widely accepted, the one he named and became known as Zinfandel.

Haraszthy finally chose Sonoma as the ideal place to realize his ambition of establishing the finest vineyards in California. He became a neighbor of the pioneer grower General Vallejo, who produced a wine of great repute, Lachryma Montis, named after his estate. The two families became friendly rivals in wine making, and became much closer than friends when the double wedding took place at Lachryma Montis in 1863, uniting Natalia and Jovita, daughters of General Vallejo, to Attila and Arpad Haraszthy, sons of the colonel.

Haraszthy had named his country place Buena Vista and here he constructed an imposing Pompeian mansion. Hundreds of acres of vines were planted and a series of tunnels dug deep in the hillside for cellar accommodation. Skilled viticulturists came to work at Buena Vista, among them Charles Krug, who was himself to become one of California's leading wine growers.

It was at Buena Vista that Haraszthy wrote his classic "Report on Grapes and Wines of California." He advised all growers to test as many varieties as possible, to cultivate those which throve the best and produced the finest wines. He was certain that California could yield "as noble a wine as any country on the face of the globe."

In 1861 Haraszthy was appointed by Governor John G. Downey to report on wine growing in Europe. From a viticultural point of view the trip was a great success. He visited all the important European winegrowing districts and collected some 100,000 cuttings from 300 grape varieties, all of which he planted on his return. Financially the journey proved a source of discord. The California Legislature refused to pay the expenses incurred, but the colonel could find consolation in being made president of the California Agricultural Society.

Haraszthy had reached the summit of his prestige. The fame of Buena Vista wines had spread far; offices of the company were operating in San Francisco, Chicago, New York, Philadelphia, and London. In October 1864 Colonel and Mrs. Haraszthy were hosts at a Vintage Ball and Masquerade, the social event of the time.

Then financial and other troubles succeeded each other rapidly. Phylloxera struck, Haraszthy suffered losses on the Stock Exchange, taxes on spirits wiped out his profit on brandy, a fire raged at Buena Vista, ruining much of the wine, credit was cut off from the bank, and financial assistance from other sources proved unavailable.

So the father of California's modern wine industry left Buena Vista, Sonoma, and California for good. He went to Nicaragua, where he obtained a government contract for the distillation of spirits from sugar and there he started a new domain. But one day, in July 1869, he vanished. It is believed that he tried to cross an alligator-infested stream by means of an overhanging branch which broke off by his weight and plunged him to his doom. The life of a great American pioneer had come to a tragic end.

In California Attila and Arpad Haraszthy continued the family wine-making tradition. Arpad became famous for his Eclipse Champagne, while Attila stayed on at Buena Vista to fight the phylloxera, which was not conquered till the turn of the century. The estate suffered a further great blow when the 1906 earthquake brought down in ruins much of the winery and caved in the storage tunnels, burying, so it is believed, much champagne beneath the debris. Buena Vista entered a dormant period in wine making which lasted till 1943.

In that year Frank H. Bartholomew, now president of the United Press, acquired a large acreage of the former Buena Vista vineyards and revived the society, restoring also the two stone wineries from Haraszthy's days.

The following high-quality wines are available under the *Buena Vista* brand:

Table wines:
  RED: Cabernet Sauvignon, Pinot Noir, Zinfandel (from the vineyards where the the wine grew to fame), Burgundy;
  WHITE: White (Johannisberger) Riesling, Traminer, Sylvaner, Green Hungarian (one of the few produced in the state), Vine Brook (rhine wine), Chablis;
  ROSÉ: Rose Brook (from Cabernet Sauvignon grapes);

Champagne (bottle-fermented): Extra Dry Champagne (from Pinot Chardonnay grapes);

Aperitif and Dessert Wines:
  SHERRY: Ultra Dry (Solera);
  PORT: Vintage Ports, marketed under governmentally certified vintage dates; 1946 and 1951 to be followed by later vintages;
  VERMOUTH: Dry and Sweet.

Hanns Kornell Cellars, Sonoma

Hanns Kornell represents the third generation of a family known in Germany since 1848 for the production of superior wines. He attended agricultural college and worked in vineyards and wineries, acquiring experience in France and Italy as well as in his native country.

When political conditions made it impossible for him to remain in Germany, he chose America as his new home. He worked in California at Los Amigos, Fountaingrove, the Gibson Wine Company, and at the American Wine Company in St. Louis, where he was the wine maker and became production manager.

His great ambition always was to manage his own winery and this he accomplished in 1952 when he took over the Sonoma Wine Company at Sonoma, which he renamed Hanns Kornell Cellars.

The great specialties of the winery are the *Sparkling wines,* bottle-fermented. These are marketed under the *Third Generation* brand and include a Brut, Extra Dry, and Sec Champagne, as well as Pink Champagne and Sparkling Burgundy.

Table and *Dessert wines* carry the *Hanns Kornell Cellars* label and include Cabernet, Burgundy, and Claret in the red table wines, Riesling, Sauterne, and Rhine in the whites as well as Pale Dry Sherry, Cream Sherry, Ruby Port, and Muscatel.

Napa & Sonoma Wine Company (Castler Cellars), Sonoma

The company has a history which dates back in San Francisco to 1896. Its president, Paul Rossigneux, operates the Castler Cellars in one of the two large stone wineries at Buena Vista, dating back to the days of Colonel Haraszthy.

Rossigneux is that rather rare type of producer in California, but usual enough in France, the vintner, who buys fine wines from vineyards not large enough to be exploited separately and then blends and ages the wines to a high standard of quality. Rossigneux prides himself on the fact that although custom demands that California wines are usually named after foreign wine types, he has developed high-quality wines of truly Californian character. Although he prefers not to use varietal names for his California wines, he markets the first-class French wines, which he imports, under their varietal grape names, which is most unusual.

The California wines of the company are marketed under the *Castler* brand as follows:

Table wines:
  RED: Rubio Castler (burgundy type);
  WHITE: Green Castler (rhine wine type), Sauterne (medium dry),
    Haut Sauterne (sweet), Chablis;
  ROSÉ: Pink Castler;

Sparkling wines (bottle-fermented):
  Dry Champagne and Sparkling Burgundy;

Aperitif and Dessert wines:
  SHERRY: Club Sherry (pale, dry) and Cream Sherry;
  PORT: Tawny Port;
  MUSCATEL: Golden Muscatel;
  VERMOUTH: Dry and Sweet.

Paul Rossigneux publishes, from time to time, recipes in card form entitled "Wine & Food Tips."

Sebastiani Winery, Sonoma

This winery, one of the largest producers in Sonoma County and the oldest wine enterprise in Sonoma Valley operated continuously by one family, was founded in 1904 by Samuele Sebastiani, who emigrated to this country from Italy at an early age. From a small beginning and in spite of many adversities Samuele Sebastiani gradually built up his enterprise through hard work, determination to succeed, and a strong faith in spiritual assistance. When Prohibition forced the closing down of many wineries, he continued to operate for the production of medicinal and sacramental wines as allowed by the dry laws. He was for many years a colorful and dominant figure, not only in Sonoma, but in the whole of the wine industry.

After Samuele Sebastiani passed away in 1944, he was succeeded by his son August Sebastiani, who now conducts all winery operations and continues the family tradition. Of historic interest at the winery is a 501-gallon tank, which represented the total wine output of the enterprise at its founding and which is still in use.

Some vineyards are owned in Sonoma Valley, but most of the wines are produced from grapes purchased from the same local growers from year to year. The winery's operation was mostly on a bulk basis, supplying bottlers throughout the United States, when it was decided in 1954 to enter the field of quality wines. The Sonoma winery specializes in table wines and champagne stock, while aperitif and dessert wines, including vermouth, are also produced.

The *S & S* and *Casa de Sonoma* brands are used for the quality wines, while *Sebastiani* is the regular brand for commercial wines of standard grades.

Table wines:

S & S: Cabernet, Pinot Noir, Barbera, Zinfandel, Burgundy, Chianti, Claret, and Red Table Wine; Riesling, Sylvaner, Sauterne, Chablis, and Rhine; Vin Rosé;

Casa de Sonoma: Cabernet (featured), Burgundy, and Sauterne; *Sebastiani:* Burgundy, Claret; Chablis, Sauterne; Vin Rosé;

Aperitif and Dessert wines:
  S & S: Pale Dry Cocktail Sherry and Sherry; Port, Ruby Port, and Tawny Port; Muscatel, Tokay, White Port, and Angelica;
  Sebastiani: Pale Dry Cocktail Sherry and Sherry; Port and Ruby Port; Muscatel, Tokay, and White Port; Sweet and Dry Vermouth.

Glen Ellen Winery & Distillery, Inc., Glen Ellen

The origin of this property goes back to 1853, when Joshua Chauvet, a Frenchman, bought a saw and flour mill from General Vallejo. The mill was located where the distillery now stands and some of the original redwood timbers are still in use. Chauvet, who owned a great part of Glen Ellen, including the Jack London ranch, built the adobe three-story winery in 1881. He went to France and purchased one of the finest continuous stills that money could buy and had it shipped around Cape Horn. It is still in operation for the production of a grape brandy.

Charles J. Pagani, who knew Jack London and used to visit him on his mountaintop above Glen Ellen, ran the winery from 1913 until his death in 1954. Louis C. Pagani, his brother, is now in charge.

Sound-quality *table wines* produced number Cabernet, Zinfandel, Burgundy, and Claret in the reds, and Semillon, Sylvaner, Riesling, Sauvignon Vert, and Sauterne in the whites. They are marketed under the *A. Pagani, Glen Ellen* and *Glen Hills* brands.

F. Mancuso Winery, Glen Ellen

Felix Mancuso, the owner, purchased the winery and vineyards in 1921, but the winery was not put into operation till 1933, when the Eighteenth Amendment was repealed. A Frenchman, Lemoine, who formerly owned the estate, planted part of the vineyards to different varieties right next to each other so that the various grapes could easily be harvested together and crushed to obtain the desired type of wine. The mansion he built is now the site of the Mancuso residence. Felix Mancuso is ably assisted in the family enterprise by his son, Peter F. Mancuso.

Red table wines, as is often the case in Sonoma, are the specialty and are typically sound "country wines." Dessert wines, including vermouths, are purchased, aged, and bottled for sale.

Under the *Mancuso* brand standard-quality wines are available, such as Zinfandel, Claret, and Burgundy and also Sauterne. The featured wine is a Special Reserve Burgundy, aged in small oak casks, which has deservedly won more than a local reputation for itself.

SONOMA COUNTY—SANTA ROSA VALLEY

The Santa Rosa Creek, after which the valley is named, empties its waters eventually in the Russian River. The city of Santa Rosa is where the Luther Burbank home is to be found. The famed botanist and horticulturist, who was also greatly interested in viticulture, lies buried beneath the cedar of Lebanon in the garden of the park.

Fountaingrove Vineyard, Santa Rosa

The romantic estate of Fountaingrove was established in 1873 by Thomas Lake Harris, preacher, philosopher, and charmer. He was the founder of the "Brotherhood of the New Life," which mixed religion, business, and love in a strange manner. His utopia attracted numerous and devoted followers, the more important of whom became so-called "pivotal figures." These included wealthy and attractive ladies, such as Lady Oliphant and Jane Lee Waring, "Dovie" to the prophet. Viticulture had been among the brotherhood's pursuits at Lake Keuka, New York, where public criticism had forced the colony's removal. Pivotals there included such men as Jacob Moore, originator of the Diamond grape, and Dr. John Hyde, expert on the Missouri Riesling. Konoye Nagasawa, a Japanese said to be of Samurai descent and who had met Harris while on a preaching tour in England, was the prophet's factotum and was to become the true creator of Fountaingrove Vineyard.

After the colony's exit from the Finger Lake district in New York, a new "Cosmos" was sought and was found in Sonoma, proved land for successful winegrowing. A few miles north of Santa Rosa, overlooking the beautiful valley from a hillside, a mansion was built in a grove near a spring. Vineyards were planted by the heavenly abode and Fountaingrove came into being. Harris orated while Nagasawa took down the golden words of the prophet, published by Dr. Hyde in the Fountaingrove Press. In their spare time Nagasawa and Hyde would cultivate the vines with great diligence. Before long the vintages of Fountaingrove achieved a national reputation. Harris had a keen eye also for business. An outlet was established in New York and Lady Oliphant set up Fountaingrove agencies in London, Liverpool, and Glasgow.

Soon new storms raged about the brotherhood. There were "betrayals," lawsuits, and much unfavorable publicity in the papers. The appearance of "Dovie" Waring in Turkish garb, complete with pipe, did not enhance the colony's reputation in the neighborhood. Other pivotals resented being ordered about by Miss Waring like slaves. Harris's young daughter took poison and died. Once again departure was the only course open to the prophet. After a hasty marriage to Jane Waring, Harris left Fountaingrove, for good. He sold most of his holdings, but kept an interest in the New York shop, continuing to discourse on the heavenliness of the Fountaingrove wines and the desirability of their prompt sale.

At Santa Rosa, Nagasawa took complete charge and after the final departure of Harris for celestial spheres he bought up all outstanding claims to the estate. Fountaingrove became his.

Nagasawa won the respect of all. He became friends with Luther Burbank, whose gardens were close by, and with the great Bioletti, viticulturist of the University of California. Then there was the library, rich in volumes written by Harris or owned by him and augmented by Herbert Spencer's collection which Nagasawa had brought over from London.

For nearly sixty years Nagasawa devoted himself to Fountain-grove and its wines. In 1934 he died, eighty years old, a great Californian and a great gentleman. A few years later the estate was purchased by Errol McBoyle, who continued Fountaingrove's tradition for fine wines. After his death in 1949 the estate passed to his widow, who later married Siegfried Bechhold. Jane Waring, it may be noted, was a painter of talent, and portraits she made of Thomas Lake Harris, which are considered outstanding, adorn the Bechhold home at Fountaingrove.

As late as 1951 Fountaingrove wines won numerous awards at the California fairs. Then it was decided, for economic reasons, to pull up the vineyards and convert the land to pasture. Fountaingrove became a cattle ranch and the winery entered a dormant period. Some of the Fountaingrove table wines and champagnes, once famous, may still be found here and there, but wine is no longer produced at what is now the "Fountaingrove Ranch."

Martini & Prati Wines, Inc., Santa Rosa

Some eight miles northwest of Santa Rosa, near Forestville, lies the extensive Martini and Prati Vine Hill winery, operated by Elmo Martini* and Edward Prati.

The Martini family have been in the wine business in Santa Rosa since the eighteen seventies. Raphaele Martini bought the present winery and vineyards shortly after the turn of the century, the enterprise being expanded at various times and later operated by his sons. In 1943 the property was purchased by the Hiram Walker interests, owners of W. A. Taylor and Company, but in 1950 the winery and vineyards reverted back to Elmo Martini, in partnership with Enrico Prati of Italian Swiss Colony fame and with the latter's son Edward. Enrico Prati passed away in 1952 and Elmo Martini is now president of the company, while Edward Prati, who also owns vineyards of his own, is secretary-treasurer.

Martini and Prati are producers of quality *table wines,* including Zinfandel, Burgundy, and Claret in the reds, and Sauterne, Chablis,

*Not to be confused with Louis Martini of St. Helena, Napa County.

and Rhine Wine in the whites. Vermouth, both dry and sweet, is also produced, while dessert wines are purchased and aged before marketing. *Martini & Prati* is the brand under which the wines are sold to the public.

Santa Rosa Winery, Santa Rosa

A small winery and family concern, owned and operated by C. B. Meda, born in San Francisco of Italian parentage. He learned the art of wine making from his father, who came from Piedmont, near Asti, and was in the wine business in Connecticut since 1893. On the latter's retirement the son took over the enterprise until the advent of prohibition.

After repeal C. B. Meda purchased the Santa Rosa winery, his main interest being to produce fine table wines and especially champagne.

Sparkling wines (bottle-fermented) are the winery's specialties. They are highly rated and include Brut, Extra Dry, and Demi-Sec Champagne, from Pinot Chardonnay and other selected grapes, as well as Sparkling Burgundy, from Pinot noir and other varieties. They are marketed under the *Grand Prize* brand.

SONOMA COUNTY—RUSSIAN RIVER VALLEY

The Russian River finds its source in Mendocino County and flows south into Sonoma, turning west past Healdsburg to empty in the Pacific Ocean some ten miles beyond Guerneville.

The lower Russian River Valley, around Guerneville, forms a small, separate winegrowing area, where some of the finest California champagne is produced. The inland or upper section of the valley takes in the area around Healdsburg northwards to Cloverdale and on into Mendocino County. In this section of Sonoma over forty wineries are located, most of the growers being of Italian descent and producing sound, robust table wines, mostly of the red types.

F. Korbel & Brothers, Inc., Guerneville

The great castlelike Korbel winery is located, among vineyards and huge tree stumps, on the Russian River a few miles east of Guerneville, just beyond Rio Nido. It is the home of champagnes, which rate among the very best and are known throughout the country and beyond.

The Korbels first produced wine here in 1881 and the story is one of enterprise which dates back to the days of the pioneers.

The Korbel brothers, Francis, Anton, and Joseph, were born in the little town of Behine in Bohemia, now part of Czechoslovakia.

They emigrated to the United States and after a stay in New York came to San Francisco in the early eighteen sixties. Ironworkers and machinists by trade, they soon found employment in the machine shops of San Francisco. Francis, the eldest, built a cigar-box factory, as he realized the need for such objects. In this he was aided by his brothers and such was the beginning of a family enterprise which led by stages to lithography, publication of *The Wasp,* lumber, a sawmill on the Russian River, and finally to the production of wine and champagne.

A younger, fourth, brother had also arrived from Bohemia, but because of his delicate health sought the outdoor life. For him the elder Korbels bought a half interest in a sawmill near Guerneville. They later took over the partnership, acquiring additional acreage and eventually owning a large tract of virgin forest on the Russian River.

When all the timber had been cut—the vast stumps of which remain an impressive sight today—the Korbels sought the advice of the University of California on what to raise on the newly cleared land. After a dairy venture which proved unsuccessful vines were planted with the purpose of selling the grapes to Sonoma wineries. When the first crop was harvested, grape prices proved so low the brothers decided to crush the grapes themselves and so landed in the wine business.

The original winery still stands and in 1886 the first section of the present winery was constructed from lumber and from brick made on the ranch property. Table wines only were produced at first, but in the nineties it was decided to make champagne as well. Shortly after the Second World War production of table wines (and of brandy) was discontinued, to concentrate on that of sparkling wines only.

The Korbels brought over from Bohemia Frank Hasek as their first champagne maker, a graduate of the Viticultural School of Melnik, near Prague, later joined by another Melnik graduate, Jan (John) Hanuska. For over forty years Hanuska, a gnomelike figure of genius, carried on as cellar master and champagne maker, a master of his trade.

In early 1954 Anton and Leo Korbel and the other members of the Korbel family sold the corporation to Adolf L. and Paul R. Heck, brothers and wine makers, originally from St. Louis and formerly president and production manager of Italian Swiss Colony. Adolf Heck became president of Korbel as well as the wine maker and Paul Heck the executive vice-president.

The four most important varieties of grapes raised at the ranch for the production of sparkling wines are Pinot noir, Pinot blanc, Semillon and Sauvignon blanc. Some White Riesling and Sylvaner are also grown.

In September 1954 the Heck brothers purchased the Santa Nella Winery, which adjoins their Korbel ranch. The Santa Nella property includes a winery, a retail establishment, and a vineyard acreage, part of which was recently replanted to select varietal wine grapes. Plans are to maintain the Santa Nella name and to operate the retail store there the year round.

The Korbel winery produces only *Sparkling wines,* bottle-fermented, and marketed under the *Korbel* brand, as follows:

Korbel Brut (very dry), Korbel Extra Dry (for Eastern markets only), Korbel Sec (medium dry), and Korbel Rouge (red champagne or sparkling burgundy and on the dry side).

A recent innovation is the clear glass bottle with transparent label in which the Korbel Pink Champagne or Sparkling Rosé is now marketed.

L. Foppiano Wine Company, Healdsburg

The winery dates back to the early eighteen seventies and was known as the Smith winery when Louis Foppiano, of Italian descent and the father of the present owner, purchased it in 1898. The company is a family concern, owned and operated by Louis Foppiano and his relatives.

Louis Foppiano was born right on the property, in the building which now houses the company's offices. Raised in the wine business since his earliest days, he has made a great success of it, including a financial one, something in which growers have not always been so fortunate.

While dessert wines and vermouth are also marketed, *table wines* are the specialty. They are of sound standard quality and are marketed under the *Foppiano* and *Sonoma Gold* brands. They include Zinfandel, Burgundy, and Claret in the reds, and Sauterne and Rhine Wine in the whites. A superior table wine is the Foppiano Vintage Burgundy. Aperitif and dessert wines include Port, Sherry, Muscatel, Tokay, White Port, and Dry and Sweet Vermouth.

Simi Wineries (Montepulciano Winery), Healdsburg

This famous old firm was founded in 1876 by Giuseppe Simi, who came over from Italy at the time of the Gold Rush and first worked in the mines. He came to Healdsburg in the early seventies, planted a large vineyard acreage and built a winery which he called Montepulciano after the place of that name in his native Tuscany. The enterprise is now managed by his daughter Isabella and her husband Fred Haigh.

The products of this winery were once featured by the fabulous old Del Monte Hotel (now the U. S. Naval Postgraduate School) at Del Monte near Monterey, California, where they achieved a wide reputation.

Table wines are still the winery's specialty, marketed both under the *Simi** and *Montepulciano* brands, sold mostly at retail at the

*Not to be confused with the *Simi Vineyard* brand of Richert & Sons, Madrone, Santa Clara County (see there).

winery's entrance. They include a varietal Carignan claret, one of the very few produced in the state, and a favorite of Mrs. Haigh.

Vercelli Brothers Wine Company (Alpine Vineyards), Healdsburg

This family enterprise, located just north of the Russian River crossing, is owned by the brothers Joseph S. and Louis J. Vercelli with Joseph (Joe) the general and sales manager. Joe Vercelli, a very popular figure in the wine industry, was born in San Francisco and has been in the wine business his entire adult life. He was at one time a pupil of the famed Dr. Bioletti. In addition to his duties concerning his own company he was named wine maker, in 1954, for Italian Swiss Colony.

In 1937 the Vercelli brothers purchased the Costa Magna Winery, established prior to the turn of the century, and two years later acquired part of the assets of the old Alpine Winery from John Greeott, who founded it in 1893. For a number of years the Vercellis specialized in varietal table wines, selling them to the larger Sonoma wineries. On account of the speculative nature of the varietal field production has more recently been concentrated on the popular generic wine types of sound standard quality.

During the Second World War, Vercelli Brothers, along with a number of other well-known California wineries, supplied wines to distant places, as far apart as Central America, Saudi Arabia and the South Sea Islands. Vercelli's wines found their way to the Free French Forces in New Caledonia, to Tahiti and Noumea in the Society Islands, and to Tientsin, Hongkong, and Macao. One faithful lady customer from Tahiti still comes yearly to purchase four barrels of wine to take back with her to Papeete.

Table wines are the specialty and are marketed under the *Vercelli, Verbro,* and *Alpine* brands. They include Zinfandel, Claret, and Burgundy in the reds, Sauterne (dry), Chablis, and Rhine in the whites, as well as a rosé, produced from either Zinfandel or from Carignane grapes.

Italian Swiss Colony, Asti

The origin of Italian Swiss Colony is in great part the story of Andrea Sbarboro, who came to San Francisco from Italy in the early eighteen fifties as a youngster to work in his brother's grocery store. Twenty years later, by working hard and saving, he bought his own store and turned builder and financier.

In 1881 he founded the Italian Swiss Agricultural Colony with the purpose of aiding Italian and Swiss immigrants to settle in their new land. Many of these were vineyardists by trade and a 1500-acre tract was chosen in Sonoma County, suitable for the planting of vines. The land was named Asti after the town of that name in Piedmont, Italy. Each immigrant was provided with room, board, and wages, in return for which a contribution was expected toward building up an equity in the land and eventually becoming an independent farmer. The immigrants objected to the last condition; they were willing to work, but not to take a chance. Sbarboro decided to operate Asti privately. He set the immigrants to work, planting vines with the idea of growing and selling grapes. The price of the latter soon dropped below the cost of production. It was then decided to press the grapes into wine. The first crush was a disaster; owing to carelessness in handling, the wine turned to vinegar.

Asti, so far, had proved a failure, but Sbarboro did not give up. He put Pietro Rossi, a San Francisco druggist who had studied wine making in Italy, in charge of the winery. This was in 1888. The first wines Rossi produced were of good quality, but the market price offered for them was unprofitable. The Colony then decided to market its wines direct and set up agencies throughout the country and abroad. Italian Swiss Colony finally came into its own. The fame of its wines soon spread and many medals were received in the United States and Europe and even in the original Asti, in Piedmont.

Sbarboro built a sumptuous mansion at Asti and, being a great practical joker, equipped the gardens with a sprinkler system, copied after the one at Hellbrunn in Salzburg. The purpose was not so much to sprinkle his plants, but his guests. The grounds of the estate became a maze of booby traps for the unsuspecting.

With the death of Pietro Rossi, thrown from his horse in 1911, one of the great figures of the Colony passed away. Management of the winery was taken over by his twin sons, Edmund and Robert Rossi, who had been taught the art of wine making by their father. Andrea Sbarboro, who among his other duties headed the Italian-American Bank in San Francisco, remained in charge of the Colony's promotion.

Prohibition was the last enemy to strike at Italian Swiss Colony. Sbarboro proclaimed endlessly that Prohibition was not the road to temperance and appeared before Congress in Washington to protest against this threat to man's liberty of action. But he realized that he was fighting a losing battle. He retired from the wine business and in 1923 he died, partly out of disgust, it is said, that his beloved Asti was bottling grape juice. It was, however, by selling grapes and grape juice that Asti was kept going during Prohibition. When Repeal came, the Rossi twins lost no time in reviving the Colony's wine industry and within a few years Italian Swiss had once again become one of the country's leading wineries.

The "experiment that nearly failed" was finally crowned with solid success. During the Second World War, Italian Swiss Colony was sold to National Distillers Products Corporation, who owned it till April 1953, when it was purchased for a record figure by the Petri family, already well known in the wine industry. The next year the Petris also acquired from National Distillers the popular Lejon and Hartley brands.*

Italian Swiss Colony owns a vast vineyard acreage in Sonoma and Mendocino counties. The main winery, for table and sparkling wines, is located at Asti itself, always a popular attraction for visitors. Other bonded premises of the company are to be found at Lodi (Shewan-Jones) and at Clovis (La Paloma Winery) for the production of aperitif and dessert wines and of brandy. Bottling plants

*In a joint deal by Italian Swiss Colony and the Midwestern distributing house of Ed. Phillips & Son, whereby Italian Swiss has the world marketing rights for both brands excepting for a few Midwestern states.

are located at Chicago, Illinois, and at Fairfield, New Jersey, to ensure adequate service for the Midwestern and Eastern markets.

Italian Swiss Colony produces a large variety of wines which enjoy a national and foreign distribution. Their quality is invariably sound and they are priced in the medium range, with *Gold Medal, Private Stock, Tipo,* and *Asti* the best-known brands in ascending order of quality and of cost.

Table wines marketed include:
   Asti: Pinot Noir, Cabernet, and Burgundy; Pinot Blanc, Dry
      Semillon, Riesling, Sauterne, Chablis, and Rhine; Vin Rosé;
   Tipo: red and white Chianti;
   Private Stock: Burgundy and Zinfandel; Sauterne (dry) and
      Haut Sauterne (medium dry); Vin Rosé;
   Gold Medal: Burgundy, Claret, and Zinfandel; Sauterne (dry)
      and Rhine.
   Italian Swiss markets a semi-sweet Vin Rosé under the I.S.C. label.

In addition Gambarelli & Davitto, an Italian Swiss Colony division, markets an inexpensive mellow *vino rosso* type under the name "Fior di California."

Sparkling wines (bulk fermented) are labeled under the *Private Stock* brand and include Champagne (medium dry) and Sparkling Burgundy.

Aperitif and Dessert wines are marketed as follows:
   Asti: Sherry (medium dry), Pale Sherry, and Cream Sherry;
      Tawny Port and Ruby Port; Muscatel;
   Private Stock: Sherry (medium dry) and Pale Dry Sherry; Port;
      Muscatel; Tokay;
   Gold Medal: Sherry (medium dry), Pale Dry Sherry, and Cream
      Sherry; Port; Muscatel; Tokay; White Port; Angelica;
   Vermouth, both dry and sweet, is available under the *I.S.C.*
(Italian Swiss Colony) and *G & D* (Gambarelli & Davitto) labels.

Separate mention must be made of the *Lejon* and *Hartley* products, made popular by that famous and colorful personality of the California wine industry, Lee Jones, of whose name the Lejon brand forms a contraction and a lasting tribute. A table wine, both red and white, is marketed under the *Chateau* Lejon brand, as are Champagne and Sparkling Burgundy (bottle-fermented), while *Hartley* Sherry and *Lejon* Vermouth, both dry and sweet, are wines familiar to many throughout the country.

Hollis M. Black Winery, Cloverdale

The Hollis Black Ranch, picturesquely situated on the Russian River, was originally the Hall Ranch, with a winery founded in 1905. Lewis Black and his son Hollis purchased the property from the Halls in 1919 and the family enterprise is now operated by Hollis M. Black, assisted by his son and daughter-in-law, Davis and Elise Black.

The ranch had been in the bulk-wine business for some forty years when it was decided, for economic reasons, to concentrate on the production and marketing of superior-quality table wines. A selection of the finer varieties has been planted in the vineyards and plans are to produce Pinot Noir, Cabernet Sauvignon, Semillon, Sauvignon Blanc, Pinot Chardonnay, White Riesling, and Sylvaner. Ruby Cabernet was planted besides and the resulting wine, when blended, has shown signs of great promise.

In the meantime, besides a home-grown Claret, a number of other *table wines* are carefully selected and then aged and bottled at the winery. These include Pinot Noir, Cabernet Sauvignon, Zinfandel, and Burgundy; White Pinot (Chenin Blanc), Sylvaner, Riesling, Sauterne (dry), and Chablis. A Pale Dry Sherry and a Port are also aged and bottled.

All wines are marketed under the *Hollis Black* brand, the label of which is artistically outstanding and the work of Mrs. Hollis Black, a portrait painter of more than local repute, who has also written for some of the better-known national magazines.

MENDOCINO COUNTY

Mendocino produces mainly dry table wines of sound standard quality, among which the reds are the more notable. There is, however, a trend away from the traditional Zinfandel and other average or better-than-average grapes toward the cultivation of the finer varietals. Popular white table types are French Colombard and Sauvignon Vert.

Calpella, Ukiah, and Hopland, all situated along the Russian River, are, from north to south, the representative wine-growing centers with Ukiah, the home of the most prominent wineries of the county.

Mendocino Grape Growers, Inc., Ukiah

This is a co-operative winery established in 1946 and owned and supported by some hundred grape growers of Mendocino County. President of the co-operative is Pete Gialdini, who also functions as general manager. In 1954 the company became a member of the Wine Growers Guild.

Table wines only are produced. These are of sound standard quality and include Zinfandel, Burgundy, and Claret, Sauterne (dry) and Chablis. The co-operative's brand is *Cal-Mendo.*

Parducci & Son, Ukiah

This family concern is owned and operated by Adolph B. Parducci and his four sons, John, George, Vernon, and Adolph, Jr., of whom John is the wine maker.

The Parduccis originated in Lucca, Italy. Adolph, Sr., born in Santa Clara County, went to Italy as a youngster, where he worked in the vineyards, returning to this country at the age of seventeen. He first entered the wine business in this country in Cloverdale and later purchased the Pine Mountain Ranch at Ukiah. With the advent of Repeal, in 1933, the present winery was built.

Parducci produces both quality and bulk table wines. Aperitif and dessert wines, including vermouth, are purchased and aged. The featured brand for all wines is *Parducci.*

Quality *table wines* include Zinfandel and Burgundy, which have also been bottled of special vintages. Plans are to produce Gamay, Pinot Noir as well as a Rosé. In the whites French Colombard and

Dry Sauterne are available, while Sauvignon Vert is a winery specialty.

B. *NAPA-SOLANO DISTRICT*

This famous district is formed by the two counties bearing those names. Napa yields some of the finest of all California wines, especially table wines, while Solano, adjoining its exalted neighbor to the east, produces table wines of greater-than-average merit. In number of active bonded wineries Napa, with thirty-eight, rates third.

From a viticultural point of view Napa County and Napa Valley are interchangeable terms, for it is from the valley and its bordering hillsides that the county's famed wines originate. Only the Mayacamas Mountains separate Napa Valley from that of Sonoma, to which it lies parallel. Napa possesses its own romantic name, for in the Indian language it is said to mean "plenty." Napa is indeed the "Valley of Plenty," one of abundant beauty and fertility. Even in ancient times grapes, though wild, are said to have grown here in profusion.

The Napa River which flows through the valley, is little more than a creek and empties, like its Sonoma neighbor, into the waters of San Pablo Bay, connecting with that of San Francisco. Dominating the valley to the north thrones Mt. St. Helena, christened after that saint by the Princess Helena Gagarin, wife of the onetime Russian Governor of Siberia and of the Russian Northern Pacific Colonies and daughter of the Czar of all the Russias.

The Napa Valley can be divided into two separate winegrowing areas, the uppper and the lower. The upper Napa Valley centers around the town of St. Helena, flanked to the north by Calistoga and to the south by Rutherford, as famed as St. Helena itself for wines of the highest quality. The vineyards are to be found both high and low on the hillsides as well as on the valley floor. The lower Napa Valley takes in the area northwest of the town of Napa in the Mayacamas Mountains toward the Sonoma County line.

NAPA COUNTY—UPPER NAPA VALLEY

California Champagne Corporation* (Schramsberg Vineyard Co.), Calistoga

This is the successor to the vineyards and winery of Jacob Schram, made famous in literature by Robert Louis Stevenson.

Jacob Schram (or Schramm, as he first spelled it) was a German barber from Johannisberg on the Rhine who did very well in his trade. In 1862 he bought the Mt. Diamond property on the steep hillsides just south of Calistoga, built himself a winery and a mansion, and had a number of cellars dug deep in the mountain. His Schramsberg wines became celebrated, not only in California, but in far-off places and are said to have been served at the Carlton Club in London.

The Robert Louis Stevensons, while honeymooning on nearby Mt. St. Helena, visited the Schrams and Stevenson related his impressions in the chapter entitled "Napa Wine" of his *Silverado Squatters*. Fanny Stevenson was entertained by the opulent Mrs. Schram on the veranda of the big house, decorated with a wondrous collection of stuffed birds, while Stevenson and his host tasted one wine after the other in the hillside cellars. He tasted them all, Red Schramsberger and White, Burgundy Schramsberger and Schramsberger Hock. There were varietal wines also and Stevenson dwells on the bouquet of Schramsberger Golden Chasselas. The charm of these wines must have been as great as that of their names, which roll so savorously over the tongue.

After Jacob Schram's death the property was inherited by his son Herman, whose family still live in California. Prohibition rendered Schramsberg useless for wine making and it was sold to a firm of investment speculators. In 1921 it was acquired by Captain Raymond C. Naylor, who used it as a summer home and one of whose daughters married John Daniel, Jr., one of the owners of Inglenook.

In 1940, Schramsberg was purchased by John Gargano, who had started his California Champagne Company in the early thirties

*Not to be confused with California Champagne Cellars (Golden State Winery) of Fresno.

and was the producer of well-known California champagnes. He wanted the property on account of the tunnels, which are among the largest hand-hewn wine-aging cellars in the state with a constant temperature of around 55° Fahrenheit. He also revived and replanted the original Schram vineyards on the mountain slopes. Gargano had great plans for Schramsberg, but was not able to carry them out, because of illness, and he passed away in the beginning of 1952.

Shortly before, in December 1951, Schramsberg and the California Champagne Company were purchased by Douglas Pringle, well known in San Francisco, who had had general experience in various wineries over a period of years. He had always liked fine wines, having a catholic taste and possessing many other qualifications, not the least of which are his enthusiasm and charm. Besides the Schramsberg Mt. Diamond property the Pringles also own the neighboring Bear Flat Ranch and the Puerta Dorada Farms. The latter was the former Henry Harris winery and vineyards, where Georges de Latour, of Beaulieu Vineyard fame, is said to have made his first Napa Valley wine. Puerta Dorada is now the Pringle home, a beautiful residence and the scene of many social events.

Douglas Pringle has revived the once-celebrated Schramsberg label for both champagnes and table wines. Among notable plantings are those of Pinot noir and Johannisberg Riesling at Schramsberg and of Sauvignon blanc at Puerta Dorada, on a sunny slope by the Silverado Trail. The famous Golden Chasselas still grows at Schramsberg, but, being Palomino, is better suited for the production of Sherry according to present tastes. George Kay, of White Russian origin and formerly of Fountaingrove, is the winemaker.

Sparkling wines (bottle-fermented):

Schramsberger Brut Champagne and *Forever Amber* Champagne.* Pink Champagne and Sparkling Burgundy are also produced, with *Tiffany* the secondary brand.

---

*The first customer of Forever Amber Champagne was, appropriately enough, the famous Sally Stanford, once a notorious hostess of San Francisco and now the proprietress of a well-known restaurant in Sausalito, Marin County.

Table wines under the *Schramsberger* label include:

Cabernet and Burgundy; Sauterne, Chablis, Riesling, and Hock; Vin Rosé.

L. Pocai & Sons, Calistoga

A small family-owned and -operated winery, producing sound Napa Valley "country" wines. Libero Pocai, the founder, came from Eglio, near Lucca, in Italy and emigrated to the United States in the eighteen seventies. He went to California, where he helped plant the vineyards and olive trees of the Korbel Ranch near Guerneville, and later produced wine on a share basis at the Junker Ranch, some seven miles east of that town. He acquired the Calistoga property in the first decade of this century and established the vineyards there, aided by his sons Frank and Henry. Except during Prohibition, when grapes were sold to private families for the purpose of making wine at home, the winery, founded in 1912, has been in continuous operation down to the present time.

Libero Pocai died in 1936 and Frank and Henry have carried on since. Most of the wine produced is sold privately. Under the *L. Pocai & Sons* label the following *table wines* are marketed: Burgundy, Claret, and Zinfandel; Sauterne and Sauvignon Vert.

Beringer Bros., Inc. (Los Hermanos Vineyards), St. Helena

A famous winery continuously operated as a family concern since its founding, in 1876, by the brothers Frederick and Jacob L. Beringer.

Jacob Beringer had learned the art of wine making in his native Rheingau in Germany as well as in France and after having come to this country his one ambition was to establish a winery and vineyards of his own, such as he had known in Europe. He found the ideal location for his purpose while on a visit to St. Helena and he persuaded his brother Frederick, who was already settled in business in New York, to come out to California and join him in his project. The result was the founding of the Beringer brothers' vineyards and winery and of a great name in the California wine industry.

The "Los Hermanos" name was aptly bestowed on the firm by a close friend of the Beringer brothers, Señor Tiburcio Parrott, a Spanish gentleman of the old school, who lived in St. Helena in a beautiful villa and was well known as a patron of the arts.

A special feature of the winery is the labyrinth of tunnels cut into the limestone hill behind it. There are a thousand feet of this tunneling, originally cut out by Chinese coolies with picks, as was the custom in the olden days. The tunnels provide an ideal storage space at a steady air-conditioned temperature for the aging of wines in fine old casks of oak.

Beringer Bros. was incorporated in 1914 with the descendants of Jacob L. and of Frederick Beringer as members. Charles Tiburcio Beringer, for long the president of the firm, died in 1954. Miss Bertha C. Beringer is now president of the firm with Miss Martha F. Beringer vice-president, Mrs. Olga Beringer secretary-treasurer, and Otto Beringer Jr. and Mrs. Agnes Beringer Young assistant secretary-treasurers. Los Hermanos carries on as of old. Miss Bertha Beringer has written the history of the winery and clearly remembers "the elegant carriage driven by a resplendent coachman, in which Señor Tiburcio Parrott and his lovely wife used to dash up the Beringer driveway to call at the winery."

The company has never closed its doors since the founding, not even during Prohibition, when a steady business was maintained for the production of sacramental wines supplied to the clergy throughout the country.

No discussion of Beringer Bros. would be adequate without mention of the manager of the winery and vineyards, Fred Abruzzini, well known also as a charming host and as an ambassador of good will.

Originally employed by the Cribaris at Madrone, Santa Clara County, as a truck and tractor driver, Fred Abruzzini soon gathered much valuable experience in the vineyards and wine cellars and he rose to become superintendent of the Cribari wine enterprise.

In July 1932, Fred, as he is familiarly known to his host of friends, became the manager of the Beringer Bros. establishment, a post he has held ever since. Soon after Repeal new buildings were erected to increase the winery's capacity. Later the Eschol winery and vineyards on the Napa Highway and the Garetto winery in the Los Amigos area of Napa were taken over by the Beringers. All three plants are under Fred Abruzzini's management, but the pride of the three naturally remains the Beringer winery itself, which Fred delights in showing to all visitors, whether they are celebrities or just plain folks.

The Beringer policy is to market well-aged wines, blended so that their character and quality remain continuous over the years. The featured brand is *Beringer Private Stock,* with *Los Hermanos* the secondary label. *Beringer Family Bottling* is used for older and more expensive wines.

Table wines:
  Family Bottling: Barenblut (a Beringer specialty, the "Blood of the Berry," made from selected dark grapes); Riesling;
  Private Stock: Cabernet, Barenblut, Burgundy, Zinfandel, Claret; Riesling, Haut Sauterne, Sauterne, Dry Sauterne, Chablis, Moselle, Hock; Rosé (mainly from Valdepeñas grapes);
  Los Hermanos: Burgundy, Claret, Zinfandel; Sauterne, Dry Sauterne, Chablis; Rosé;

Sparkling wines (carbonated): Beringer Sparkler Burgundy and Sparkler Moselle;

Aperitif and Dessert wines:
  Family Bottling: Port
  Private Stock: Pale Dry Sherry, Sherry; Port; Muscatel, Malvasia Bianca (a specialty); Tokay, White Port, Angelica;
  Los Hermanos: Pale Dry Sherry, Sherry; Port; Muscatel; Angelica.

Beringer Bros. has been in the Sacramental Wine business since the end of the last century. Pure Altar Wines (available only to the clergy) include:

Table wines: Cabernet, Barenblut, Burgundy, Zinfandel, and Claret; Riesling, Haut Sauterne, Sauterne, Dry Sauterne, Chablis, Hock, and Moselle;

Sweet wines: Sherry and Pale Dry Sherry; Port; Muscatel and Malvoisie; Tokay, White Port, Angelica; Beringerber (a madeira-type wine).

L. Brendel, St. Helena

A small winery and vineyard owned and operated by one man, Leon Brendel. Only one wine is produced, a Grignolino, marketed, appropriately enough, under the *Only One* brand.

Leon Brendel was born at Equisheim, near Colmar in Alsace, France, and comes of a family of winegrowers who also made only one wine, in their case Traminer. He studied chemistry at Besançon and Rouffach in France and at Aschaffenburg in Bavaria. With Dr. Goettler he helped to organize a school for distillers in Basel, Switzerland. He went to Mexico at the request of the family of President Madero and became the wine maker and chemist for the Madero winery and vineyards at Parras, Coahuila, Mexico.

At the time of Repeal, Brendel came to Southern California, where he established himself as a chemist and wine consultant. Later he became connected with the Ahern wine enterprise and was the wine maker and chemist at Freemark Abbey.

In the meantime Leon Brendel had decided to establish his own winery and vineyards and chose his present location in St. Helena. He wanted to make only one kind of wine and after experimenting with many grape varieties he finally chose Grignolino, probably the only one made in Napa Valley. His Grignolino wine is darker in color than most other California Grignolinos and has a distinctive flavor and charm of its own. The grapes are crushed at Freemark Abbey, but the wine is aged at the Brendel winery and clarified naturally.

Leon Brendel can relate most interestingly his adventures in Mexico and elsewhere. He is also the inventor and perfecter of various tools useful to the wine industry. Among these are an electromechanical wine-hose-cleaning unit and a bench budding gadget which simplifies the grafting of vine cuttings and is used by growers both in this country and abroad.

Freemark Abbey, St. Helena

A family concern devoted mainly to the production and marketing of quality table wines. Michael Ahern is general manager in charge of the plant at St. Helena, while executive offices are maintained in Santa Monica. A retail store is operated by Freemark Abbey in San Francisco, featuring only Freemark Abbey wines and wine jellies, probably the only outlet of its kind in a metropolitan area in the United States owned and run by a winery.

Freemark Abbey was purchased by the Ahern family in 1939 and at that time was a corporation of which the members were Albert M. Ahern (nicknamed *Abbey*), Charles *Free*man, and *Mark* Foster, from whose names that of the winery was derived. Before purchasing the St. Helena winery the Ahern family had owned vineyards in Southern California, where they still have other agricultural interests.

Table wines are the specialty, marketed under the *Freemark Abbey* brand. These include: Pinot Noir, Zinfandel, Burgundy, and Claret in the reds, and Semillon, Traminer, Chablis, and Sauterne in the whites, as well as a Vin Rosé.

Chateau Freemark is the brand name used in marketing a medium-dry bottle-fermented Champagne and Sparkling Burgundy. *Aperitif and Dessert wines,* including Pale Dry Sherry, Ruby Port, and Dry and Sweet Vermouth, also carry the *Freemark Abbey* label.

A special feature of Freemark Abbey is the production of *jellies* made from Freemark Abbey wines, which was started in 1951. Made in a factory directly behind the winery, these wine jellies come in the following varieties: Pinot Noir, Zinfandel, Burgundy, and Claret; Semillon, Traminer, Sauterne, Chablis, and Rhine Wine; Vin Rosé; Sherry and Port.

Charles Krug Winery (C. Mondavi & Sons), St. Helena

Cesare Mondavi and his sons, Robert and Peter, are the worthy successors to Charles Krug, one of the great figures in the development of the California wine industry.

Charles Krug was born in Trendelburg, Prussia, in 1825 and emigrated to America as a young man. He returned to his fatherland to take part in the democratic uprising of 1848 and, on the failure of that movement, returned to the United States for good. He came to California and devoted his energies to a study of viticulture with the aim of establishing his own vineyards and winery. During this period he worked for General Vallejo and Colonel Haraszthy in Sonoma and became convinced of the desirability of planting European grape varieties. In 1858 he purchased some acreage of his own and made viticultural history by producing, from the grapes of John Patchett of Napa, some 1200 gallons of wine with a small cider press, the first wine obtained in Napa County by more modern methods. The press is preserved at the Krug Ranch today, a treasured memento of its founder.

Krug built his original winery at St. Helena in 1861. The fame of his wines soon spread throughout the country and beyond. By 1880 the Krug Ranch was considered one of the most beautiful and productive in the Napa Valley and Krug himself was well established as a leader of the wine industry. Such men as Carl Wente and the Beringer brothers worked with him and obtained valuable experience at his winery.

After the death of Charles Krug in 1894, the ranch was purchased by his close friend and admirer, James K. Moffitt, who used the residence and gardens as a country home. The vineyards and winery were leased until Prohibition forced them into a dormant period.

When Repeal came the Moffitt family was willing to sell the ranch, but only to some wine-making family capable of reviving the fame and prestige of the Krug wines. With a feeling of accomplishing this purpose the property was sold, in 1943, to Cesare Mondavi and his sons, the present owners.

Cesare Mondavi came to America from Ancona, Italy, and also personifies the story of successful enterprise. He first went to work in the ore mines of Minnesota. There he was chosen by a group of Italian home wine makers to select and buy grapes for them in California. He stayed on and engaged in the wine-grape-shipping business, expanding his operation later to include fruits. After Repeal he entered the wine-making field, first producing dessert wines at the Acampo Winery in Lodi. Later he began to produce dry table wines in St. Helena at the Sunny St. Helena winery. Anxious to concentrate on the production of high-quality wines the Mondavi family found in the Krug Ranch the worthy means to achieve their goal. His sons, Robert Mondavi, the general manager of the company, and Peter Mondavi, the production manager and wine maker, have been familiar with the wine industry since their earliest years and both are graduates of Stanford University, majoring in viticulture and enology. Cesare Mondavi, their father, remains president of the firm.

Since 1943 the Mondavis have renovated the whole Krug plant, modernizing the winery and cellars and re-equipping the buildings. Gradually the older vines on the ranch were replaced, always with the finest varieties. The name of Charles Krug was revived and maintained in order to restore it to its honored place in the California wine industry. Actually the names of Charles Krug and of C. Mondavi & Sons are interchangeable today.

The main accent of the Krug (Mondavi) production is on that of fine *table wines*. A few Aperitif and Dessert wines are also included. The finest-quality wines are marketed under the *Charles Krug* brand, while *Napa Vista* is used for the winery's medium-priced vintage table wines and *CK* for table and dessert wines of commercially competitive grades.

The *Charles Krug table wines* include:

RED: Cabernet Sauvignon, Gamay, Zinfandel, Burgundy, and Claret;

WHITE: Traminer (limited production and generally recognized as outstanding, Johannisberger Riesling, Grey Riesling, Riesling, Rhine Wine; White Pinot (Chenin Blanc), Chablis; Dry Semillon, Haut Sauterne, and Dry Sauterne;

ROSÉ: Vin Rosé (from the Gamay grape)

The *Aperitif and Dessert wines* under the *Charles Krug* label include Sherry, Port, and Muscatel.

The Charles Krug Winery, from time to time, "uncorks and

pours" an informative and chatty pamphlet entitled "Bottles and Bins."

Louis M. Martini, St. Helena

The wines produced by Louis Martini rate among the very best of California. Born in Pietra Ligure on the Italian Riviera, Louis Martini came to San Francisco as a boy and first assisted his father, Agostino Martini, in his mussels, clams, and fish business. In 1906, the year of the earthquake, the decision was made to enter the wine-making field. A small plant was built in San Francisco, some forty by seventy-five feet, the modest forerunner of the modern Martini winery in St. Helena today.

Louis Martini returned to Italy to study wine making at the University of Genoa and in Piedmont, and then returned to this country to practice the knowledge he had acquired. He worked for various wine makers, including the famous Secundo Guasti, founder of the Italian Vineyard Company at Guasti in the Cucamonga district. Later Louis Martini acquired a plant of his own at Fresno for the making of grape juice, and then built a winery and distillery at Kingsburg in the southern part of the San Joaquin Valley for the production of sweet wines and brandy. His ambition, however, had been steadily directed toward producing top-quality table wines. When he sold the Kingsburg plant for a good price, he settled in St. Helena to fulfill his ambition, armed with the necessary know-how, drive, and capital.

Martini's St. Helena winery was built in 1933 and he successively acquired three vineyard complexes. The Villa del Rey, or St. Helena vineyard, is situated on light, well-drained soil along the Mayacamas foothills near St. Helena and is planted mostly to Cabernet Sauvignon, Napa Valley Gamay, Chenin blanc (for White Pinot) and Sauvignon blanc. The Napa, or La Loma, vineyard, part of the former Rancho Rincon de los Carneros, lies on the rolling, gravelly, southern end of the Mayacamas range, southwest of the town of Napa. It specializes in Cabernet Sauvignon, Pinot noir, and Zinfandel.

Most famous of the three vineyards is, undoubtedly, the one formerly called Goldstein, planted in the early eighteen eighties, and by Martini renamed Monte Rosso after its red volcanic soil. It is situated at an altitude of over 1000 feet on the crest of the Mayacamas Mountains in Sonoma. In this cool location most wine grape varieties attain their peak of perfection. The Monte Rosso varieties include Cabernet Sauvignon, Barbera, Zinfandel, and White Riesling, Gewurztraminer, Sylvaner, Pinot Chardonnay, Folle blanche, and Semilllon. The wines produced from these grapes are truly "mountain" wines and usually carry that designation on the label.

Louis Martini, a colorful, vital, and forceful figure, is president of the Louis M. Martini Corporation. He is ably assisted in the family enterprise by his son Louis P. Martini, the vice-president, and a graduate of the viticultural department of the University of California at Davis, Yolo County.

The Martini wines are marketed under the *Louis Martini* brand and include the following:

Table wines:

RED: Cabernet Sauvignon (vintage, one of the great California clarets, and available in especially fine years as Cabernet Sauvignon Special Reserve), Mountain Pinot Noir (also bottled in magnums), Mountain Barbera (vintage), Napa Cabernet, Mountain Zinfandel (vintage). "Monte Rosso," named after the Sonoma vineyard, is a specialty, a red chianti type of top quality, put up in the traditional Italian *fiaschi*. Generic red wines produced are: Napa Burgundy, Mountain Claret, Mountain Chianti, and Mountain Red.

WHITE: Mountain Johannisberg Riesling (vintage), Napa White Pinot (vintage), Mountain Folle Blanche (vintage), Mountain Sylvaner (vintage), Mountain Dry Semillon (vintage) in the varietals, and Dry Sauterne, Napa Chablis, Mountain Rhine, and Mountain White in the generics.

ROSÉ: Napa Gamay Rosé.

A number of older-vintage varietal table wines are also available at times, but in very limited quantities. They have been set aside on account of their special distinction and carry the words "Private Selection" on the label. Such vintage specialities have included Cabernet Sauvignons, both from the Monte Rosso and Villa del Rey vineyards, Zinfandels from Monte Rosso and La Loma, Gewurztraminers from Monte Rosso, and from the same vineyard Pinot Chardonnay, Folle Blanche, and Sylvaner.

Aperitif and Dessert wines:

Port, an older Tawny Port and a Muscatel. At one time a light Moscato was produced and it is entirely possible that such a Moscato Amabile will again be marketed.

An outstanding aperitif is the Pale Dry Sherry with the character of a Spanish Fino and the product of Louis Martini's own adaptation of the Solera system.

Each year a so-called "annual blend" is made on the basis of aroma and taste to duplicate, as closely as possible, the sherry of previous years and to supply continuity of character and quality. This annual blend, produced in a quantity sufficient to meet the current year's estimated requirement, is then in turn blended with an equal volume of the previous year's blend. About one half of the resulting master blend is set aside to be bottled during the year and the balance is retained as the base to which the following year's blend will be added.

Any annual blend is composed of some thirty-five different-aged sherries, each with its own particular character, ranging in age from six to twenty years. Together they compose the Solera system. As certain types used in the blend become depleted, they are replaced by others of the same general character. To ensure continuity, a system of sub-Soleras has been developed for the various types. Important among the latter are the *flor* sherries, which contribute their typical *flor* character to the final product.

Stony Hill Vineyard, St. Helena

Some seven hundred feet above the floor of the Napa Valley, on the steep hillsides between Spring and Diamond mountains, lies the Stony Hill Vineyard, the name of which speaks for itself. They are planted mainly to three varieties, all white: Pinot Chardonnay, Pinot blanc, and White Riesling.

Frederick H. McCrea, vice-president of the internationally known advertising agency of McCann-Erickson, Inc., for long had the ambition to see what he could do about producing good wines in small quantities. He purchased the Stony Hill property in 1943 and built a small but very modern winery in 1951. Crushing of the grapes is done by hand power and the wine is fermented in fifty-gallon barrels.

Production is limited to a small output, some of it going to Souverain Cellars across the Napa Valley. Pinot Chardonnay, Pinot Blanc, and Johannisberger Riesling are bottled under the *Stony Hill* brand, carrying the vintage on the label as well as the Napa Valley appellation of origin.

Souverain Cellars, St. Helena

On the slopes of Howell Mountain, overlooking the upper Napa Valley from the east, are to be found the ranch and vineyards of J. Leland (Lee) Stewart. It was in 1943 that Lee Stewart, always appreciative of fine wines, decided to enter the winegrowing and wine-making fields himself. Originally headed for Ukiah, he happened to detour by way of Napa and St. Helena and ended up by purchasing the old Peter Stark place above the Silverado Trail. Gradually he modernized the winery and replanted the vineyards. His aim is to combine the best traditions of the European winegrower with the most modern California methods. A feature of the winery is the handsomely carved entrance door, depicting a vintage scene, the work of Merrill Abbott of St. Helena.

What had first started out as a hobby soon became a steady business. The accent of production is on the choice *table wine* varieties, for which Cabernet Sauvignon, Grenache, and Zinfandel are grown on the Howell Mountain property. Lee Stewart feels that certain varieties like the Rieslings, Pinot blanc, and Gamay are of superior quality when grown on the opposite side of the valley. Three of his friends, who came to the Napa Valley about the same time and with the same desire to own vineyards of fine varietals, are, to quote Lee Stewart, "enthusiastically growing these varieties on such steep and rock-lain slopes as would scare less timid souls out of their wits." And so the Al Menasco, Jerry Draper, and Fred McCrea Spring Mountain vineyards contribute to the Souverain Cellars vintages every fall.

The name Souverain Cellars owes its origin to the simple fact that it headed the list of suggestions submitted to Lee Stewart at the time he was looking for a suitable brand and name. It rang true and was adopted forthwith.

Souverain is the brand name for all the choicer wines, with *Villa LeGlen* the secondary label.

The following *Souverain table wines* are produced:

RED: Cabernet Sauvignon, Gamay, Mountain Zinfandel; Burgundy;

WHITE: Johannisberger Riesling (featured), Pinot Blanc, Sylvaner, Green Hungarian (one of the very few produced), Dry Sauterne;

ROSÉ: Grenache Rosé.

Beaulieu Vineyard, Rutherford

A true California chateau with a name for its wines as great as it is justified.

It was just before the turn of the century that a young Frenchman, Georges de Latour, came to California, desirous of producing table wines comparable in quality and character to the finer ones of his native France. He had heard much about California's favorable climate and soil and he came to see for himself. He stemmed from a family well known in both the Bordeaux and Burgundy regions and was already familiar with many of the problems of viticulture and of the difficult art of wine making. He was, besides, gifted with an exceptionally fine taster's palate, an attribute of primary importance to all those engaged in the wine business, and especially in the producing end of it.

Georges de Latour traveled through California searching for the ideal location suited to his purpose and found what he sought in the Rutherford area in the Napa Valley. It was here, in 1900, that he founded the Beaulieu estate and vineyards, as he named them so appropriately. Beaulieu, enlarged and modernized at various times, has remained in the family's hands ever since and is today one of the show places of the valley.

For some forty years Georges de Latour devoted his energies to the production of the finest wines the favored climate and soil of the Napa Valley were capable of yielding. He proved himself eminently successful in his endeavor and established a solid reputation for the Beaulieu wines throughout the United States and abroad.

During Prohibition the winery continued to operate, producing sacramental wines, to which a part of the Beaulieu industry is still actively devoted.

Beaulieu is one of the few wineries in California where the accent in wines and wine production is very distinctly inspired by the French taste; the whole atmosphere is that of *"la belle France,"* completely at home in the Napa Valley.

After the death of Georges de Latour in 1940, Madame de Latour presided over Beaulieu in her husband's place. Known to so many for her grace and charm, she had become the *"grande dame"* of California viticulture. With her demise, in 1951, another great figure had passed on.

Today Beaulieu is owned by the daughter of its founders, Hélène de Pins, who, together with her husband, the Marquis de Pins, continues the great tradition set by the De Latours. The Marquis de Pins is a landed proprietor in France; he has a thorough knowledge of fine vintages throughout the world and is known in this country and in France as an outstanding connoisseur and judge of wines. The De Pins divide their time between Beaulieu and San Francisco, where they are leaders of society, and periodically visit France, often touring the various French winegrowing districts. Their daughter Dagmar, a wine expert in her own right, is married to a prominent San Francisco real estate investor, Walter H.

Sullivan, Jr., and Beaulieu's distinguished heritage will continue through them and their children.

The reputation of Beaulieu's wines has progressed with the times, their quality the result of a happy blending between the traditional subtleties of French taste and know-how in the modern California manner. To this philosophy fully subscribes French-trained André Tchelistcheff, who joined Beaulieu in 1938 and is the production manager in charge of the winery and vineyards. He skillfully adapts New World techniques of quality-wine production to his store of Old World wine-making experience.

There are four Beaulieu vineyards, two of them located at Rutherford and the other two at Oakville, each being planted with the grape varieties best suited to its particular soil and location.

The brand name under which all wines are marketed is *Beaulieu Vineyard*. As some have difficulty in pronouncing the name, the labels also carry the letters *B V,* and it is by this name that the wines are also widely known. All table wines are labeled with the Napa Valley appellation of origin.

The Beaulieu (*B V*) family of *table wines* includes the following:
RED: Georges de Latour Private Reserve (a vintage Cabernet Sauvignon, produced exclusively from that grape only in the better years, and considered by many to be the premier claret of California), Beaumont (a vintage Pinot Noir produced exclusively from that grape and only in the favorable years), Cabernet Sauvignon (a vintage wine principally from that grape, but, as is the case with many of the better Red Bordeaux of France, with small proportions of Merlot and Petit Verdot added), Burgundy (from Pinot noir, Napa Valley Gamay, and Mondeuse de Savoie);
WHITE: Chateau Beaulieu (a vintage sweet Sauterne from late-picked Sauvignon blanc and Semillon grapes with a touch of Muscadelle du Bordelais added), Pinot Chardonnay (a vintage wine from that grape, the production of which is very limited), Beauclair (a vintage Johannisberger or White Riesling), Dry Sauternes and Sweet Sauternes (both from Semillon and Sau-

vignon blanc grapes), Chablis (from Pinot Chardonnay, Chenin blanc, and Melon de Bourgogne), Riesling (from Johannisberger or White Riesling and Sylvaner);

ROSÉ: Beaurosé (from Cabernet Sauvignon mainly);

Sparkling wines (bottle-fermented):

The Beaulieu Champagnes (dry and medium dry in character) became available for the first time in 1955; a Sparkling Burgundy of high quality is also in production.

Aperitif and Dessert wines:

Although Beaulieu's renown has primarily been based on its table wines, some very good *Aperitif and Dessert wines* are also produced at the winery. These include: Pale Dry Sherry, Sherry XXX (medium sweet), Cream Sherry (sweet); Port XXX; Muscatel XXX and Muscat de Frontignan (from the vines of that name, cuttings of which were imported by Georges de Latour from France in the early part of the century).

The Beaulieu Vineyard Pure *Altar Wines* (available only to the clergy) include:

Table wines: Cabernet Sauvignon and Burgundy in the reds, and Chateau Beaulieu, Sweet Sauternes, Dry Sauternes, Riesling, Rhine, and Chablis in the whites;

Sweet wines: Muscat de Frontignan and Muscatel XXX, Tokay XXX and Angelica XXX.

Inglenook Vineyard Company, Rutherford

The great, castlelike, vine-covered winery of Inglenook, home of its famed vintage table wines, lies in the heart of the Napa Valley at Rutherford, with Beaulieu its immediate neighbor.

Founder of Inglenook's viticultural renown was that colorful Finnish seafarer, fur trader, and winegrower, Captain Niebaum. Gustave Ferdinand Nybom (later Americanized to Niebaum) was born in 1842 in Helsinki, Finland, at that time under Russian domination. He went to sea as a boy and received his master's papers when only nineteen. Two years later he had his own command and in 1864 sailed for Alaska, then also part of the Russian Empire.

For three years he ranged Alaska, the Aleutian chain, and the Asiatic shore as far as Kamchatka, bartering for furs and acquainting himself thoroughly with the region. Negotiations by the United States for the purchase of Alaska had been started and Niebaum realized that America would have economic as well as political interests in the territory. He decided to make full use of his opportunities and amassed a vast collection of sealskins and other valuable furs. When the sale of Alaska to the United States was completed in March 1867, Niebaum lost no time in loading his precious furs aboard a ship bound for San Francisco. He was no more than twenty-six when he sailed through the Golden Gate, the owner of a cargo worth well over half a million dollars.

Captain Niebaum's knowledge of the seal country was invaluable to the Alaska Commercial Company, organized to obtain exclusive fur-sealing rights in the Alaskan waters and he became their youngest partner. The company proved so successful that it paid the United States Government considerably more in rights than the total cost of the Alaskan purchase.

The captain was now ready for a less rigorous mode of life, and as Mrs. Niebaum did not share his love for the sea he turned his thoughts to the land and to an enterprise they both could enjoy.

On his various trips to Europe in the interests of the Alaskan company he had become increasingly interested in viticulture and wine making. He had visited many of the European winegrowing regions and collected a large number of books on the subjects. His hobby finally became his life's destiny. With enough time and money to accomplish his purpose he decided to attempt to produce in California wines comparable to Europe's finest.

After a thorough search for the most suitable location Captain Niebaum purchased, in 1879, a portion of the old Mexican Caymus Rancho grant, extending from Rutherford up the slopes of Mt. St. John, highest peak of the Mayacamas range. The property had already been called Inglenook (Scottish for fireside corner) by the former owner, W. C. Watson. The name appealed to Niebaum and he retained it.

Niebaum devoted the following years to planning, building, and planting. Further trips to the winegrowing regions of Europe were made, where he studied every aspect of viticulture. Cuttings of the choicest wine grape varieties were shipped home. At Inglenook he established the vineyards with the utmost care and always with due regard to the beauty of nature. The cellar and winery were built according to the most modern specifications. Inglenook had become Captain Niebaum's ship and the vineyards his sea.

By 1890 Inglenook had become a model winery and vineyard. So particular was the captain that he used to inspect the cellar wearing white gloves and woe the culprit if the least speck of dirt was observed. In wine production his motto was "quality and not quantity." Inglenook's vintages soon achieved the highest reputation.

When Captain Niebaum died, in 1908, Inglenook was inherited by his widow. John Daniel, her niece's husband, ably directed operations for her until the advent of Prohibition. His knowledge, in turn, was passed on to his son, John Daniel, Jr., who has been in charge of the winery and vineyards since Repeal, first on behalf of Mrs. Niebaum and, after her death in 1936, on his own behalf and that of his sister, Mrs. Hawkins.

Inglenook was the first winery to label many of the better-known varietals as such, pioneered such wines as White Pinot (known at one time as White Zinfandel), Red Pinot, and Charbono and was one of the earliest producers of Vin Rosé in the state.

John Daniel, Jr., is as justly proud of Inglenook today as his great-uncle, Captain Niebaum, was in his day. Production is concentrated on high-quality varietal vintage table wines; with a few exceptions each is the product of the single grape whose name it bears. The policy is to give the vintage designation greater value than simple age dating, the practice being to eliminate any wine of a given variety which does not live up to the Inglenook standard.

The following *table wines* are produced, all derived from the

single grape unless otherwise noted. They are marketed under the
Inglenook brand and carry the Napa Valley appellation and the
vintage year on the label.

RED: Cabernet Sauvignon, Pinot Noir, Red Pinot (from the Pinot
St. George grape and fuller-bodied than the Pinot Noir), Gamay
(from the Napa Valley Gamay), Charbono (from the grape of
that name and one of the very few produced);

WHITE: Pinot Chardonnay, White Pinot (from the Chenin blanc
grape), Traminer, Riesling (from the Franken Riesling or
Sylvaner grape), Semillon (principally from that grape),
Navalle White Wine (a medium-dry blend to be vintaged
again);

ROSÉ: Navalle Rosé (predominantly from the Napa Valley Gamay
and named, like the Navalle White Wine, after the creek which
winds through the Inglenook vineyards).

Inglenook also markets a few *Aperitif and Dessert wines,* which
are purchased, blended, and aged in its cellars and include a Dry
Sherry and a Ruby Port.

The Inglenook Palomino Sherry, produced entirely from Palomino grapes grown in its own vineyards, has become a collector's
item, as its production has been discontinued until such time as
separate facilities for its renewed production have become established.

NAPA COUNTY—LOWER NAPA VALLEY

The Christian Brothers (Mont La Salle Vineyards), Napa

The Mont La Salle Vineyards and Novitiate of The Christian
Brothers are located high in the hills of the southwestern part of
Napa County in the so-called Napa Redwoods district, some eight
miles northwest of the town of Napa.

The "Brothers of the Christian Schools," as The Christian Brothers are officially called, form a congregation of the Roman Catholic
Church, dedicated to the education of young men and boys. The
order was founded in 1680 at Reims, France, by Jean Baptiste de la

Salle, for the purpose of educating the underprivileged. Its head-quarters are in Rome. Although not priests, the brothers lead dedicated lives, having taken the vows of poverty, chastity, and obedience.

The Christian Brothers first came to the United States before the middle of the nineteenth century. At present they operate one hundred and ten institutes of learning in the country, such as Manhattan College in New York City, La Salle Military Academy on Long Island, New York, St. Mel's High School in Chicago, Christian Brothers College in St. Louis, St. Mary's College at Moraga near Oakland in California.

Mont La Salle at Napa is The Christian Brothers' Novitiate for California and the Western States. Here young men are trained for the work of the congregation, while a school is maintained for boys of high-school age and a home for brothers who have retired after a lifetime of service. Here also the brothers proudly follow their wine-making tradition, a heritage dating back many centuries.

In California The Christian Brothers started making wine in 1879, at first for sacramental use only and later, with the growing demand by lay circles, for the public. Profits are exclusively used for the maintenance of Mont La Salle and in furtherance of the congregation's educational work. No personal compensation is received by the brothers, whether engaged in teaching or in wine-making activities. Brother Alfred (George Brousseau) is the visitor or president of the institute. Brother John is general manager for the wine and brandy production and Brother Timothy is the wine maker.

Besides the Mont La Salle winery and distillery The Christian Brothers operate the famed Greystone Cellars at St. Helena, a land-mark once known as the largest winery of the world and now principally used for the aging of The Christian Brothers' table wines, though some altar wines as well as aperitif and dessert wines are aged there and a small amount of red table wine is produced there every year. In addition a winery and distillery is maintained at Par-lier, near Reedley, in Fresno County.

All commercially available table wines as well as the even better-known aperitif and dessert wines are marketed under *The Christian Brothers* brand.

Table wines (mostly produced at the Mont La Salle winery and aged in oak casks):

RED: Cabernet (mostly from Cabernet Sauvignon), Burgundy, Claret;

WHITE: Sauterne, Dry Sauterne, Haut Sauterne, Riesling (mainly from Sylvaner), Rhine, Chablis;

ROSÉ: Napa Rosé (slightly sweet, containing, unlike many rosés, a small amount of residual sugar).

Aperitif and Dessert wines:

Cocktail Sherry (aged longer in fifty-gallon oak barrels), Dry Sherry, Golden Sherry, and Cream Sherry; Treasure Port (an older Tawny aged in fifty-gallon oak cooperage), Ruby Port, and Tawny Port; Muscatel and Tokay; Vermouth: "Starlight Dry" and "Aperitif Wine," sweet.

Altar wines:

The Christian Brothers produce a full range of sacramental wines, available only to the clergy. These are bottled under the *Mont La Salle* label and include:

Dry wines: Cabernet and Burgundy, Haut Sauterne, Dry Sauterne, and Chablis;

Sweet wines: Sherry, Port, Muscatel, Tokay, and Angelica. Two specialty altar wines are St. Benedict (medium sweet with a slight sherry character) and La Salle Special (high-quality sweet wine similar to muscatel).

Mayacamas Vineyards, Napa

High in the Mayacamas Mountains, on top of Mt. Veeder, an extinct volcano some twelve miles west of Napa in the Lokoya district, lies one of the smallest wineries devoted to fine wines, the Mayacamas Vineyards. According to local authorities, Mayacamas means "Howl of the Mountain Lion" and comes from the language of the Lokoya tribe of Indians, who formerly inhabited the Maya-camas region.

Mayacamas Vineyards is strictly a family affair, owned and oper-ated by Jack F. M. and Mary Catherine Taylor. Jack Taylor, an Englishman and a graduate of the University of Cambridge, was for many years with the Shell Oil Company and contributed much to its development in California. He is still oil consultant for various Central and South American countries. Mary Taylor, who comes from an editorial family, has published two books on that charming form of song called rounds, and has recently written the story of the Mayacamas Vineyards. Among her other talents she is an extremely gifted cook, a true "Cordon Bleu."

The Taylors became winegrowers for the simple reason that they had always liked fine wines. They decided, in 1941, on the Mt. Veeder property because of its beautiful setting, its perfect grape-growing location, and because there was an old winery and distill-ery, dating back to 1889, known for a number of years as Mount Veeder Vineyards.

The distillery, completely remodeled, is now the hospitable Taylor home. The old vineyards were all ripped out, terraced at great ex-pense, and replanted mostly to Pinot Chardonnay, yielding the wine in which the Taylors specialize, with justified pride.

The Taylors are ably assisted in their enterprise by their daughter Judith (Judy) and her husband Rodney Revett (Rev) Cant.

The following *vintage table wines* are produced either from home-grown grapes or from Napa Valley selected varieties and carry the *Mayacamas* brand with the Napa County appellation of origin on the label:

WHITE: Chardonnay (nearly exclusively from that grape with a slight addition of Pinot blanc to bring out the full flavor), White Pinot (from the Chenin blanc);

ROSÉ: Gamay Rosé (from the Napa Valley Gamay).

Two *table wines* of Napa County origin are aged at the winery and marketed under the *Lokoya* brand: Lokoya White (of the rhine wine order) and Lokoya Red (a light claret type).

To round out their wine list, Mayacamas Vineyards selects a number of wines which they like in other wineries and market them under the *Lokoya* brand with the California designation:

Table wine: Zinfandel;

Sparkling wines (bottle-fermented): Pinot Champagne (from Pinot varietals) and Sparkling Burgundy;

Aperitif and Dessert wines: Black Muscat, Dry and Sweet Vermouth.

SOLANO COUNTY

Cadenasso Wine Company, Fairfield

Adjoining Napa County to the east lies the county of Solano and here, at Fairfield, in the Suisun district, is to be found the Cadenasso winery, producer of some of the finest grignolino and zinfandel in the state.

The Cadenasso wine enterprise was founded in 1906, when Giovanni Cadenasso, who had emigrated from Italy shortly before, started his own vineyard and winery on the Rutherford ranch in Green Valley, north of Cordelia. In 1916 Cadenasso moved to Fairfield and planted vineyards on the site where the Solano County Hospital now stands. With Prohibition wine making came to an end and the winery was dismantled in accordance with the Eighteenth Amendment. Cadenasso sold his property to the county, but wine making remained in his blood. And so, undaunted, in 1926 he started a third vineyard, across the road from his former location in the belief that Prohibition would be repealed. He had judged rightly and soon after Repeal his vineyards were prospering once more.

Giovanni Cadenasso is still the president of the company, but his son Frank is now the wine maker and vineyard manager. Other members of the Cadenasso family are the senior Mrs. Cadenasso, Louisa, and the couple's other children, Leo Cadenasso and Mrs. Mae Balestra. Giuseppe Cadenasso, a brother of Giovanni, was the well-known painter who taught art at Mills College.

Table wines only are produced, from grapes grown on the home ranch as well as from others purchased in Solano and Napa counties. The featured brand is *Cadenasso* and the wines include the following:

RED: Grignolino (the house specialty), Zinfandel; Burgundy (from Petite Sirah and others), Claret (mostly from Carignane, blended with Zinfandel);
WHITE: French Colombard, Sauvignon Vert, Dry Muscat; Sauterne and Haut Sauterne, Chablis;
ROSÉ: Vin Rosé (dry) and Chateau Rosé (semi-sweet).

A number of *Aperitif and Dessert wines* are purchased, aged and bottled at the winery for local marketing.

C. *LIVERMORE—CONTRA COSTA DISTRICT*

This district, as famous in its own way as that of Napa-Solano, consists of a number of separate wine-producing areas located in Alameda and Contra Costa counties.

Celebrated throughout the country and beyond is Alameda County's Livermore Valley, home of unsurpassed California wines of the Sauterne types. Some red table wine is also produced as are sparkling wines and aperitif and dessert wines of great merit. The Livermore Valley, actually not so much a valley as a wide basin, comprises two neighboring winegrowing areas, the famed vineyards centering around the town of Livermore, with their gravelly vineyards, and separated from them only by some low hills to the west, the sector around Pleasanton.

Second only in importance to the Livermore Valley is southern Alameda, close to the southern tip of San Francisco Bay. With its winegrowing centers of Mission San Jose and Irvington it actually forms an extension of the adjoining wine-producing areas in Santa Clara County. In southern Alameda the red table wines vie with the whites in quality and here sparkling wines and aperitif and dessert wines of note are also produced.

Western Alameda boasts one winery at Hayward, although no grapes are grown there and real estate developments are fast encroaching on the area.

Contra Costa County is best known for its table wines and especially for its Gamay. The county's more important winegrowing areas are located south of the city of Martinez and by Mt. Diablo, which rises so majestically east of San Francisco to a height of nearly four thousand feet.

THE LIVERMORE VALLEY

Concannon Vineyard, Livermore

An old firm with a famous name, strong in Roman Catholic traditions, and known for its high-quality wines. The main accent in production is on table wines of the sauterne family, as is to be expected in the heart of the Livermore district. Sacramental wines form a major factor in the winery's business.

James Concannon, the founder, was born in the Aran Islands, County Galway, Ireland, in 1847, into a family descended, according to an ancient tradition, from the Milesian Kings of Spain. As a youth James helped his family raise the customary potatoes, but he soon determined to carve out a career for himself in what he called "that shining land across the seas."

He saved enough money for his passage to Boston, where he found a job with the Singer Sewing Machine Company. He moved to Augusta, Maine, where he worked as a bellboy in the Mansion House, attending school at night, and rose to become the hotel's manager. By 1874 he could afford to marry and a year later brought his bride to San Francisco.

In the West James Concannon found full opportunity to apply his energy and resourcefulness. He managed a sheep ranch in Oregon, sold books from door to door, and pioneered the rubber-stamp business, a new industry which proved highly profitable. He became agent for the whole of the Pacific coast and included Mexico in his travels. In Mexico City he criticized the then prevailing sanitary conditions in no uncertain terms with the result that the famed dictator of Mexico, Porforio Díaz, sent for him. Díaz took a liking to the forthright and energetic young Irishman and entrusted him with full authority to remedy the situation. For a number of years Concannon was in charge of the city's hygienic rehabilitation, eventually disposing of his franchise to a syndicate on profitable terms.

The rubber printing stamp, however, backed by his pioneering spirit, was what made Concannon's fortune. By 1883 he had amassed sufficient capital to settle down with his family and farm. It was at the advice of his friend, the colorful Archbishop of San Francisco, Joseph S. Alemany, that James Concannon decided to produce wines for religious use and that he purchased, in the Livermore Valley, a suitable ranch from Horace Overacher, a homesteader. Concannon's success as a vineyardist and wine maker became rapidly established and the high tradition he set has been carried on down continuously to the present day.

After James Concannon passed away in 1911, management of the winery passed to his son, Joseph S. Concannon, the present head of the firm. "Captain Joe," as he is known to all, is a figure of profound charm, energy, and wit. A former U. S. Cavalry officer, the military touch at Concannon is nearly as evident as that of the master wine-grower and the fact that he is a devout son of the Roman Catholic Church. Concannon wines are familiar to Catholic dioceses near and far, including the Vatican.

Captain Joe has managed the winery for more than forty years with the sole exception of the period 1916–18, when he joined the cavalry to take part in General Pershing's expedition against Pancho Villa in Mexico. During Prohibition Concannon Vineyard continued to operate, producing altar wines as permitted by the dry laws.

Today the third generation of the Concannon family is gradually taking over control. Captain Joe continues as president, aided by his two sons, Joseph Jr., a Notre Dame graduate, and James, who graduated from St. Mary's College in California. Two daughters complete the picture of the family-owned business, of whom Nina Concannon is vice-president of the firm.

Concannon produces the following *table wines* commercially

under the *Concannon Vineyard* brand and with the Livermore designation of origin on the label:

WHITE: Sauvignon Blanc (Concannon's prize white vintage table wine and a great wine indeed), Chateau Concannon (sweet sauterne from late-picked Semillon and Sauvignon blanc grapes), Haut Sauterne (similar to a French Graves), Dry Semillon (vintaged), Dry Sauterne, Chablis (a blend of Folle blanche and other grapes), Moselle;
RED: Cabernet Sauvignon (vintaged and similar to a red Graves in character owing to the gravelly soil on which it is grown), Zinfandel (exclusively from that grape), Burgundy and Claret;
ROSÉ: Cardinal Rosé.

A few *Aperitif and Dessert wines* are also produced under the same brand and with the Livermore appellation: Pale Dry Sherry and Sherry, Port, and a vintage Muscat de Frontignan (sweet and soft and with a very perfumed bouquet and aroma).

The Concannon Vineyard altar wines (available only to the clergy) include:
Dry wines: Chateau Concannon, Haut Sauterne, Dry Sauterne, and Chablis; Cabernet, Zinfandel, Burgundy, and Claret;
Sweet wines: Muscat de Frontignan, Port, Tokay, and Angelica.

Cresta Blanca Wine Company, Livermore

A great name in the California wine industry, Cresta Blanca is owned by Schenley Industries. Since 1941 this company has operated the winery and tended the vineyards, which nestle in the gently sloping hills in the southeast corner of the Livermore Valley. Lucas Hat, whose family has been interested in growing grapes and making wine for generations, is in over-all charge of the vineyards and winery. The wine maker is Myron Nightingale, who has been closely associated with some of the industry's important experiments and achievements. A bonded winery is also maintained in Tulare County, right across the county line from Delano, Kern County. All

Cresta Blanca wines are marketed through the CVA Corporation of San Francisco.

Founder of Cresta Blanca was the celebrated California wine pioneer Charles A. Wetmore, who purchased part of the old Rancho El Valle de San Jose in Livermore in 1882, planted his vineyards with selected imported cuttings, and built the Cresta Blanca winery in 1883. He named his winery and his wines after the limestone ridge which still dominates the vineyards and where a landslide at one time exposed a great white crest, sliced off the mountainside as by a giant's carving knife.

Charles Wetmore was born in Portland, Maine, in 1847 and came to California with his parents when he was nine years old. After attending public schools in Oakland he entered the newly established University of California, graduating with its very first class, of which he was valedictorian. He worked as a reporter on various newspapers, including the *Alta California* and the San Francisco *Chronicle*. Deeply interested in viticulture, he was appointed in 1878 as a delegate of the California State Vinicultural Society to visit the Paris Exposition. During this trip he made a thorough study of French winegrowing methods. On his return he organized the Board of State Viticultural Commissioners and served on it with prominence for a number of years. As an official of the California wine industry, as a winegrower, and as the author of treatises and articles on viticulture and wine production, Charles Wetmore was an outstanding authority on California wines for over half a century.

Wetmore considered that the gravelly soil at the mouth of the Canyon of the Arroyo del Valle in Livermore Valley offered every condition essential for producing the finest wines of the Bordeaux types. In Cresta Blanca he planted vines brought over from France, among them cuttings from Château d'Yquem in Sauternes and from Château Margaux in Médoc. He was a perfectionist in his methods, and the reputation of his Cresta Blanca wines became solidly established within a short time and their fame spread far and wide. The "Grand Prix" awarded to Cresta Blanca at the Paris Exposition of 1889 is said to mark the first time that California was officially recognized by France as a competitor in the production of fine table wines.

Clarence J. Wetmore, also a University of California graduate, became associated with his brother Charles in Cresta Blanca at an early date. In 1893 Clarence purchased the property from his brother and retained his connection with Cresta Blanca for over forty years, operating it until 1920, when he sold Cresta Blanca to L. B. Johnson. During Prohibition business was carried on, as allowed by the dry laws, for sacramental and medicinal purposes. With Repeal the corporation was reorganized with Clarence Wetmore once more as president and Johnson as general manager. With the death of Clarence Wetmore in 1936 Johnson became the sole owner. In 1941 the latter disposed of Cresta Blanca to Schenley.

Cresta Blanca produces table, aperitif, dessert, and sparkling wines of high quality, some of which are outstanding. The winery has continued to feature its white table wines grown in the Livermore Valley and also emphasizes its red table wines from grapes grown in the Napa and Sonoma valleys. Cresta Blanca has been a leader in the field of high-quality California sherries and also developed a *flor* sherry which will be marketed in the near future. High-quality ports and vermouths have been produced; some special port wines have not as yet been put on the market.

All wines are marketed under the *Cresta Blanca* brand, some with the added *Souvenir* labeling.

Table wines:
  WHITE: Dry Semillon, Sweet Semillon, Sauvignon Blanc, Chateau Sauterne, Haut Sauterne and Sauterne, Grey Riesling and Riesling, Chablis;
  RED: Cabernet, Pinot Noir and Red Pinot, Burgundy and Claret;
  ROSÉ: Vin Rosé.

Sparkling wines (bottle-fermented):
  Champagne (medium dry, available also in magnums), Brut Champagne (quite dry), Pink Champagne (medium dry), and Sparkling Burgundy;

Aperitif and Dessert wines:
  Dry Watch Cocktail Sherry (pale, dry) and Triple Cream Sherry (golden, sweet), aged in small cooperage and outstanding sherries

both, Palomino Sherry (pale, dry) and Souvenir Sherry (medium dry); Tawny Port and Ruby Port; Golden Muscatel; White Vermouth (Triple Dry) and Sweet Vermouth.

Wente Bros., Livermore

Bearing one of the greatest and most respected names in the whole of the California wine industry, the brothers Wente are the producers of some of the finest white table wines of the country, notably of the sauterne and white burgundy varieties.

Carl H. Wente, the founder of the firm, was a native of Hanover, Germany, and came to this country in 1880. He received his first experience in California wine making under the personal supervision of Charles Krug, the great pioneer viticulturist of Napa Valley. Carl Wente soon branched out for himself and purchased, late in the fall of 1883, some vineyards in the Livermore Valley south of the town of Livermore. On this land the original Wente winery still stands.

From the beginning Carl Wente specialized in the production of the finest-quality table wines, for which he found a ready market and at prices considerably higher than the average at that time. Both the Semillon and Sauvignon blanc grapes of the Sauternes region in France soon proved themselves to be particularly well suited to the Livermore soil and climate, and so, later on, did the Pinot Chardonnay of white burgundy and champagne fame.

Gradually the Wente holdings were extended, first by the founder and later on by his sons, Ernest and Herman Wente, the present owners.* An important acquisition was that of the neighboring El Mocho vineyards. When that highly regarded winegrowing pioneer of the Livermore Valley, Louis Mel, retired at an advanced age, he sold his treasured El Mocho property to the Wentes. Mrs. Mel-de Bire was a friend of the contemporary Marquis de Lur-Saluces, owner of the world-renowned Château d'Yquem in Sauternes, near Bordeaux in France, and when Charles Wetmore, as delegate of the California Vinicultural Society and the founder of Cresta

*Another son, Carl Wente, became president of the Bank of America.

Blanca, was charged with obtaining cuttings of the finest European vine varieties, she gave him a letter of introduction to the proprietor of Yquem. Wetmore returned with cuttings of the Semillon, Sauvignon blanc, and Muscadelle du Bordelais vines from the vineyards of Château d'Yquem itself and naturally gave some to Louis Mel, who propagated them in his El Mocho vineyards. When the present Marquis de Lur-Saluces visits California, he never fails to call on the Wentes to enquire how his California Yquem children are doing and to taste with appreciation what California is capable of producing in the way of sauternes.

The Wentes have never ceased to concentrate on creating the very best. Ernest Wente is more the farmer and winegrower, while Herman specializes in the wine making and sales end of the enterprise. Much of the soil of the Wente vineyards is alluvial deposit, washed down from the hills to the east and containing considerable heavy gravel, well suited to the finer grape varieties that like to mature the hard way. The sight of these gravelly vineyards is a perpetual source of wonderment to the novice.

The grapes are picked, variety by variety, at the peak of ripeness for wine making. The juice is pressed in small batches; the wines racked in small cooperage, then aged in oaken puncheons, and finally aged again in the bottle to full maturity.

Herman Wente, unassuming and simple in his ways, is one of the great wine makers in California today and there are many who say he is the greatest.

The famous specialties of the Wente brothers are their white table wines, which are generally and rightly considered unsurpassed in California. Only *table wines* are produced at the Wente winery and mostly varietals. These are marketed under the *Wente Bros.* brand and all but one carry the vintage date on the labeling. The generic wines, white, red, and rosé, are labeled with the *Valle de Oro* brand, the romantic name the Spaniards gave to the Livermore Valley.

Wente Bros. white wines:

Dry Semillon (similar to a French Graves though less sweet, vintaged), Sweet Semillon (produced from late-picked grapes to ensure the maximum richness and sweetness, non-vintaged), Sauvignon Blanc (from that grape, vintaged); Grey Riesling (a very popular wine, the demand for which far exceeds the yearly supply, vintaged), Pinot Blanc and Pinot Chardonnay (from those grapes and both vintaged);

Valle de Oro white wines:
Chateau Wente (from a judicious blending of Semillon and Sauvignon blanc grapes with the addition of a little Muscadelle du Bordelais, and as fine a sweet sauterne as produced in California); Chablis;

Valle de Oro red wine and rosé:
Burgundy, Rosé.

Note: A little-known Wente wine is the Wente Bros. Claret, available only in larger containers at the winery and in nearby localities. It is an ideal wine for daily use by the home bottler who likes to have an inexpensive but more than pleasing red wine at dinnertime.

Garatti Winery, Pleasanton

Frank Garatti, a native of the Italian province of Lombardy, founded this firm in 1902. He planted the vineyards and operated the winery until his death in 1948. Since then his son-in-law, F. W. (Bill) Brenner, has been in full charge.

Most of the firm's business is derived from the sale of generic and varietal table wines in bulk to other wineries, including wines such as Semillon, Sylvaner (Franken Riesling), and White Pinot in the whites. Some fine red table wines and aperitif and dessert wines are also produced. A little wine is marketed directly to consumers under the *Garatti* brand.

Ruby Hill Vineyard Company, Pleasanton

Ruby Hill is a beautiful winegrowing ranch with tall and stately palms lining the driveway to the residence, with vineyards stretching out on all sides. The great winery, which lies beyond the residence, was built in 1887 by John Crellen, later succeeded by C. L.

Crellen, and by whose family name the estate was known for many years. In 1921 the property was purchased by Ernest Ferrario, the present owner and wine maker.

Ernest Ferrario was born near Lake Como in Italy and came to this country in 1901, first to New York, and then to California. He worked on the railroads in San Raphael and in the brickyards in San Francisco. Accustomed to wine in his native country, he had always been interested in wine making, but what made him go into the wine business in California, according to his own story, was Prohibition. The reason for this had to do with the high prices obtainable for grapes grown for home wine makers, as allowed by law. During the dry period he also made wine for medicinal and sacramental purposes.

Since Repeal Ernest Ferrario developed Ruby Hill into a magnificent vineyard property and established a more than enviable reputation for his wines. He does all of his own wine making, selling most of his production to other wineries. At the same time Ruby Hill is a very popular place for those who like to buy their wines at the winery itself, be it small quantities or by the barrel.

Ruby Hill produces only *table wines,* all of high quality and mostly of the white types. They are marketed for the public under the *Ruby Hill* brand and include:

White wines: Semillon (semi-dry), Malvasia Bianca or White Malvasia (a specialty of the house), Pinot Chardonnay, Riesling, Haut Sauterne, and Sauterne;

Red wines: Barbera (another specialty and one of the finest of its kind in the state) and Burgundy.

Southern Alameda

Los Amigos Vineyards, Mission San Jose

Edward P. Werner and Edwin A. Grau were the founders of this once-famous vineyard, now the victim of encroaching real estate development. Werner was a Bavarian who married his girl against his parents' wishes and Grau was from Austria, the son of a winegrower. The two met in California, where Werner became cellar master for the Gallegos family near Mission San Jose and Grau was with Salazar, who operated the Los Cerritos Cellar in that town. Together they purchased from the Gallegos family a beautiful hill site, commanding a sweeping view of the surrounding countryside and of San Francisco Bay. They established their vineyards in 1888 and named their property "Los Amigos" in honor of their close friendship.

The Los Amigos wines attained a national and international fame and were produced by Werner and Grau until the advent of Prohibition, which forced the winery to close down. They kept the vineyard, however, and sold the grapes. Neither of the *amigos* lived to see the coming of Repeal and after the death of Mrs. Werner the estate passed into various hands. Not till Robert S. Mayock bought it in 1936 did Los Amigos and its wines come into their own once again.

Bob Mayock, an attorney and realtor of Beverly Hills, California, had for long been interested in good wines. In Southern California he had been in the wine business, selecting fine wines and selling them, but he wanted to get in the producing end of it. Once the owner of Los Amigos, he replanted the vineyards to Cabernet Sauvignon and Pinot noir and successfully revived the great tradition set by the founders. In this he was ably assisted by his wife, Ann Mayock, who continued to operate Los Amigos and its vineyards for some years after he passed away in 1945.

Now that new housing developments have invaded the privacy of Los Amigos, its vineyards are no more, but the winery continues to operate and the *Los Amigos* brand is still on the market with the well-known Sherry Sack, a first-class dry and very pale sherry of the Amontillado type, blended and aged at the winery.

Ann Mayock is enthusiastically aided in her enterprise by her children as far as their other duties allow them to do so. Sally Ann, a graduate of Mills College and now Mrs. Hollis Hartley, studied wine chemistry, worked in the winery, and has often acted as hostess at Los Amigos. Douglas, the elder son, helps in the business as much as his operatic career permits, while Robert Stoney, Jr., now of the Marine Corps, will probably return to the wine business after he has completed his service.

Besides the Sherry Sack, which will continue to be produced, a few choice *table wines* are still available under the *Los Amigos* label, be it in small quantities soon to be exhausted. Gone are the older vintages of Cabernet Sauvignon and Pinot Noir, the Grenache Rosé of 1944, the very special Black Pinot from Pinot Meunier grapes, the Tawny Port, to be found only in some prize cellar perhaps and now collectors' rarities, but still on the market are the Cabernet Sauvignon 1945, the Pinot Noir blend of 1949–1950, and the Riesling 1946 (from Johannisberg Riesling and Franken Riesling grapes).

Weibel Champagne Vineyards, Mission San Jose

A relative newcomer to the California wine industry, Weibel Champagne Vineyards, founded in 1939, is an up and coming concern, producing high-quality table, sparkling, aperitif, and dessert wines which have established an excellent reputation for themselves. The best proof is that they not only market their wines for the public but also supply many a winery. It is a family enterprise, owned and operated by Rudolph Emile Weibel, Sr., and his son Frederick E. Weibel, Jr., natives of Münsingen, canton of Bern, Switzerland.

Rudolph Weibel, Sr., had been engaged in the wine and champagne business in Switzerland and France since 1904 and came to this country in 1934 as an importer of wines and brandies. He traveled all over the United States and when he came to California, observed its climate and soil, the fine wine grapes which could be grown, and the quality of the wines which could be produced—comparing them type by type and bottle by bottle with those of the old country—he made up his mind to immigrate to the United States and devote himself in California to the production of the finest wines he could produce. Sampling of the Beaulieu Vineyard wines was an important factor in his final decision. And so he came to this country for good in 1936, accompanied by his son Frederick, better known as Fred.

Production of high-quality champagne was always the main ambition of the Weibels and for that reason the enterprise was called as it is, a name to which they have done full justice.

The Weibels first settled in San Francisco, making champagne from purchased wines while looking for a suitable vineyard property and winery. This they found in their ranch near Mission San Jose and Warm Springs. Their holdings are part of the old Rancho del Agua Caliente and of the once-famous ranch of Josiah Stanford, brother of Leland Stanford, railroad builder, governor, senator, founder of Stanford University, and a great California wine pioneer. Leland Stanford purchased a square mile of land at Warm Springs back in 1869 and soon afterwards his brother Josiah planted a large acreage of vines there and constructed both a winery and distillery. For a number of years a flourishing wine business was conducted in Warm Springs and large quantities of wine labeled "Stanford" were sold. Leland Stanford then deeded the Warm Springs vineyard to his brother and, encouraged by Josiah's success in wine making, embarked on his vast winegrowing project at Vina, in Tehama County, which was to become the largest vineyard in the world for the time, an enterprise which lasted well into the twentieth century.

The Weibels purchased their ranch in 1945 and devoted the next three years to replanting the vineyards and modernizing the winery. Rudolph and his son Fred are partners in the firm, the latter being also the wine maker.

The following wines are produced and marketed under the *Weibel* brand:

Sparkling wines (bottle-fermented):
Grand Cru Select Champagne Brut (the specialty champagne of the house, from Pinot Chardonnay grapes), Grand Cru Pink Champagne, and Grand Cru Champagne Rouge (from a blend of Pinot Noir and Cabernet Sauvignon); Weibel Champagne:

Brut, Extra-Sec (medium dry), Sec, Pink, and Sparkling Burgundy;

Sparkling wines (bulk process):

Two specialty wines are the Sparkling Malvasia (one of the very few if not the only one produced in the state) and the Sparkling Muscat.

Note: Bulk-process champagnes, excellent in their class, are marketed under a number of various brands such as Chateau du Chevalier, Chateau Lafayette, Chateau Alameda, and Chateau Louis d'Or. They are all of the same quality and include Brut, Demi-Sec, and Sweet types as well as Pink Champagne and Sparkling Burgundy.

Table wines:

WHITE: Pinot Chardonnay, Pinot Blanc, Haut Sauterne, Grey Riesling, Dry Semillon, Dry Sauterne, and Chablis;
RED: Pinot Noir, Cabernet Sauvignon, Zinfandel, Burgundy, and Claret;
ROSÉ: Grenache Rosé and Vin Rosé;

Aperitif and Dessert wines:

Sherries: featured are the Solera *flor* Sherries, the Cocktail (dry), the Golden (medium), and the Cream (sweet); regular sherries include Pale Dry, Cream Sherry, and Sweet Sherry;
Black Muscatel (also marketed as Black Muscat and as Cream of Black Muscat, and a top-flight specialty dessert wine), Ruby Port, and Tawny Port, Muscatel;
Vermouth, Dry and Sweet; an herb-flavored white aperitif wine of the Dubonnet Blonde type and an aperitif called "Compare-It," of the Italian Campari type.

WESTERN ALAMEDA

Paul Rhodes Winery, Hayward

Paul Rhodes is a fifth-generation wine maker with vineyard and wine-making experience along the Rhine and Moselle rivers in Germany, in the Sauternes and Burgundy regions of France, in

Brazil and Argentina in South America, on the Niagara Peninsula in the province of Ontario, Canada, as well as in the United States. He is convinced that if the 2000 years of European know-how in wine making are used, even better wines can be produced in California because of the excellence of the grapes grown, notably in the coastal counties. He joins many in wishing that the average American family will take fine dry wines into their everyday living to add to their mealtime enjoyment.

In this country Paul Rhodes was connected with the Monarch Wine Company in New York and Atlanta, Georgia, and was superintendent of Cresta Blanca in Livermore under L. B. Johnson's ownership before he founded his own winery at Hayward in western Alameda County.

There are no vineyards around Hayward and the Paul Rhodes wines are either produced from grapes grown in nearby areas or are selected, blended, and bottled at the winery. Paul Rhodes, with his years of wine-making experience, is also a gifted vintner who blends and ages wines to a high standard of quality.

Table wines are the specialty, but a full line of aperitif and dessert wines, including vermouths, are also marketed, all under the *Paul Rhodes* brand. An important part of the enterprise is the retail outlet at Hayward.

Table wines, aged mostly in white-oak cooperage, include:

RED: Cabernet, Burgundy, and Claret; WHITE: Semillon, Sauternes, Moselle, and Chablis.

CONTRA COSTA COUNTY

J. E. Digardi Winery, Martinez

Of the Contra Costa wineries that of Joseph E. Digardi is the best known and most representative. The winery was founded in 1886 by Frank Digardi, a native of Sicily, where the Italian branch of the family still owns vineyards in the neighborhood of Palermo. Frank Digardi planted his vines on the slopes of Mt. Diablo and later acquired and developed other vineyards in the county.

The family enterprise is owned and operated today by Joseph

(Joe) E. Digardi, son of the founder and a well-known personality in the wine industry, and by his own two sons, Francis and Ernest. Holdings include vineyard property in the Clayton, or Diablo, Valley, in the shadow of the mountain by the latter name, and in the Vine Hill area, south of Martinez.

Red table wines are the specialty, with *Digardi* the top brand for fine-quality wines and *Diablo Valley* for those of standard grade. *Digardi table wines* include:

RED: Mountain Gamay (from Gamay Beaujolais grapes, and is a famous California wine), Zinfandel, Burgundy, and Claret. Plans are to produce varietals, such as Pinot Noir and Cabernet Sauvignon, from Napa Valley grapes.

WHITE: Sauterne, Chablis, and Rhine.

ROSÉ: Vin Rosé.

A few *Aperitif and Dessert wines* are also marketed, and there are plans to produce Solera *flor* Sherries and a Solera Port from the Trousseau grape.

Gopher Gulch Ranch Wine Cellars, Walnut Creek

This is an excellent example of a small private winery operated simply for the pleasure of making wines as a hobby and serving them to one's friends, and for that reason is treated much more extensively than its size would warrant. It is permissible by law to operate a non-commercial winery producing not more than two hundred gallons yearly.

Owner of Gopher Gulch Ranch is that well-known former journalist, James Pomeroy Howe, who since his retirement has made quite a name for himself in his hobby, that of wine making.

Jim Howe was born in Atchison, Kansas, on the Missouri River, where his father, Ed Howe, ran the Atchison *Globe*. Ed Howe, known as the "Sage of Potato Hill" wrote several books, the best known being *The Story of a Country Town* which Mark Twain liked so much he penciled a nine-page letter about it, now a treasured document of the Howe family.

Perhaps the fact that the Brenner brothers in Atchison, when

Jim Howe was a youngster, made dry red wines from their Doniphan vineyards inspired the budding journalist's later hobby. Jim Howe first followed his father's footsteps and worked with newspapers all over the country, including the *Journal* in New York, the *Times-Democrat* in New Orleans, the *Oregonian* in Portland, the *Bulletin* in Honolulu. At one time he ran the *Index* at Emmett, Idaho. He joined the Associated Press in 1914 and was an army correspondent during the First World War. He traveled extensively all over the world, including Russia, and was stationed at one time or another in London, Paris, Berlin, Peking, Tokyo, and Singapore.

In 1910 he acquired his Walnut Creek property, located on what is called Poverty Heights. During his lengthy absences a caretaker was in charge of the property and Jim Howe will hardly forget the day when he returned and found that the caretaker had moved house and all from the top of the hill, where he had left it, down to the bottom, its present location.

Jim Howe's winery is, as he himself calls it, an experimental one. He obtains grapes from well-known winegrowers, such as the Wente Bros. of Livermore, John Daniel, Jr., of Inglenook, L. K. Marshall of the Wine Growers Guild, and the University of California at Davis, or they give him the grapes to see what can be accomplished with them for purposes of comparison. Some wines turn out better than others and some are fine indeed. On the whole he has had better luck with the whites than with the reds.

The resulting wines are labeled with the *House of Howe* name, with indication both of the grower who supplied the grapes and of the particular variety. Thus there is, for example, a House of Howe Pinot Chardonnay, Vintage 1952, Grapes from Wente Bros., produced and bottled by Gopher Gulch Ranch Wine Cellars.

Among the *white table wines* Jim Howe has experimented with are: Pinot Chardonnay, Pinot Blanc, Gewurztraminer (one of his most successful vintages), Emerald Riesling, and French Colombard. The *reds* include: Cabernet Sauvigon, Pinot Noir, Gamay Beaujolais, Ruby Cabernet, Barbera, and a delightful Aleatico. The rosés number most of the usual types and also a Merlot Rosé from the Napa Valley.

A feature of the cellars of Gopher Gulch Ranch—scene of some grand parties—is the truly fabulous collection of vintage wines, both European and Californian. Here can be seen—and, if one is a lucky guest, tasted—such vintages, all of the better years, as Romanée Conti, Château Latour, Château Cheval Blanc, Martin Ray, Beaulieu, and many others of the top-flight class. Jim Howe has a passion too for magnums, a bottle seen and cultivated only too rarely in California. Many an expert has said with reason that a great wine achieves its ultimate greatness when bottled in the imposing and comfortable magnums.

D. *SAN FRANCISCO DISTRICT*

A number of wineries are located in San Francisco and the city is therefore treated as a separate district.

California Wine Association, San Francisco

This famous old company has a long history, dating back to 1884, when a number of California's well-known wineries joined to form the original California Wine Association. Membership has varied over the years, but the company has always played an important part in the California wine industry. In 1929 it was reorganized as Fruit Industries, Ltd., but reverted back to its former name in 1951.

For many years A. R. Morrow was the dominant figure of the company. The memory of this "grand old man" of California viticulture will always be cherished and his name is perpetuated in one of the company's well-known brands. Sydney C. Wortley is president of the California Wine Association, Fred Snyde is chairman of the board, while Mario Perelli-Minetti, of the well-known wine-growing family, is general manager.

The California Wine Association is composed of eleven cooperative and other wineries to which some 1200 winegrowers contribute their grapes. The wineries are located in the four major wine districts, one in Sonoma, specializing in dry table wines

(Sonoma County Cooperative Winery at Windsor), six in the Lodi-Sacramento district, mostly for sherry, tokay, and brandy (Cherokee Vineyard Association at Acampo; Community Grape Corporation, Lodi Winery, Inc., Rancho del Oso Winery, all at Lodi; Florin Winery Association at Florin; Woodbridge Vineyard Association at Elk Grove), two in the Fresno-San Joaquin district, especially for muscatel and grignolino (Delano Growers Cooperative Winery and A. Perelli-Minetti & Sons, both at Delano), and one in the Cucamonga district for port and other sweet wines (Cucamonga Growers Cooperative Winery at Ontario).*

In this manner the Association can produce the various types of wine where it is most advantageous to do so with regard to regional suitability and quality. The main offices of the Association are in San Francisco, together with a vast winery for blending, finishing, aging, and bottling purposes.

California Wine Association is one of three largest wine producers of the state and its wines enjoy a national distribution, the brands varying somewhat according to region and locality.

The Association's top-quality table and dessert wines are marketed under the *Ambassador District* brand. These wines derive not less than 75 per cent of their volume from grapes grown in the district designated on the label, assuring that they are produced from vines famed for each particular type. Sound standard-quality table and dessert wines are marketed under various brands, of which *Eleven Cellars,* so named because of the eleven winery members of the Association, is the most prominent. Other brands for sound standard-quality table and dessert wines are *Guasti, Ambassador Reserve, F.I.,* and *Greystone.*

The more important of the featured wines of California Wine Association are the following:

Table wines:
  Ambassador District RED: Cabernet, Grignolino, Zinfandel, and
    Burgundy; WHITE: Dry Sauterne, Sauterne, Haut Sauterne,
    Riesling, Rhine, and Chablis; ROSÉ: Grignolino Rosé;

*An eleventh winery, the Mokelumne Winery at Lodi, burned down in 1954.

Dolly Madison: Red and white specialty wines produced from 100 per cent vinifera grapes and marketed mostly in the East; *Eleven Cellars* RED: Zinfandel, Burgundy, and Claret; WHITE: Sauterne and Chablis; ROSÉ: Vin Rosé;

Sparkling wines (Bottle-fermented):
Ambassador Champagne and Sparkling Burgundy;

Sparkling wines (Bulk process):
Ambassador Champagne, Sparkling Burgundy, and Spumante;
Greystone Champagne and Sparkling Burgundy;
Calwa Champagne and Sparkling Burgundy;

Aperitif and Dessert wines:
Ambassador District: Pale Dry Sherry, Sherry, and Creme Sherry (sweet), Port, Muscatel, and Tokay;
Eleven Cellars: Pale Dry Cocktail Sherry, Sherry, and Cream Sherry, Port and Ruby Port, Muscatel, Tokay, and White Port;
Ambassador—F.I.: Dry and Sweet Vermouth.

Pacific Coast Brands, San Francisco and Livermore

Steve Forni, the founder of this enterprise, was born in Capronno, Varese Province, Lombardy, Italy, in 1898. He came to the United States as a youngster and started in San Francisco as a bus boy at twenty dollars a month. He worked in that capacity and as waiter and cook in various well-known San Francisco restaurants, steadily working his way up. He then went into the restaurant business for himself and for some years ran the Fly Trap on Broadway, which enjoyed the patronage of many of the city's judges and attorneys.

Later Steve Forni branched out into the wine business and founded his Pacific Coast Brands in 1932, first operating a winery in Stockton with a finishing plant in San Francisco. In 1945 he purchased vineyards and a winery in Livermore which he now operates in conjunction with a San Francisco winery which he acquired in 1941. He is assisted in the family wine business by Mrs. Forni and their son Raymond.

Table wines from Livermore Valley grapes are the specialties, while Champagne (bulk process) is also produced. Aperitif and dessert wines are purchased, aged, and marketed, of which the Vermouths, dry and sweet, are featured.

The quality wines are marketed under the *Forni* brand and include Sauterne, Chablis, Burgundy, Zinfandel, and Claret from the Livermore Valley as well as Champagne and Sherry, Port and Muscatel. Secondary brands are *Blanco Vista* and *Cal-Best* for table and dessert wines, the latter also for Champagne.

Signature Vintners, San Francisco

Signature Vintners, part of the Petri Wine Company, was established for the marketing of the highest-quality table, aperitif, and dessert wines.

A panel of three connoisseurs and experts personally selects the wines, which bear the *Signature* brand with the added *"Tasters' Selection"* indication on the label. The panel is composed of:

Harold Price, well-known winetaster and judge, founder and past president of the San Francisco Wine and Food Society;

Morrison Wood, wine connoisseur of long standing, founder of the Wine and Food Society of Chicago, author of the syndicated newspaper column on unusual cookery "For Men Only!" and of the popular wine cookbook *With a Jug of Wine;*

Russell S. Codman, Jr., co-founder of Boston's famous gourmet society "Club des Arts Gastronomiques," president of the French Center in New England, author of *Vintage Dinners,* and consultant on foreign and American wines.

The table wines selected are all produced from California's northern coastal region and can come from any of the fine table-wine-producing sections such as Sonoma Valley, Napa Valley, Livermore Valley, Santa Clara Valley, Contra Costa County, and others. The sparkling and aperitif and dessert wines originate in the San Joaquin Valley region.

Signature Tasters' Selection wines include:

Table wines:

RED: Cabernet Sauvignon, Gamay, Red Pinot, Zinfandel, and Burgundy;

WHITE: White Pinot, Grey Riesling, Dry Sauterne, Haut Sauterne, Rhine Wine, and Chablis;

ROSÉ: Vin Rosé.

Aperitif and Dessert wines:

Royal Velvet Port (with extra aging in oak casks) and Tawny Port; Pale Dry Sherry, Amorino Sherry (medium sweet, of the Spanish Amoroso type), and Cream Sherry; Marsala (medium sweet, darker than sherry, somewhat spicy in character and one of the few produced in the state); Golden Muscatel (from the Muscat of Alexandria grape).

To this group of wines also belong the *Louis IV* brand Vermouths, both dry and sweet. Although not selected like the others by the tasters' panel, this brand is used for certain high-quality specialty wines.

Signature Sparkling wines (bulk process):

Champagne and Sparkling Burgundy.

E. *SANTA CLARA—SANTA CRUZ AND CENTRAL COASTAL DISTRICT*

The neighboring counties of Santa Clara and Santa Cruz, with the Santa Cruz Mountains forming the border between the two, are usually grouped together as one winegrowing district. Extensions of this district include the winegrowing areas in San Benito County and in the central coastal counties of Monterey and San Luis Obispo.

Santa Clara County, with some thirty-seven active bonded wineries, rates fourth in number in the state. It can be divided into three winegrowing areas, spreading west and east from the Santa Clara Valley floor to the adjoining hills and mountains.

West of the Santa Clara Valley, in the foothills, lies Los Gatos, and higher yet, in the hills beyond, Saratoga, together forming the Los Gatos-Saratoga area. Here are the homes of some of the finest table wines and champagnes of California, while excellent aperitif and dessert wines are also produced there.

To the east of San Jose lies the hillside Evergreen area with its vineyards stretching onto the slopes of Mt. Hamilton. From this section hail a number of superior table wines.

The southern part of Santa Clara County and of its valley is noted for an important winery section, centering around Madrone, San Martin, and Gilroy, with good wines of all types being produced from the neighboring hillsides. Many a sound "country" table wine also is produced in the small wineries, run mostly by Americans of Italian descent, in the section west of Gilroy up toward the Hecker Pass and in the Uvas area.

Santa Cruz County is noteworthy for its wines although the number of active wineries has been reduced to only two. Some excellent table wines are produced above Felton and some good ones at Soquel. Besides there are scattered vineyard areas in the county including Vinehill, toward Los Gatos, Bonny Doon, southwest of Ben Lomond, Boulder Creek, north of that Scottish-named elevation, the Laurel area in the mountains toward the Santa Clara County line, and the Casserly section, up toward Mt. Madonna.

San Benito yields some well-known table wines south of Hollister, and Monterey County can boast, in the Salinas River Valley foothills above Soledad near Pinnacles National Monument, some very fine vineyards from which champagne has been produced with marked success.

San Luis Obispo County, where Paderewski once grew his wine grapes and almonds, is noted for its hillside table wines of sound quality and especially for its Zinfandel.

SANTA CLARA COUNTY

SANTA CLARA VALLEY—LOS GATOS—SARATOGA AREA

Almadén Vineyards, Los Gatos

About midway between Los Gatos and the former mining village of Almadén, some six miles south of San Jose, are to be found the winery and domain of Almadén, overlooking the undulating hills toward Loma Prieta and the Santa Cruz Mountains. Here some of the finest champagnes and sherries of California are produced as well as table wines and other aperitif and dessert wines of great merit.

Founder of Almadén was the Frenchman Etienne Thée, a farmer from Bordeaux who is said to have come to California lured by the Gold Rush but who turned to less elusive and more permanent pursuits, grape growing and wine making. To this end he purchased from the Guadalajara pioneer José Augustín Narváez part of the old Rancho San Juan Bautista, securing for himself a fertile tract of land along the creek called Guadalupe River. Here he planted his first vines in 1852 and later, on a high knoll with its sweeping valley and mountain view, built his home, which still stands today.

Thée was soon joined in his enterprise by a neighbor and compatriot, Charles Lefranc, once said to have been a tailor in Passy, the suburb of Paris. The vineyards were enlarged and planted to cuttings of choice varieties imported from the districts of Champagne, Bordeaux, Burgundy, and the Rhône Valley in France. Lefranc married Thée's daughter Adèle and eventually inherited his friend and father-in-law's property. He named it Almadén, after the nearby quicksilver mines of New Almadén, so called by the Spaniards in honor of the well-known quicksilver mining town of that name in the province of Ciudad Real in New Castile, Spain.

Lefranc prospered together with his vineyards and by the end of the eighteen seventies could boast that they contained more vines than any other in the county and, what was even more important, that his wines rated with the very best in all the West. The finest cooperage was imported from France around Cape Horn, some of it to continue in use down to the present. Many were the famous guests who enjoyed Lefranc's warm hospitality, among whom are said to have numbered Admiral Farragut, Generals Sherman, Halleck, and Ulysses S. Grant.

The French influence and atmosphere were dominant at Almadén and this tradition was strengthened when Lefranc hired a young Burgundian to help in the office and winery. This was Paul Masson, who was to make his own name great in the California wine industry and also followed another precedent by marrying Lefranc's daughter Louise. Paul Masson eventually became associated with

Lefranc in the production and merchandising of champagnes and table wines in a jointly owned business, Lefranc-Masson. He never owned any interest in the Almadén vineyards, but established himself on his own property, which he acquired and developed in the hills above Saratoga. Eventually Almadén was inherited by Charles Lefranc's son Henry and after the latter's death in 1909 the property was held in trust for the family until it was sold to Charles Jones. With the advent of Prohibition Almadén entered a dormant period as far as wine making was concerned.

In 1941 Louis A. Benoist, well-known San Francisco businessman and social leader and president of the Lawrence Warehouse Company, national field-warehousing concern, purchased Almadén at the advice of the noted wine authority Frank Schoonmaker. As wine maker and plant manager, Oliver J. Goulet was engaged, one of the foremost experts in the field. Since 1954 Goulet is ably assisted by A. C. (Al) Huntsinger, formerly general manager of the Napa Valley Cooperative Winery at St. Helena.

Under the direction of Ollie Goulet the winery and other buildings were renovated and the original vineyards brought back into shape. Additional acreage was acquired, including a tract high up in the mountains near Eagle Rock, planted to Johannisberg Riesling and Traminer vines, and another a few miles south of the Almadén ranch where Cabernet Sauvignon, Pinot Chardonnay, and Pinot blanc are grown. There are also important vineyards of Pinot noir.

At Almadén, Louis Benoist revived the tradition of hospitality set by Charles Lefranc. A charming host, he receives with elegance in the villa built by Etienne Thée over a hundred years ago. Excellent luncheons and dinners are given, preceded by the traditional aperitif, Almadén Brut Champagne, and accompanied by a selection of the ranch's choice vintages.

The policy of Louis Benoist and Ollie Goulet is to produce only wines of the highest quality. Recent winery expansions include a new champagne cellar and an additional sherry room featuring six Soleras, making Almadén's Solera operation the most modern and probably the largest in the country.

All wines (with the exception of the Vermouths) carry the

Almadén brand on the label, many with the Santa Clara Valley appellation of origin. They include the following:

Table wines:

RED: Cabernet Sauvignon and Pinot Noir, Burgundy, and Chianti; Mountain Red Burgundy and Claret in the low-price range;

WHITE: Johannisberg Riesling, Pinot Chardonnay, Pinot Blanc, and Traminer, Dry Semillon, Sylvaner, Grey Riesling, and Chablis; Mountain White Sauterne and Chablis in the low-price range;

ROSÉ: Grenache Rosé (outstanding of its type and extremely popular).

Sparkling wines (bottle-fermented):

Almadén Brut Champagne (the *spécialité de la maison* available also in magnums, very dry and full-flavored without acidity, ranking with the very best), Almadén Extra-Dry (medium dry), Pink Champagne, and Sparkling Burgundy.

Aperitif and Dessert wines:

Solera Sherries (all outstanding *flor* sherries, produced from Palomino grapes and matured in small oak butts brought over from Spain): Cocktail Sherry (very pale and very dry, on the *Fino* order), Golden Sherry, and Cream Sherry;

Solera Ports (probably the only ones produced in the U.S.A. by a Solera system): Ruby Port and Tawny Port;

Vermouths (marketed under the *Nob Hill* brand): Dry and Sweet.

Lone Hill Vineyards, Los Gatos

Owners of the Lone Hill Vineyards are the four brothers Arthur H., Rodolphe A., Clovis T., the wine maker, and Ambroise N. Mirassou. Their father, Herman Mirassou, is the younger brother of the late Peter Mirassou of the Mirassou Vineyards at Evergreen, near San Jose (see there), and the grandson of Pierre Pellier, one of the pioneer winegrowers of Santa Clara County.

The Lone Hill Vineyards, originally set out in 1864 by a former

New Yorker, David M. Harwood, were purchased by this branch of the Mirassou family in 1936. In order to get a longer marketing period for their grapes the four brothers built their winery in 1946.

Lone Hill concentrates on making available to the public better-than-average table wines at a competitive price to get the maximum number of people interested in wine consumption. Much of the business is devoted to supplying very inexpensive wines to customers bringing their own gallon jugs to the winery, saving thereby bottling and merchandising costs.

Table wines are also bottled under the *Lone Hill Green Label* and the *Lone Hill Reserve Label,* mostly Burgundy, Sauterne, Vino Rosso (medium-sweet red table wine), and Vin Rosé (a blend). Dessert wines are also available.

The *Lone Hill Gold Label* is reserved for a few quality wines, such as Pinot Noir, Pinot Blanc, and Riesling, produced from neighboring vineyards which have since been replanted to other crops. When these wines are exhausted this label will be used for bottling other varietal table wines.

Clovis Mirassou is the inventor of a five-gallon barrel with interior plastic compartments from which five different wines can be poured from separate spigots.

Novitiate of Los Gatos, Los Gatos

In the hills above Los Gatos lies the beautiful and magnificently situated Seminary of the Sacred Heart Novitiate of the Society of Jesus. Here young men begin their training for possible missionary work in the Orient, teaching positions in schools operated by the Jesuits in California, or for parochial duties in some of the dioceses along the West Coast.

Since its founding the Novitiate has maintained the tradition for producing fine altar wines in strict accordance with the Canon Law of the Roman Catholic Church. Once the needs for sacramental wines had been met, the remainder of the production was made available to the public through commercial channels.

The Jesuit fathers have full charge of the production of the wines, while the Jesuit brothers supervise or carry on the actual work in the vineyards and winery. The novices and the junior students pick most of the grapes each fall. Many of the vines were originally imported from France, notably the muscats from the region of Montpellier near the Mediterranean.

President of the Novitiate is Father John F. X. Connolly, S.J., while Father Ralph J. Deward, S.J., is the general manager, Brother Michael Walsh, S.J., the wine maker, and Father James E. Ransford the chemist in charge.

Both *table wines* and *aperitif and dessert wines* are produced, marketed for the public under the *Novitiate* brand. They include:

Table wines:
RED: Cabernet Sauvignon, Zinfandel, Burgundy;
WHITE: Pinot Blanc, Sauvignon Blanc, Dry Semillon, Chateau Novitiate (Sweet Sauterne), Dry Sauterne, Chablis;
ROSÉ: Grenache Rosé.

Note: In the future Pinot Noir and White Riesling may also be produced.

Aperitif and Dessert wines:
Dry Sherry, Cocktail Sherry (medium dry), Sherry (medium sweet), and Golden Sherry (sweet); Port; two specialty wines from muscat grapes, the famed Novitiate Black Muscat (from Muscat Hamburg grapes exclusively) and the Muscat Frontignan (all from that grape, the vines of which were originally brought over from Frontignan); Tokay and Angelica.

Novitiate Altar wines, available only to the clergy:
Dry wines: RED: Manresa (Burgundy); WHITE: Villa Joseph (medium-dry sauterne), Vin Doré (slightly sweet sauterne); San Carlos (chablis type).
Sweet wines: Villa Maria (medium-sweet sherry), Novitiate (port), San Jose (black muscat), Guadalupe (golden muscatel), San Ignacio (tokay), and l'Admirable (angelica).

Paul Masson Vineyards, Saratoga

A great name in the history of the California wine industry and a national enterprise, founded by that famed Frenchman from Burgundy, Paul Masson.

Paul Masson first worked for Charles Lefranc in the latter's winery at Almadén and while employed there looked for the best place to establish vineyards and a winery of his own. He decided on a location in the mountains above Saratoga where the soil and climate were eminently suited to the growing of the finer wine grape varieties. He acquired lands there, named "La Cresta," in the eighteen eighties and planted them to cuttings of choice imported vines. He married Charles Lefranc's daughter and established a business partnership with his former employer for the merchandising of their wines, known as Lefranc-Masson. On the death of LeFranc, Paul Masson acquired the latter's interest in their joint business, merged it with his Saratoga holdings and the Paul Masson Champagne Company succeeded the partnership, champagne having become the principal product.

The original winery Paul Masson had built on his Saratoga property was destroyed by the 1906 earthquake, but was rebuilt by him in the following years, using some of the sandstone from old St. Joseph's Church in San Jose, which had been destroyed in the same disaster.

Paul Masson made his name forever famous by producing champagnes and table wines of the highest quality. For over half a century he worked in his steeply sloping mountain vineyards and in his wine cellars establishing a great name for his wines and becoming somewhat of a legendary figure himself. In 1936 he retired from his vineyards and passed away four years later, a greatly respected personality and a true modern pioneer of the best that can be produced in California wines.

Before he retired Paul Masson had sold his vineyards and winery to Martin Ray, a native of the village of Saratoga at the foot of the hills where Masson had created his domain. Martin Ray operated the enterprise with skill and success, following the tradition of producing only the best in champagne and table wines. A disastrous fire occurred in 1941, wrecking the winery and causing great losses, but Martin Ray, with energy and determination, rebuilt both the winery and his business. Two years later he sold the enterprise to Joseph E. Seagram's, the distillers, later establishing another domain of his own even higher up in the mountains. Seagram's held the Masson winery and vineyards only a short while, disposing of the business in 1945 to a company in which Alfred Fromm and Franz Sichel are the partners and who have operated it since that time.

Both the Fromm and the Sichel families have been in the wine industry for a great number of years, the former for five generations and the latter for seven. The Fromms are winegrowers from Bingen on the Rhine in Germany since 1864 and the Sichel name is a familiar one in the wine industry both in Mainz, Germany, and in Bordeaux, France, as well as in this country as importers. Max Fromm, the father of Alfred, was a famous wine blender in Germany and is still active, though in his eighties, and continues to advise his sons Alfred and Norman in their California wine enterprise.

Kurt G. Opper, one of the best-known wine makers in the country, is the winery manager, while Hans Hyba, the champagne master, is one of the foremost champagne makers. Hyba, a very modest person, has contributed notable improvements to the production process of bottle-fermented champagne and experts of famous French champagne houses have visited him to observe his methods, which are available to anyone wanting to use them.

The main Paul Masson winery is located on the Saratoga property, while the champagne winery and cellars are to be found in Cupertino. A third winery, at Mountain View, Cupertino, is used as a bottling plant and storeroom.

Paul Masson Vineyards produces both *table wines* and *sparkling wines* of superior quality as well as some notable *aperitif and dessert wines*. Their champagnes rate among the very best of the state and of their table wines the finer varietals are the more notable.

The table wines, both red and white as well as the rosé, and the sparkling wines are marketed under the *Paul Masson* brand, while the aperitif and dessert wines carry the *Masson* label.

Table wines:
RED: Cabernet Sauvignon, Pinot Noir, Gamay Beaujolais, and Burgundy;
WHITE: Pinot Chardonnay, Pinot Blanc Vrai, Chateau Masson (Sweet Semillon), Dry Semillon, Dry Sauterne, Riesling, and Chablis;
ROSÉ: Vin Rosé Sec.

Sparkling wines (bottle-fermented): Brut Champagne (predominantly from Pinot blanc, Folle blanche, and Johannisberg Riesling grapes, the *cuvées* having been additionally aged), Extra Dry Champagne, Oeil de Perdrix (Partridge's Eye) Pink Champagne (Triple Red), and Sparkling Burgundy (Cuvée Rouge).

Aperitif and Dessert wines: Marketed in special heart-shaped decanters: Rare Cream Sherry and Rare Tawny Port, both outstanding wines of their types; Pale Dry Sherry and Rich Golden Sherry, Rich Ruby Port, Choice Muscatel (all also available in magnums); Vermouths: Double Dry and Sweet.

Martin Ray, Inc., Saratoga

High above the Saratoga foothills rises Mt. Eden to an altitude of some two thousand feet, commanding a grandiose view of the whole of the Santa Clara Valley. It is here on the very summit of the mountain that Martin Ray devotes his skill to the production of the finest and costliest California wines, of which the Pinot Noir champagnes and table wines especially rank as supreme achievements, comparable to the finest wines of France.

Born into a farming family of Saratoga, Martin Ray first became a stockbroker, a trade he followed with sufficient success to start, at a relatively early age, the wine-making career he ambitioned. He had set his heart on Paul Masson's winery and vineyards above his native village and in 1936 he accomplished his desire, purchasing them from that great man when the latter retired from his life work. Martin Ray operated the enterprise with success and distinction, and then, desirous of a more restricted field of operations, sold it in 1943 for a good price. He then bought, built, planted, and developed his present domain, which is adjacent to his former property but is situated on even loftier heights.

Martin Ray, or Rusty, as he is known to his friends, is a dynamic and forceful personality, an excellent showman, deeply devoted to his art, and as profoundly appreciative of truly fine wines as he is impatient with any other. His vineyards, planted on the eastern and southern exposures of the mountain slopes, are planted to three varieties only: Pinot noir, Cabernet Sauvignon, and Pinot Chardonnay. An underground concrete pipe system with strategically located pumps ensures proper drainage during the rainy season and preservation of the topsoil. All of the work done in vineyards; wine making, bottling, and shipping is accomplished by Martin Ray and his family or under his immediate supervision. The wines are clarified by racking and decanting, not by filtering or fining; the wines sometimes throwing a deposit when maturing, as do many of the great European vintages.

Martin Ray's wines are all 100 per cent varietal vintage wines and of the best years only. Any wine not measuring up to the highest standards is disposed of and sold in bulk. The policy is to produce only the very best and to improve wherever possible, regardless of cost. Production is in a small scale, the wines being destined for gourmets and connoisseurs and for the best restaurants and clubs. It is not surprising that their cost is high.

The *Martin Ray* wines include the following *champagnes* and *table wines,* which are available in the vintages indicated, to be succeeded by later vintages:

Champagnes (bottle-fermented): Madame Pinot Champagne (Blanc de noir), made entirely from the free-run juice of the Pinot noir grape, vintage 1950; Sang-de-Pinot Champagne (Rosé de noir), a coral-pink champagne, made from the first light pressing of the Pinot noir grape, vintage 1949.

Table wines (all marketed in champagne bottles with champagne corks for better aging, a Martin Ray trademark since 1936):

RED: Pinot Noir, vintage 1941, one of California's greatest wines, produced from Martin Ray's old vineyards, available only in limited quantities and easily the costliest California table wine; Pinot Noir, vintage 1951, the first great Pinot Noir vintage from his present domain; Cabernet Sauvignon, vintage 1947, his finest Cabernet Sauvignon to date; Cabernet Sauvignon, vintage 1946, a great full-bodied wine, is available in very limited quantities for laying-down purposes; Cabernet Sauvignon, vintage 1948 and similar in character to the 1947, is developing well. *Note:* A small amount of La Montana Woodside Cabernet is still available. This is a non-vintage Cabernet Sauvignon (marketed in the traditional claret-type bottle), produced from Woodside vineyards in San Mateo County, which Martin Ray used to farm.

WHITE: Chardonnay, vintage 1952, a true Mountain Chardonnay produced from Pinot Chardonnay grapes only.

ROSÉ: Pinot Noir Rosé, vintage 1952, coral pink, and the only rosé produced in California from the Pinot noir grape.

SANTA CLARA COUNTY
SANTA CLARA VALLEY—EVERGREEN AREA

Mirassou Vineyards, San Jose

The type of operation at Mirassou Vineyards, a very special one, consists in producing varietal table wines and champagne stock of superior quality and in supplying these in bulk to other wineries. A little bottling is also done under private labeling.

The enterprise is co-owned by the brothers Edmund (Ed) A. and Norbert G. Mirassou, fourth-generation winegrowers, who are continuing the tradition started in the Santa Clara Valley by their great-grandfather Pierre Pellier in 1853.

The Pelliers were farmers from the region of La Rochelle in France. When Pierre Pellier first came to California in 1850, he realized the vast agricultural potentialities of the fruitful Santa Clara Valley. He started a nursery in what is now the heart of the city of

San Jose, but soon decided that what was needed for propagation was the highest-quality European rootstock. Accordingly he went back to France, accumulated thousands of cuttings of choice *vinifera* vines, roses, and fruit trees and sailed with them for California. The voyage around Cape Horn was a long and rough one. Water gave out and many of his precious cuttings withered away. Pierre was desperate, but finally purchased all the available potatoes aboard, inserted in them the ends of his cuttings, and in this original manner saved part of his valuable stock. Included in this shipment was what is believed to have been the first French prune tree to make its way to California.

In 1862 Pierre Pellier purchased a large hillside acreage on the west side of the Santa Clara Valley, a portion of the old Rancho Yerba Buena, once granted the Chaboya family by the King of Spain. Here he planted the choicest vines from his San Jose nursery and made his first wine, the forerunner of a long and famous series of vintages.

Henrietta Pellier, Pierre's eldest daughter, married another French winegrower and immigrant, Pierre Mirassou, who was put in charge of the Pellier vineyards and winery. The eldest of their sons, Peter, became the father of the present owners of the Mirassou vineyards, while the second son, Herman, is the father of the four Mirassou brothers who operate Lone Hills Vineyards at Los Gatos (see there).

Pierre Mirassou died while still quite young and Henrietta later married Thomas Casalegno, who continued operation of the vineyards, assisted by his three Mirassou stepsons, Peter, Herman, and John. When phylloxera attacked the vines at the turn of the century Casalegno procured some twenty thousand disease-resistant roots of the *Rupestris St. George* variety, which were planted in the vineyards and to which the surviving *Vitis vinifera* vines were grafted with success.

In 1909 the three brothers purchased the enterprise from their stepfather and formed a partnership. They expanded the vineyard acreage in Evergreen in the rolling foothills between the Santa Clara Valley and Mt. Hamilton, including the location of the present winery and of the home Peter Mirassou built for his family and where his sons were born, Norbert and Edmund.

Prohibition led to the dissolution of the partnership and to a division of the property. Peter Mirassou's share included the Evergreen tract and, although vineyards were thought to be worthless by some, Peter refused to replant to any other crop. His judgment proved sound, as grape prices soon rose, and he then began to supply Eastern markets both with grapes from his own vineyards and with those he purchased elsewhere.

The grape-growing business was continued till 1937, when Peter Mirassou informed his sons that if they desired he would back them to revive the family tradition of fine wine making. This proposal was accepted and carried out with an enthusiasm and a devotion which have continued on to the present. In 1942, when Peter Mirassou retired, Norbert and Edmund formed a co-partnership and purchased their father's interest in the business. Since then further land for the planting of choice varieties has been acquired and the winery enlarged.

Mirassou Vineyards specializes in superior-quality varietals, especially the whites. Available under the *Mirassou* label, with the Santa Clara appellation of origin, are the following *table wines:*

WHITE: White Riesling, Pinot Blanc, Sylvaner, Semillon (dry), Sauterne (dry), and Chablis;
RED: Cabernet Sauvignon, Zinfandel, and Burgundy;
ROSÉ: Grenache Rosé.

SANTA CLARA COUNTY—LOWER SANTA CLARA VALLEY

Richert & Sons, Madrone

A small winery and one of the latest to be launched. It was founded in November 1953 by Walter S. Richert and occupies a portion of the premises, formerly the home of Madrone Vineyards, a concern once famous for the quality of its wines, but which was dissolved in 1951.

Walter Richert first entered the wine industry in 1937 and has been connected with different wineries in various capacities, including as chemist, production manager, sales representative, and general manager. He served as technical editor for the publication *Wines and Vines* and is prominent in the American Society of Enologists.

The Richert winery is located in the front section of the former Madrone plant, as is a retail outlet. The policy is to produce fine wines at very reasonable prices. The first crushing of the winery's own grapes took place in the 1954 harvest season and, as the business expands, more and more of Richert's own wines will be produced, as distinct from those which are selected, purchased, and bottled. Walter Richert has great plans for the future, including that of his sons, Bob, Eric, and Scotty, who already form part of the company's name in spite of their extreme youth.

The featured brand is the well-established one of *Simi Vineyard,** acquired by Walter Richert, along with other assets and interests, from C. Schilling Company of Cloverdale, Sonoma County, when Richert & Sons was formed.

The main accent at the Richert winery is on the production of *table wines,* while sparkling wines and aperitif and dessert types are also marketed. Available under the *Simi Vineyard* label are the following:

Table wines:
> RED: Cabernet, Zinfandel, Burgundy, and Claret; WHITE: Dry Semillon, Haut Sauterne, Sauterne, Riesling, and Chablis; ROSÉ: Vin Rosé.

Sparkling wines (bulk process):
> Champagne, Pink Champagne, and Sparkling Burgundy.

Aperitif and Dessert wines:
> Pale Dry Sherry and Cream Sherry, Ruby Port; Dry and Sweet Vermouth.

Walter Richert publishes, from time to time, witty and chatty "Reports," informing his friends and customers both of the progress

*Not to be confused with the *Simi* brand of Simi Wineries (Montepulciano) of Healdsburg, Sonoma County.

made by his winery and its products and of the family doings in general.

San Martin Vineyards Company, San Martin

This well-known enterprise is owned by the close-knit Filice family, which originally came from the province of Cosenza in Calabria, Italy, and members of which are spread all over Central and Southern Europe. The Italian firm of Bozzo and Filice of Donnici claims to have been in the wine business since 1700.

A branch of the Filice family settled in California in the Santa Clara Valley in the early eighteen nineties and planted considerable land there in the early part of this century. Bruno Filice, who had wine interests in Italy, acquired in 1932, with the passing of Prohibition, the old San Martin Winery and Vineyards, which had been founded some forty years before.

The family concern is now owned and operated by Bruno Filice's four sons and by his son-in-law. Michael J. Filice is the vineyard manager and also acts in a general managerial capacity along with his brothers John M. and Peter C. Filice and his brother-in-law, Pasquale Lico. The last is also the wine maker, while another Filice brother, Frank C., is the bottling superintendent. Michael Bo is the chemist.

The Filices have a considerable vineyard acreage under cultivation, most of which was planted by members of the family. The vineyards are located on the sunny western hillsides of the Santa Clara Valley, many of them on the slopes of Mt. Madonna, dominating the Hecker Pass, and include Glen Loma and Castlewood, planted to the choicer varietal vines.

Table wines, sparkling wines, and aperitif and dessert wines of fine quality are produced, with *San Martin Private Reserve* the leading brand. Available are the following wines:

Table wines:
  RED: Cabernet, Pinot Noir, Zinfandel, Burgundy, and Claret;
  WHITE: Riesling, Malvasia, Chablis, Rhine Wine, and Sauterne;
  ROSÉ: Rosé.

Sparkling wines (both bottle-fermented and bulk-process):
Champagne, Pink Champagne, Grenache Pink Champagne, and
Sparkling Burgundy.

Aperitif and Dessert wines:
Flor Sherries, including Golden Palomino and Pale Dry Sherry,
Sherry (medium), and Cream Sherry; Port and Tawny Port,
Muscatel, Tokay, White Port, and Angelica.

A number of high-quality varietal table wines are also produced
under the *Castlewood* brand, some of which carry the vintage year
on the label. These include: Cabernet Sauvignon, Pinot Noir, Zinfandel, Grignolino, and Barbera in the reds, as well as Semillon and
Pinot Chardonnay in the whites, and Grenache Rosé. A specialty
will be Montonico, a mild, tawny-pink sweet table wine (12 per
cent alcohol by volume), produced from grapes of that name imported from Calabria. Both Emerald Riesling and Ruby Cabernet
will also be available.

The mellow type of red Italian table wine is represented by the
San Martin Vino Rosso, by a Mellow Claret, as well as by a wine
named Hostess Burgundy.

Both Dry and Sweet Vermouth are produced, the latter being
aged in small chestnut barrels.

A special building for the development of *flor* Sherries has been
constructed and is now in production.

Santa Clara Valley is the home of some of the finest strawberries
of the West Coast and San Martin markets a well-known Strawberry Wine which has captured the full flavor and delicacy of that
fruit. Other *berry wines* marketed include Loganberry and Blackberry.

Bertero Winery, Gilroy (Hecker Pass)

A small winery in the western foothills of the Santa Clara Valley
in the Hecker Pass area, and included here on account of the excellent quality of its Grenache Rosé.

Alfonso Bertero, the owner, was born in the neighborhood of

Turin in Italy and came to this country in 1911. He first worked for the Standard Oil Company and in 1919 went into the wine business, selling grapes to home wine makers and to other wineries for the production of sacramental wines. He moved to his present location in 1924, where he built the winery and his home. The property is part of the old Los Alamos grant and some of the original Spanish wooden stakes survive.

Bertero, who is getting on in years, is assisted in the family enterprise by his son Angelo, who in turn is aided by his son, Angelo, Jr., whose brother, Carl, will rejoin the family and the business when he has completed his term in the Navy.

Table wines only are produced, all from local grapes, including Zinfandel, Carignane, Grenache, and French Colombard (for the Sauterne). Wines are marketed under the *Bertero* brand and are sold at the winery in large glass containers although they can be bottled on special order.

Burgundy and Claret are produced as well as Sauterne, but the outstanding product is the winery's Grenache Rosé, made exclusively from that grape. It is a full-flavored, brilliant-colored wine which can easily compete with the finest Grenache in the state.

Bonesio Brothers, Gilroy (Uvas district)

A winery well known in the surrounding counties, producing sound "country" Santa Clara table wines. It is located in the hilly Uvas district west of Gilroy near the Hecker Pass, *uvas* being Spanish for grape and the region so named because the Spaniards, presumably, already raised or found grapes there. The property forms part of the former Solis Rancho, and the Bonesio residence, over a hundred years old, was once the headquarters of the Solis Rancho grant.

Pietro (Peter) Bonesio, the founder of the winery, came from an Italian wine-raising family and was born in Cardona near Asti in Piedmont. Now in his seventies, he came to the United States at the turn of the century and worked in subway construction in New York City. He later farmed in Louisiana, and then moved to Oakland, California, where he was engaged in the concrete business. In 1915 he reverted to the traditional family occupation, first starting a winery in the Rucker district, north of Gilroy, and then moved to his present location on Solis Rancho in Uvas Canyon.

Peter Bonesio is still active, but turned the business over in 1932 to his sons Louis and Victor, the present owners and general managers, who were brought up in the enterprise since their earliest days, being taught the trade by their father. Victor Bonesio is also the sales manager, while Louis is the wine maker and chemist, and Peter Bonesio the vineyard manager.

The Bonesio wines are made from home-grown grapes which include Zinfandel, Grignolino, Grenache, French Colombard, Golden Chasselas, and Sauvignon vert.

The featured brand is *Uvas,* under which the following *table wines* are marketed:

RED: Burgundy (full of flavor, full-bodied, practically straight Zinfandel) and Claret (from mixed grapes);

WHITE: Sauterne (from the Golden Chasselas and others);

ROSÉ: Grignolino Rosé (with plans to produce also a Grenache Rosé).

A number of aperitif and dessert wines are purchased and marketed.

SANTA CRUZ COUNTY

Hallcrest Vineyard, Felton

Some 400 feet up the slopes of the Santa Cruz mountains, overlooking the San Lorenzo Valley above Felton, lie the Hallcrest vineyards and winery, devoted solely to the growing of Cabernet Sauvignon and White Riesling grapes, and to the production of these two 100 per cent varietal table wines.

The vineyards are planted on the crest of a hill and were for that reason named Hallcrest by their owner, Chaffee E. Hall, who purchased the property in 1941. A corporation attorney by vocation, practicing in San Francisco for many years, Chaffee Hall is also an enophile, knowing and appreciating truly fine wines, having developed his taste during his numerous trips to the wine lands of Europe. It is at Hallcrest that he fulfills one of the great ambitions of his life, that of producing, with knowledge and lavish care, Santa Cruz County table wines which compare in elegance, bouquet, and taste with the very finest of California.

Chaffee Hall is his own wine maker and all operations in vineyards and winery are either accomplished personally or supervised closely by members of the Hall family. The utmost care is taken, both of the vines and of all stages of wine production. The first vintages were of 1946 and these, as well as the succeeding ones, have been remarkably successful.

Cabernet Sauvignon and White Riesling are marketed under the *Hallcrest* brand, with indication of the vintage year and with the Santa Cruz County appellation of origin. They are bottled in elegant fashion, with lead-foil caps imported from the Netherlands and with wire-mesh covering procured in France.

Bargetto's Santa Cruz Winery, Soquel

The founders of this family firm were the brothers Philip and John Bargetto, sons of Giuseppe Bargetto, winegrower and wine maker from the neighborhood of Asti in Piedmont, Italy. Giuseppe came to this country, but later returned to his native land. He must have inspired his sons differently, for they both came over to stay. Philip came in 1887 and worked for some twelve years in the famed old Delmas Winery near San Jose. John Bargetto immigrated in 1909 and first engaged in the produce and grape-shipping business. In 1933 Philip and John founded the Bargetto Winery in Soquel, which is now owned and operated by John Bargetto and his two sons, Lawrence and Ralph, the former being the wine maker, chemist, and general manager, and the latter having charge of sales. Two daughters of Philip complete the family membership of the enterprise.

The Bargetto wines are produced from grapes purchased from vineyards scattered over Santa Cruz and Santa Clara counties. *Table wines* are the specialty, while aperitif and dessert wines, including a Marsala and Dry and Sweet Vermouths, are purchased, aged, and marketed to round out the line.

Fine-quality table wines are featured under the *Bargetto* brand, with *Winemaster's Bouquet* the label for those of the regular grade. *Bargetto* table wines include the following:

RED: Cabernet Sauvignon (from Vinehill-area grapes), Barbera, Malvasia (from the Black Malvoisie grape, and one of the very few produced in the state), Zinfandel (from grapes purchased in the Bonny Doon area), Burgundy, and Claret;

WHITE: Sauvignon Blanc (their premium white wine), Dry Muscat (a light, dry muscat wine made from the Alexandria variety), Moscato Amabile (a light, sweet muscat wine from the same grape), Sauterne;

ROSÉ: Grenache Rosé (dry), Grenache Rosé (semi-sweet), Grignolino Rosé.

Note: A dry Vin Rosé made from local Zinfandel grapes is also marketed under the *Winemaster* brand.

The plans are eventually to produce other varietal table wines of quality, including Pinot Blanc, depending on the availability of the desired grape varieties. A red table wine of the vino-rosso type will also become available.

SAN BENITO COUNTY

Valliant Vineyards, Hollister

Two separate hillside vineyard complexes form the Valliant Vineyards of today. The one, and the more historical, is located in the so-called "Vineyard District" valley and the other in the Cienega, or Grass, Valley. The two neighboring valleys are situated some ten miles southwest of the city of Hollister in the picturesque Gavilan (Sparrow Hawk) Mountain Range which separates the Salinas and the San Joaquin valleys. Both the Cienega and the "Vineyard District" vineyards, be it noted, are planted to *vinifera* vines growing on their own roots, no phylloxera ever having penetrated into the region.

The "Vineyard District" was first planted to vines by Théophile Vaché,* surnamed Vaca, a Frenchman who cleared the chaparral brush and trees in 1849 or earlier and started what were to become famous vineyards. William Palmtag, a German immigrant who became mayor of Hollister, where he also owned a bank, acquired the property in 1883 and greatly extended the vineyards, importing choice European varieties. He established a winery and his Palmtag Mountain Vineyard wines won many prizes at national and international wine competitions.

During the first decade of the twentieth century Captain Jules Jacques St. Hubert and his partner, John Dickinson, formerly a Chicago grain broker, bought out Palmtag and incorporated as the San Benito Vineyards and increased the vineyard acreage in the surrounding mountains. After about five years Captain St. Hubert, the wine maker, left and Dickinson continued to operate the enterprise until Prohibition forced the winery to close down. The property then passed through various hands until the advent of Repeal, when Edwin Valliant, Sr., took it over and began operating the old winery. The Valliant family, with E. P. Hickman as partner, revived the tradition of producing fine-quality table wines. The Valliant brand was retained when the Hiram Walker interests purchased the property in 1943 to assure a continuous supply of fine California wines for their subsidiary, W. A. Taylor & Company, the well-known New York importing firm and the present operators of Valliant Vineyards.

The story of the Cienega, or Grass, Valley vineyards was quite different. In 1908 Professor Bioletti, the great viticulturist and enologist of the University of California, interested Dr. Harold Ohrwall, a San Francisco physician, in developing an experimental vineyard in this area, considered exceptionally well suited to the

*The same Théophile Vaché who landed from France in Monterey in 1830 and whose nephews, in 1883, founded the Vaché winery in Redlands, San Bernardino County, predecessor of the present Brookside Vineyard Company of Ontario in the Cucamonga district (see there).

production of fine table wines. Bioletti's association with the enterprise lasted only a couple of years, but the Ohrwall family operated the winery and vineyards continuously until their acquisition, in 1944, by W. A. Taylor & Company and the Hiram Walker interests. Dr. Ohrwall's son, John P. Ohrwall, a graduate of the University of California, who has been associated with the Cienega Valley property all his life, is now the manager for both vineyard ranches.

The winery, which has been completely rebuilt, is located on the "Vineyard District" property and contains cool cellars, oak and redwood cooperage, and modern and efficient equipment to produce the best wines from the grapes of this famous locality. Production manager Lloyd A. Searing and A. G. Hoelscher, who has had long experience in the quality-wine field (he and his brothers formerly marketed the well-known I. De Turk wines), zealously guard the development of the Valliant wines.

While *white table wines* are the specialty, some red table wines and first-class *vermouths* are also produced, all marketed under the *Valliant* brand.

Table wines:
> WHITE: Riesling (for which the vineyards are perhaps the best known), Johannisberg Riesling (a wine for which this winery has been famous and which will be available again), Rhine Wine, Dry Sauterne, Sauterne, and Chablis; Vin Rosé;
> RED: Cabernet, Burgundy, and Claret.

Aperitif and Dessert wines: Palomino Dry Sherry and Cream Sherry, Ruby Port; Dry and Sweet Vermouth (produced from the special formulas of the well-known wine maker and chemist Charles Altair of Carmel-by-the-Sea).

MONTEREY COUNTY

F. W. Silvear, Soledad

F. W. (Bill) Silvear owns and operates some very fine vineyards above Soledad (meaning solitude) in the Salinas Valley, from which quite special champagnes have been produced at various times. For that reason his operation is included in the *Guide,* although no winery is connected with his vineyards.

The origin of Bill Silvear's family is uncertain but romantic. His grandfather Charles Silvear was raised in a nunnery on the Azores Islands until he was eight, and then the youngster went to sea. He came to California in 1849 and settled in Watsonville, where he raised potatoes. One of his three sons, Tom, went to Oregon and there Bill Silvear was born.

Bill and his wife Agnes, a San Franciscan, have both always had a strong feeling for the finer and more romantic things in life. What led Bill to the acquisition of his ranch above Soledad was his love for California wild flowers and his interest in minerals. Looking for flowers near the Pinnacles National Monument he came across some Iceland spar, a doubly refracting mineral, the best of which is found in Iceland. This find eventually led to champagne rather than to mining and riches. Emery Smith, assayer and geologist, who had studied viticulture in France, told Bill Silvear about a Frenchman named Tamm, who had traveled far and wide to find soil similar to that of the Champagne region in France, as his ambition was to produce California champagne which would be as close as possible to the French wine in character. This soil he had found in the hills near the Pinnacles, where he had planted vineyards some two thousand feet up on a bench of the Chalone Mountain in the Gabilan Range. The age of the soil had since been estimated at millions of years, if not older, one of the oldest types of soil known. Tamm had died in the beginning of the century, before he could accomplish his ambition, but the soil and climate were as promising as ever. So Bill Silvear decided to buy a ranch next to Tamm's former place and to set it out in vineyards.

This was in 1919. He planted his vines, but Prohibition effectively closed the door to new wine enterprises. Bill Silvear rented his ranch, but took it back after Repeal. He gradually replanted the vineyards to the champagne varieties, Pinot Chardonnay, Pinot blanc, and Pinot noir and grafted them to disease-resistant rootstock. This took him into the early nineteen forties. Soon he could prove that Tamm, the Frenchman, had been right, that the Pinot grapes did exceptionally well in this area with ideal conditions of average rainfall, ocean breezes, plentiful sunshine, no extremes in temperature, and in soil consisting of decomposed granite overlaid with marl of lime.

As Bill Silvear did not own a winery he made arrangements with an old friend, Oliver J. Goulet of Almadén Vineyards at Los Gatos, to make small *cuvées* of his Pinot Champagnes for him. And so Bill Silvear's excellent *Soledad* Champagnes came into being, available only in small quantities and in a few places, among them the retail outlet which Bill and his wife operate in that little village just north of Watsonville in Santa Cruz County, which is now known as Freedom but was once more forcefully known as Whiskey Hill.

San Luis Obispo County

York Brothers, Templeton

Representative of good wine making in San Luis Obispo County is the winery owned and operated by the York family, located just below the peak of York Mountain on the eastern slopes of the Coast Range, overlooking Templeton and the valley below.

The ranch property was acquired in 1882 by Andrew York, grandfather of the present owners. Born in Indiana, Andrew York came out West from Missouri in the eighteen fifties and settled in San Luis Obispo County after having first spent some time in the Napa Valley. A proud family possession is a valuable document, the original deed to the land, dated 1875—made out to Jacob B. Grandstaff, from whom Andrew York bought it—and signed by U. S. Grant, President of the United States.

Andrew York found that the grape vines he had planted to supplement his apple orchard yielded more grapes than he could market, and so, with the help of his sons, Walter, Thomas, and Silas, built a small winery to take care of the surplus. Shortly after the turn of the century additional land was purchased and a large vineyard planted of Zinfandels, selected because they mature early and usually miss the danger of early winter frosts. About that time the winery also was enlarged, using bricks molded and burned on the place in the ancient traditions of the Babylonians.

The York place is a historic one, as time goes, and many tales are told of how the lumber to build the original houses and winery was carted over the rough mountain roads all the way from Cayucos on the Pacific Ocean, at one time a small, flourishing harbor. Indians used trails running through the property on their way to the hot sulphur and mud baths in what is now Paso Robles, some twelve miles distant. Nearby also is the San Ygnacio Ranch, once owned by Ignace Jan Paderewski, the great Polish patriot and world-famous pianist, who raised wine grapes and almonds there.

After the death of Andrew York in 1913 his sons Walter and Silas took over the enterprise, which became the York Brothers winery. The present owners and operators are the third-generation wine makers, Wilfrid S. York and Howard A. York, the sons respectively of Walter and of Silas.

Only one wine is produced, a fruity, zestful, and nearly 100 per cent varietal Zinfandel. It is made in small quantities and is available in barrels for family use and bottled commercially under the brand which is also the name by which the area is known, *York Mountain*.

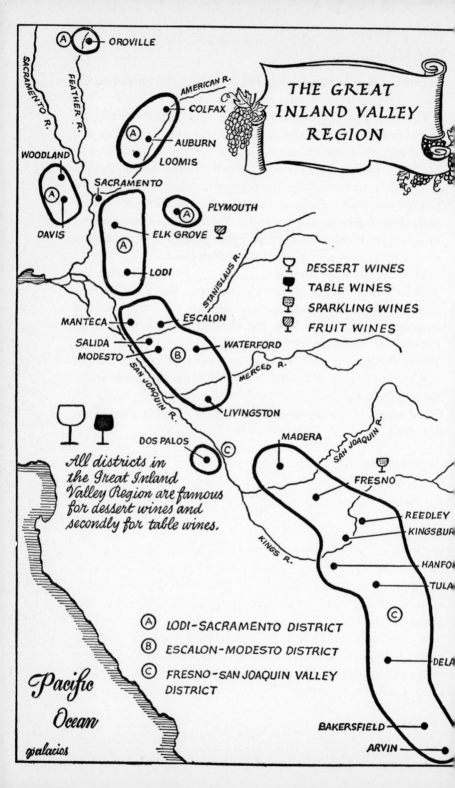

X

THE GREAT INLAND VALLEY REGION

*T*HIS VAST VALLEY REGION sweeps down in a fairly narrow band parallel to the coast line, from which it is separated by the mountains of the Coast Range. Some three hundred miles long, it stretches from north of the city of Sacramento down south beyond Bakersfield in Kern County. Its climate, moderately warm in the northern areas, becomes progressively hotter the farther south one comes.

The region takes in the territory of both the Sacramento and the San Joaquin river valleys. It is the home of the great California dessert or sweet wine production, for which the climate and soil are especially well suited. Table and sparkling wines are also produced, often blended with wines made from grapes grown in northern coastal counties vineyards. Most of the inland valley region vines, especially in the warmer climatic zones, are cultivated by irrigation methods.

The three great and equally famous winegrowing and wine-producing sections of the great inland valley region are, from north to south, the *Lodi-Sacramento,* the *Escalon-Modesto,* and the *Fresno-San Joaquin Valley* districts.

A. *LODI—SACRAMENTO DISTRICT*

This district takes in the wine-producing areas of Sacramento County and of the northern part of San Joaquin County.

In Sacramento County there is a winegrowing area which stretches east of the city of Sacramento down southward, where both table and dessert wines are produced. Elk Grove is a center famous for its production of berry and fruit wines.

Northern San Joaquin County contains the famed winegrowing area of Lodi, which spreads out from that city in all directions to a surrounding region some ten miles deep. Lodi is on the Mokelumne River, which flows into the San Joaquin and is sometimes referred to as lying in the upper reaches of the San Joaquin Valley. It can also be said to be situated at the juncture of the Sacramento and San Joaquin valleys and in what is known as the Central Valley.

Lodi is especially noted for its dessert wines although table wines are also produced there. It is the center of a vast Flame-Tokay vineyard district, spectacular in the fall on account of the brilliant coloring of the grapes. The Flame Tokays are mainly used as table grapes, but are also employed in many of the dessert wines produced by the Lodi wineries including the wine called tokay.

SACRAMENTO COUNTY

Mills Winery, Sacramento

The winery, situated east of Sacramento and just south of the American River, was founded in 1910 by the Silver brothers, who operated it until the thirties. The present owner, Paul Kershaw, Jr., who is president and general manager of the enterprise and also his own wine maker, took over in 1945, modernizing the winery and adding a large distilling plant for the production of brandy.

Most of the grapes used in the winery are from non-irrigated vineyards, some of them originating in the hillsides north of the American River toward the Mother Lode country, and others from the north coast counties. For the production of the dessert wines grapes from the inland valley region are also used.

Both *table* and *dessert wines* are produced, mostly on a bulk basis, destined for other wineries, but some bottling is also done for sale at the winery under the *Mills* and *Beaumille* brands. The featured wines are the Burgundy in the table wines and the Port in the dessert types, both of a dark red, nearly purple color. The Burgundy is produced from a blend of Carignane, Mataro, Petite Sirah, and Zinfandel grapes, all from non-irrigated vines.

Gibson Wine Company, Elk Grove

The Gibson Wine Company, with its winery at Elk Grove, California, and offices at St. Helena and Palm Desert, California, is a subsidiary of the parent corporation, the Gibson Wine Company of Nevada, with principal offices in Cincinnati, Ohio.

A large and modern bottling plant is maintained in Covington, Kentucky, just across the river from Cincinnati, to which the company ships its bulk wine from California to be bottled and marketed throughout the Middle West and the East.

President of both the California company and the Nevada corporation is Robert H. Gibson, who after spending ten years in the stockbrokerage business in Cincinnati and New York turned to the production of wines.

He felt that many people would enjoy the taste of wines made from types of fruit other than grapes, and experimented for some years in the production of berry and fruit wines. His faith was fully justified and he succeeded in developing a large market in this field. Berry and fruit wines have found their own customers and the Gibson Wine Company has become one of the largest producers of these wines in the world.

Robert H. Gibson, known to his many friends as Bob, spends most of his time at St. Helena and Palm Desert, where he maintains his summer and winter homes as well as offices. On his St. Helena ranch he raises rare pheasants, of which he is a well-known breeder, supplying them to zoos throughout the world. He and his entire family also have a hobby of raising and showing fine quarter-breds and he is the proud possessor of one of the outstanding strings of these horses in the West.

The trade-mark of the corporation is the Golden Pheasant, which appears on many of the labels and is blown into most of the company's bottles.

The Elk Grove winery, where nearly all of Gibson's berry and fruit wines, as well as the table and dessert wines, are produced, was originally built in 1912 as a gas-engine works where plane engines were built for the First World War. In 1934 it was converted into a winery by the Elk Grove Fruit Growers Association, a co-operative, and when Gibson secured it in 1943, it was known as the Sunny Crest Winery. The name was changed to the Gibson Wine Company of California and extensive rebuilding and modernization took place. From a small plant it grew into a large and modern winery, producing the finest berry and fruit wines in the state.

The following wines are produced and marketed under *Gibson's* brand:

Berry and Fruit wines (12 per cent alcohol by volume): Old Briar Blackberry of the Boysenberry Variety, Boysenberry, Cherry, Elderberry, Loganberry, Raspberry, and Red Currant;

Berry and Fruit wines (20 or 21 per cent alcohol by volume): Apple, Blackberry, and Grape;

Light Sweet wines (12 or 13 per cent alcohol by volume): Light Sweet Red, White, and Muscat; American Concord;

Sparkling wines (from 100 per cent California wines and fermented in the bottle): Yellow Label Champagne (Brut, Extra-Dry, and Sec), Red Label Sparkling Burgundy;

Vermouth: Sweet and Dry.

The quality brand for table and dessert wines is *Gibson's Golden Pheasant* and under this label the following varieties are produced and marketed:

Table wines:

 RED: Cabernet, Burgundy, and Claret; WHITE: Sauterne, Riesling, Rhine, and Chablis;

Aperitif and Dessert wines: Palomino Sherry, Pale Dry, Golden, and Cream Sherries, Tawny and Ruby Ports; Muscatel and Tokay.

Numerous other Gibson brands and labels exist, of which *Gibson's Private Stock Pheasant Brand* is the most prominent and is used for wines in the economy field. These include:

Table wines: Burgundy, Claret, and Sauterne;

Aperitif and Dessert wines: Pale Dry Sherry, Sherry, and Cream Sherry; Port; Muscatel, Tokay, and White Port.

NORTHERN SAN JOAQUIN COUNTY

Acampo Winery and Distilleries, Acampo

The winery is named after the town of that name, just north of Lodi. The owner, general manager, and wine maker is Dino Barengo, a graduate of the University of Nevada at Reno. He has been active in the wine industry for many years and worked among others for that colorful and legendary personality, Lee Jones, formerly head of the Shewan-Jones Company, which he founded after Prohibition, and who maintains his residence not far from Lodi.

Dino Barengo has been associated with the Acampo Winery since the early forties, when it was a stock corporation of which Cesare Mondavi, who later took over the Charles Krug Winery, was president. In 1943 the Acampo Winery was acquired by the Gibson Wine Company, now of Elk Grove, and Dino Barengo managed it for that concern. Barengo then leased the winery and finally purchased it in 1946, when he became the sole proprietor.

Both table and dessert wines of sound standard quality are produced, with *Barengo* and *Barengo Reserve* the featured brands with *Royal Stag* for northern Nevada, where Dino Barengo has retained many connections.

The most popular of the Barengo *dessert wines* are the Port (mostly from the Zinfandel grape), Sherry (from Palomino and Mission), Muscatel (from the Muscat of Alexandria), and Tokay (mainly from the Flame Tokay).

East-Side Winery, Lodi

The well-known East-Side Winery, one of the largest in the district, is a farmers' co-operative, founded in 1933. Its name was adopted because that section of the Lodi area where the winery is located, directly east of the city, is known as an area of particularly rich soil yielding high-quality grapes.

The co-operative is formed by some hundred winegrowing stockholders, to whom all returns revert after costs and taxes have been paid. E. J. Mettler is the president, Ed Preszler the vice-president, and K. T. Anderson the general manager. The wine maker is Herman Ehlers, R. Gianelli is the chemist, and W. Ehlers the bottling superintendent.

Both table and aperitif and dessert wines are produced, which rate among the finest of the inland valley wines.

The featured brand is *Royal Host* for quality wines, with *Gold Bell* the secondary label for those of competitive grade.

The *Royal Host* wines include the following:

Aperitif and Dessert wines: Pale Dry Sherry (featured), Sherry, and Cream Sherry; Port (another featured wine, of the Ruby type) and Tawny Port; Flame Tokay (produced 100 per cent from the Flame Tokay grape); Marsala (medium sweet, with a high percentage of Palomino with the addition of Angelica); Muscatel, White Port, and Angelica; Dry and Sweet Vermouth;

Table wines: WHITE: Rhine Wine (a house specialty of exceptional quality), Dry Sauterne, and Haut Sauterne; RED: Burgundy, Zinfandel, and Claret;

Light Sweet wines: Light Sweet Red and White.

A red table wine of the mellow Italian "vino rosso" type is marketed under the *Buon Vino* label, while another specialty is the so-called "Palomino Beige," an aperitif wine of the sherry order, very dry, made exclusively from the Palomino grape and containing 18 per cent alcohol by volume.

Under the *Gold Bell* brand a full line of sound standard-quality wines is marketed as follows:

Aperitif and Dessert wines: Pale Dry Sherry and Sherry, Port, Muscatel, Tokay, White Port, and Angelica;

Table wines: Burgundy, Zinfandel and Claret; Dry Sauterne, Haut Sauterne, and Rhine Wine.

Wine Growers Guild, Lodi

The Wine Growers Guild, one of the largest producers of the California wine industry, was incorporated as such in 1943, succeeding California Wine Sales. The Guild is actually a federation of separate co-operative wineries, composed in turn of numerous individual growers. The crushing is done by the member wineries, who crush the grapes belonging to their members and produce the wines. The Guild is for central bottling and merchandising only, returning to the member wineries the gross proceeds of the sales, less all costs of blending, bottling, freight, advertising and sales and administrative expenses. The member wineries return to the growers the gross return from the sales of the wines, which is the figure returned to them by the Guild less actual production costs and including the administration of the producing plant. Both the Wine Growers Guild and all of the Guild producing units are strictly non-profit co-operatives.

The following are the member wineries of the Guild:

Cucamonga Pioneer Vineyard Association at Cucamonga (also known as Cucamonga Cellars of Wine Growers Guild), Lockeford Winery at Lockeford near Lodi, Del Rio Winery, Inc., at Woodbridge near Lodi (also known as Woodbridge Cellars of Wine Growers Guild), Bear Creek Vineyard Association at Lodi (also known as Lodi Cellars of Wine Growers Guild), Mendocino Grape Growers, Inc., of Ukiah, Mendocino County.

The location of the member wineries in the prime grape-growing areas enables the Guild to produce and market Zinfandels, Burgundies, and Clarets from the Cucamonga district, red table wines from Mendocino County in the Northern Coastal Region (such as used in their Vino da Tavola), and Palomino Sherry, Pale Dry Sherry, Port, White Port, and Zinfandel from San Joaquin County in the inland valley region.

L. K. Marshall, one of the great men of the California wine industry, with a knowledge and charm which only equal the respect in which he is held by one and all, is the president of the Wine Growers Guild. He is at the same time the general manager of Bear Creek Vineyard Association of Lodi, a well-known enterprise in its own right, founded in 1934, and a Guild member. Lawrence Quaccia is the Guild's wine maker.

One of L. K. Marshall's hobbies is the growing and developing of special varietals, and many an experimental wine has been made under his direct supervision. The purpose is to test out favorable varieties for which there seems to be a need under local climatic and soil conditions. Most the varieties are available to anyone interested in growing them. Varieties grown successfully by Marshall include the Tinta Madeira, a wonderful grape for the production of fine port wine, and Ruby Cabernet, which may have a great future before it in the claret field. The most intensive search at the present time is for a suitable variety to replace the Zinfandel, which in some localities is so subject to diseases that it is fast dying out.*

A committee of outside experts yearly classifies and grades each cuvée or batch of Guild wine produced.

The top-quality brand is *Ceremony,* which is reserved for the older and vintage wines. These include:

Aperitif and Dessert wines: Palomino Pale Dry Sherry and Palomino Cream Sherry (excellent sherries both, produced from the grape of that name and aged in oak puncheons, available also in decanters), Tawny Port (from the Grenache and other grapes, also available in decanters), Golden Muscat;

*It may be noted in this connection that the University of California has recently developed a cross between the Zinfandel and the Refosco vines which appears to show great promise, being disease-resistant and producing higher yields and wines of better quality and color than the Zinfandel.

Table wines: Burgundy and Sauterne;

Sparkling wines (bulk process): Champagne and Sparkling Burgundy.

The brand for the sound standard-quality wines is *Guild* and these include the following:

Aperitif and Dessert wines: Pale Dry Sherry, Sherry, and Cream Sherry; Port, Tawny Port, and Ruby Port; Muscatel, Tokay, White Port, and Angelica; Dry and Sweet Vermouth;

Light Sweet wines: Lite Sweet Red, White, Amber, and Muscat;

Table wines: RED: Vino da Tavola, Burgundy, Zinfandel, Chianti, and Claret; WHITE: Sauterne and Rhine; ROSÉ: Vin Rosé.

The Guild has been especially successful in the promotion of its "Vino da Tavola" (or table wine), often called "Tavola" for short. It is a wine of the Italian "vino rosso" type and, in the words of L. K. Marshall: "not as light as a Rosé, not as heavy as a Burgundy, not as tart as a Claret and possessing a 'soupçon' of sweetness." It is deservedly an extremely popular wine, one of the very finest of its kind, and is available in all sizes, from gallon containers to splits.

B. *ESCALON—MODESTO DISTRICT*

This district covers the winegrowing areas and wineries of the southern part of San Joaquin County, from Stockton south and southeast to Manteca and Escalon; it takes in Stanislaus County from Salida on down to Modesto and also includes the Livingston area in northern Merced County.

The Escalon-Modesto district, located in the northern San Joaquin Valley, is best known for its dessert wines, but table and sparkling wines are also produced. Some of the California wineries with the largest distribution are located in this district.

SOUTHERN SAN JOAQUIN COUNTY

Franzia Brothers Winery, Ripon

This family concern, located about halfway between the towns of Manteca and Escalon in the southernmost part of San Joaquin County, is owned and operated by the five Franzia brothers. They are the sons of the late Giuseppe Franzia (Joe Sr.), a native of Genoa, Italy, who immigrated to this country, settling first in San Francisco and then moving to Stockton. He purchased the Franzia ranch in Ripon in 1906 and was for many years prominent in the grape-shipping business and from 1933 until his death in 1952 in the wine-producing field.

Giuseppe Franzia's sons carry on the family wine-making tradition, Joseph, the youngest son, better known as Joe, Jr., being the president of the firm, John the secretary and treasurer, and Frank, Louis, and Salvador vice-presidents in charge of the various departments. Fernando Quaccia is the wine maker and chemist.

The Franzia policy is to produce and market sound standard-quality wines at popular prices. The dessert wines are all produced exclusively from San Joaquin Valley grapes and so are the white table wines. The red table wines are blends of San Joaquin Valley and north coast counties wines, the latter mostly from the Napa Valley.

The main brand is *Franzia Special Reserve* and is used for the following wines, of which the Port and the Burgundy are especially featured:

Aperitif and Dessert wines: Port and Tawny Port; Pale Dry Sherry, Cocktail Sherry, Sherry, and Cream Sherry; Muscatel, Tokay, White Port, and Angelica;

Table wines: RED: Burgundy, Zinfandel, Chianti (a select, light Zinfandel), Claret, and Barberone; WHITE: Sauterne and Haut Sauterne (from the Palomino grape mostly), Rhine Wine, and Chablis.

The *Franzia* labeling is used for the featured Vino Rosso da Famiglia of the mellow Italian red table type, for the marketing of Champagne (Extra-Sec) and Sparkling Burgundy (produced according to the bulk process) and for Vermouth, both Dry and Sweet.

Petri Wineries, Escalon

Petri Wineries (and Mission Bell Wineries at Madera, Madera County, see there) are the operation and production names of Allied Grape Growers, a co-operative winery association composed of some three hundred members, owners of medium-sized or small wine-grape vineyards in the San Joaquin Valley. It was to this organization that Louis Petri, the youthful president of Petri of California, sold the Petri and Mission Bell Wineries in 1951, retaining the exclusive marketing rights for the whole of the co-operative's output. Two north coast counties wineries are owned and operated for the production of dry table wines, the Forestville Wineries at Forestville and the Northern Sonoma Wineries at Geyserville, both in Sonoma County.

The organization of Allied Grape Growers was created to permit both the grower and winery to share in the profits and risks of wine-growing and wine marketing. The arrangement made available to the growers a nationally advertised brand of wine in which millions of dollars were invested in advertising and sales promotion. With Allied Grape Growers producing the wine and Petri Wine Company selling it, the growers dispose of a complete sales organization headed by a family of experts and, in acquiring the wineries, the growers have come in as partners.

For the marketing of top-quality wines the Petris established Signature Vintners of San Francisco (see there). In that city, also, the headquarters of the various Petri enterprises are located. In 1953 the Petri interests acquired from National Distillers the famed Italian Swiss Colony at Asti, Sonoma County (see there) in a wine-history-making transaction.

The Petri Wine Company, which markets one of the most popular of the nationally advertised brands of sound standard-quality wines under the Petri labeling, is headed by Louis Petri as president with Angelo Petri, his father, the chairman of the board. Albert Petri, Paul Petri, L. N. Bianchini, and Clair N. Fishell are vice-presidents and B. Mortara is secretary-treasurer. Plant manager of the Petri Wineries at Escalon is James Gott while Thomas Leong is the chief chemist.

The Petri story is one of enterprise and success, the result of hard work coupled with the necessary flair for accomplishment. Founder of the family enterprise in California was Raphaelo Petri, a native of Tuscany, Italy, who came to San Francisco in the early eighteen eighties, bringing with him the family tradition for hospitality, good food, and wine. He first entered the hotel business and his Toscano Hotel on Broadway and later his Cosmopolitan on Green Street became popular meeting places where good meals and wines could be obtained at reasonable prices. Raphaelo Petri also started a wine enterprise, buying a small winery in San Joaquin Valley and founding the Petri Wine Company in 1886. He shipped wine to numerous members of the Italian-American colony in California and elsewhere, including New York City. Gradually his wine business expanded until it claimed the major share of his business attention. In 1916 he purchased a large vineyard in Escalon, near the site of the principal Petri winery at Alba Station.

With the coming of Prohibition Raphaelo Petri retired from the wine business and his son, Angelo, concentrated his energies on the Petri Cigar Company, founded by Raphaelo's brother, Amadeo. During Prohibition the Petris had another interest, the manufacturing of Italian-style boots in Tennessee.

Repeal saw the return of the Petris to the wine industry. Vineyards and wineries were acquired in various parts of California and wine stocks were built up. The third generation of the family now entered the wine picture. Louis Petri, born in San Francisco in 1913, the son of Angelo, had planned to become a doctor. He had studied chemistry and physics at Stanford and at the University of California and Repeal found him a medical student at St. Louis University. He decided to use his chemistry training in the family tradition of wine making and joined his father and grandfather in rebuilding the Petri wine enterprise. He started at the bottom, rolling barrels in the firm's San Francisco warehouse, but soon rose "from dirt to decanter." In 1945, at the age of thirty-two, he was president of the company.

During the first years after Repeal the Petri Wine Company confined its activities to shipping wines in bulk, according to specifications of other firms and bottlers. It was then decided to bottle at the winery and to reintroduce the Petri brand and label to the public, reviving the tradition set some fifty years previously by Raphaelo. By 1941 the Petri name was starting to become a familiar one on the retailers' shelves. In the early fifties the Petri organization, while retaining the family's name and label and brand, decided to devote its main energies to the merchandising end of the business, using modern advertising and marketing techniques, leaving the production end of the business to a co-operative, as described above.

Under the *Petri* brand a full line of sound standard-quality table, sparkling, and aperitif and dessert wines is marketed:

Table wines:
> RED: Burgundy, Zinfandel, Chianti, Claret, Barberone, and Sweet Burgundy;
> WHITE: Sauterne, Dry Sauterne, and Haut Sauterne, Chablis, Rhine Wine, and Muscat Wine;
> ROSÉ: Grenache Vin Rosé;

Sparkling wines (bulk process): Champagne (medium sweet) and Sparkling Burgundy;

Aperitif and Dessert wines: Pale Dry Sherry, Cocktail Sherry, Sherry, and Cream Sherry; Port, Ruby Port, and Tawny Port; Marsala, Muscatel, Tokay, White Port, and Angelica; Dry and Sweet Vermouth.

A featured table wine is the Vino Rosso Pastoso, one of the earliest wines of the mellow red Italian type produced, which is marketed under the *Marca Petri* label. Other *Petri* wines are: *Light Sweet wines* (Petri Party wines): red and white; *Berry wines:* Blackberry, Currant, Loganberry, and Strawberry.

Solera Cellars (Bianchi Cellars, Inc.), Escalon

While Solera Cellars so far has not marketed its wines directly to the public, it is included in the *Guide* because of its specialized operation, the large-scale production of *flor* Solera sherries, and the first California winery to have done so.

Solera Cellars is part of Bianchi Cellars, producers of table and dessert wines, owned by C. G. Bianchi & Company, of which Chauncey G. Bianchi is president and general manager. The Bianchi wine dynasty in California was founded by Giuseppe Bianchi, a native of Lucca, Italy, who came to this country in 1889 and farmed near San Jose in Santa Clara County. He had vineyards near Saratoga, but sold out when Prohibition came. He later bought vineyards in Manteca, San Joaquin County, and went into the grape-growing business. After his death in 1932 his son, Chauncey G. Bianchi, took over the enterprise and, together with his brothers Rinaldo, Joseph, Enrico, and his son William, went into the wine business at Lodi. The company bought what was known as the Village Winery at Escalon in 1950, which became Bianchi Cellars. In 1946 the Village Winery had started Solera Cellars in conjunction with Parrott & Company, the well-known wine- and liquor-distributing firm. Solera Cellars, in turn, was purchased by Bianchi Cellars, Inc., in 1951.

In the production of the winery's *flor* Solera Sherries, Palomino grapes only are used, grown on the Bianchi ranches in the triangular area formed by the cities of Manteca and Escalon in San Joaquin County and Modesto in Stanislaus County to the south.

The grapes, picked at the proper stage of ripeness, are crushed within six or eight hours, depending on the temperature. The wine is then drawn off and allowed to ferment completely dry in vats—with the fermentation temperature held at 65° Fahrenheit by refrigeration—and brought up 15.5 per cent alcohol by volume through the addition of brandy. It is then moved to the special *flor* vats, where the *flor* yeast does its miraculous work, covering the wine with a thick flower crust and imparting the typical nutty flavor of true *flor* sherries. When fully matured the wine is brought up to the traditional strength of 20 per cent alcohol by volume and moved for full aging and blending to the Solera system.

The Solera consists of four superimposed rows of large oak barrels or butts reclining on their sides. Three times a year, when sufficiently matured, approximately half the wine contained in the lowest row of barrels is drawn off for bottling purposes. These barrels are then replenished with sherries contained in the row immediately above it, and so on to the top row, which in turn is filled with wine brought over from the *flor* vats.

The first Solera was started by the Solera Cellars in 1946 with sherries that had already been aged. The average age of the sherries is about four years, including approximately six months under *flor* film and the balance in the oak butts or puncheons. Three types are produced, the very dry, pale, Cocktail type, the medium-sweet Golden, and the sweet Cream sherry. The Cream sherries are aged longer to impart more oak character to the wine and the sweetness is achieved by adding sufficient blending wine to accomplish the purpose.

A small amount of Angelica, produced from the Palomino grape exclusively and also aged according to the Solera method, is probably the only of its kind. This light golden, liqueurlike wine is very sweet, brandy having been added during the early stages of fermentation, as is usual with this type, the wine thereby retaining the natural sweetness of the grape.

The *flor* Solera Sherries and the Angelica produced by this winery easily rate among the finest of the state. Much credit is due to the well-known wine maker Leonard J. Berg, who is also the plant manager, and to Julius Fessler, the chemist.

STANISLAUS COUNTY

F. Pirrone & Sons, Inc., Salida

Located in Salida, some seven miles north of Modesto, this winery was founded by Frank Pirrone, Jr., and Frank I. Pirrone, his son.

Frank Pirrone, Jr., was born in Sicily and came over to this country as a youngster, becoming an architect at the age of twenty-one in Garfield, New Jersey. In 1919 he purchased some vineyards near Salida as an investment and went into the grape-shipping business as an avocation, while practicing architecture. In 1936 he built the winery and the family went into the wine-producing field.

Frank Pirrone, Jr., is president and general manager of the enterprise, while his three sons are also active in the business, Frank I. being vice-president and sales manager, Alfred F. vice-president and wine maker, and Joseph P. the bottling foreman. Until 1950 all bottling was done in Garfield, New Jersey, but since then this operation has been transferred to the Salida winery.

The main brand is *Pirrone,* under which a full line of the regular dessert and table wines is marketed, with distribution in the East as well as in California. Port and Burgundy are the featured wines and the company was among the first to market a red table wine of the "home-made type" under the brand name of "Vino Naturale" back in 1937.

Table wines: RED: Burgundy, Zinfandel, Chianti, Claret, Barberone, and Vino Naturale; WHITE: Sauterne and Rhine; ROSÉ: Grenache Rosé.

Aperitif and Dessert wines: Pale Dry Sherry, Sherry and Mellow Cream Sherry; Ruby Port and Tawny Port; Muscatel, Tokay, White Port, and Angelica.

Since 1949 F. Pirrone & Sons also produces altar wines, notably Angelica, for which they have the ecclesiastical approbation from the Roman Catholic Church.

E. & J. Gallo Winery, Modesto

An up-and-coming concern, producing and marketing sound standard-quality wines of the table, aperitif, and dessert types, which have become increasingly popular and enjoy a national distribution.

The story is a recent one, as time goes, of vision and enterprise, which goes back to a spring day of 1933 at Modesto, heart of the historic county of Stanislaus, with its winegrowing tradition dating back to about 1854, when George H. Krause, a native of Germany, laid out what was to become his famed Red Mountain Vineyard on part of the old Mexican grant El Rancheria del Rio Stanislaus.

Some eighty years later, on that spring day of the last year of Prohibition, two youthful brothers, Ernest and Julio R. Gallo, visualized the coming rebirth of the California wine industry, dormant during the dry years. They thought of creating a modern winery and imagined that someday in the future homes throughout the nation would proudly serve wines from shiny bottles bearing their family name. Wine also had not had the chance to catch up with the progress of modern American marketing ways and this was the ideal time to do something about it.

It was an ambitious plan for the brothers Gallo; Ernest was twenty-four and Julio a year younger. They had been brought up in the tradition of good wine, born as they were in the third generation of a California winegrowing family, whose forebears had cultivated vineyards and made wine in Italy's famed province of Piedmont. The brothers had been educated in the public schools of Modesto and knew about viticulture firsthand, having worked in the family's vineyards. Ambitious as they were, they lacked the necessary funds to start a winery.

Ernest and Julio Gallo were determined to go ahead with their plans. They borrowed and scraped enough dollars together to rent a warehouse in Modesto to house a few casks and a grape crusher and to serve as a winery until they could build a cellar of their own. They bought their equipment on credit. In the old warehouse the first Gallo vintage was crushed and fermented that same year, 1933.

A few months later they built a small wine cellar on the outskirts of Modesto. This first concrete structure on the bank of the Dry Creek was carefully planned as the first unit of the modern winery the brothers envisioned. It was built and ready for use in 1935.

At first the Gallos made only red and white table wines, selling them in bulk to wholesale bottlers. They still lacked wine-aging facilities and bottling machinery, but were planning for the future and the day when they could perfect and mature their products. In 1937 they were able to build an extension to their cellar and to install further equipment. They began to produce port, sherry, and muscatel in addition to their table wines. They studied modern developments in viticulture and wine making and searched for the best types of cooperage and other winery equipment. Julio Gallo devoted himself increasingly to the development of the most suitable grape varieties in the family's vineyards and to the production of the wines, while Ernest Gallo studied consumer and trade problems and marketing.

In the Gallo vineyards at Modesto, which the family had owned since 1925, new varieties were grafted onto old rootstocks. Additional vines were planted to grow the choicer varieties suited to local soil and climatic conditions including Petite Sirah, Palomino, Mission, and Salvador. The Gallos gradually increased their vineyard acreage, planting vines in the Keyes district of Stanislaus County and acquiring a vineyard near Livingston in Merced County.

The brothers realized that, while in San Joaquin, Stanislaus, and Merced counties a wide assortment of choice grapes for all wine types was grown, Fresno and other southern San Joaquin Valley areas yielded many varieties desirable for the sweeter dessert wines, while such districts as Napa and Sonoma in the north coast counties provided the best grapes for dry table wines. Accordingly they selected grapes from each of these several regions to complete the assortment of varieties grown on their own vines.

It took seven years before the Gallo brothers felt that they were producing wines of the quality they wanted to market in bottles under the Gallo family label; it was 1940 when they first appeared on the market. A following of consumers soon developed and Gallo advertising began.

From a small beginning in California and Louisiana the Gallo wines steadily gained acceptance. The company concentrated on trying to please the consumer. The Gallo brothers and their staffs interviewed buyers of their wines to learn the exact qualities of wine flavor, of dryness or sweetness, and of color that pleased householders. They talked to retailers and salespeople to learn what their customers wanted and they strove to get their wines efficiently displayed and stocked. In this manner Gallo wines were introduced market by market in the various parts of the country.

The assortment of Gallo wines was broadened. A more complete line of aperitif and dessert wines was established in addition to the expanded selection of table wines. A Concord wine was added, made from *labrusca* grapes grown in the Pacific Northwest. In recent years a light and mellow wine of the "vino rosso" type was developed with success, the Gallo "Vino Paisano," and in 1953 a Rosé was marketed with promising results, made from Grenache grapes grown in the Gallo family vineyards.

The selection of grapes from different viticultural areas was continued. The Gallos entered into long-term arrangements with other wineries, beginning with the Napa Valley Cooperative Winery of St. Helena and Calistoga in Napa County, owned by some 150 growers. The brothers also provided an outlet for grapes and wines produced by their neighboring growers; in 1953 the Gallo winery began to receive the entire vintage of the Modesto Cooperative Winery produced by its sixty farmer members. Similar arrangements were made with the Del Rey Cooperative Winery Association of Fresno, owned by eighty-five growers; with Frei Brothers of Santa Rosa, Sonoma County; with Vella Brothers Winery of Salida, Stanislaus County; with the St. Helena Cooperative Winery, comprised of thirty-five Napa County growers. In all the Gallos provide an outlet for the crops of almost a thousand California wine-grape-growing farmers.

To these other wineries the technical advice of a highly trained staff of enologists is available. The Gallo experts, headed by production manager Charles E. Crawford, a graduate of Cornell University and of the University of California, assist in solving vineyard and winery problems for the growers and in maintaining the required rigid specifications of quality.

In 1954 the Gallo brothers decided to eliminate the hundred-mile transportation of grapes from the southern San Joaquin Valley to

Modesto. They acquired the historic Las Palmas winery, situated in the famous vineyard district near Clovis, Fresno County, and initiated a remodeling program to bring the winery buildings and equipment up to modern standards.

By that year, 1954, the Gallo production and marketing principles had proved their value and the brothers had come a long way since that day in 1933 when they first formulated their farsighted plans.

Much credit is due to the Gallo brothers, along with the other producers of nationally advertised brands, to bring sound wines—mostly of the generic types—to the American public at a very reasonable cost and creating thereby many new customers for the wine industry. The Gallo principles are as sound as their wines; their production and marketing methods modern and their advertising efficient.

The Gallo brothers consider their work as having only begun. Another generation of the Gallo family, the fourth in California, is being prepared to carry on the wine-making tradition. Ernest Gallo's two sons, Joey and David, still in their teens, work in the vineyards and winery during vacations, and Julio's sons, Bob and Phil, are also preparing to carry forward. A younger brother of the founders is also active in the firm, having charge of the family's vineyards.

In October 1954 the Gallos announced the undertaking of an extensive, long-term research program for the development of improved viticultural practices, broader markets, and better returns for the products of California wine-grape growers.

The *Gallo* brand wines available include the following:

Table wines: RED: Burgundy, Chianti, Claret, Zinfandel, and Barberone;

WHITE: Sauterne, Haut Sauterne, Rhine, Chablis, Light Dry Muscat;

ROSÉ: Grenache Rosé (an outstanding wine of its type);

Aperitif and Dessert wines: Pale Dry Sherry, Cocktail Pale Dry Sherry, Sherry, and Cream Sherry; Port, Tawny Port, and Ruby Port; Marsala, Muscatel, Tokay, White Port, and Angelica; Dry and Sweet Vermouth;

Berry and Fruit wines: Blackberry, Loganberry, and American Concord Grape Wine (from grapes grown in the Pacific Northwest).

A featured wine, and one of the best of its kind, is the popular "Vino Paisano di Gallo," an "old country style" table wine of the "vino rosso" type.

C. FRESNO—SAN JOAQUIN VALLEY DISTRICT

This great district coincides with the lower San Joaquin Valley. It is famous especially for yielding wines of the sweeter dessert types, some of which have achieved great excellence. Table wines and bulk-fermented sparkling wines are also produced.

The district takes in the following counties, from north to south:

Madera, with the city of Madera the main sector;

Fresno, with its many famed wineries located in the city of Fresno and in the surrounding towns, with other famous wineries to be found in Sanger, Reedley, Parlier, Fowler, Selma and Kingsburg;

Kings, with its Hanford area;

Tulare, with the main winery centers in Dinuba, Cutler, Tulare, Lindsay, and on the Kern County line right across from Delano;

Kern, with Delano and the sector east of Bakersfield down to Arvin the wine-production areas.

A number of well-known wineries located in this district do not produce wines directly for the public under their own brands and are, for that reason only, not discussed in this *Guide*.

MADERA COUNTY

Ficklin Vineyards, Madera

A small and unique operation, the only California winery to produce no other wines than port and the first time in the United States that port wines made entirely of choice Portuguese grape varieties became commercially available. The Ficklin Ports rate as the finest produced in California, being unsurpassed in quality and character with a full richness of flavor.

The Ficklin wine concern is still a young one, being founded in the middle of the nineteen forties, but is rapidly and deservedly making a great name for itself throughout the nation wherever fine dessert wines are consumed. It is a family enterprise, the principal owners and operators being David (Dave) B. Ficklin, the wine maker and a well-known wine judge, and his brother Walter C. Ficklin, Jr., the vineyardist. Their father, Walter C. Ficklin, Sr., a charming gentleman familiar with all the better things of life, has an interest in the winery and vineyards.

The senior Ficklin first came to California as a young man in 1911, making his home in Fresno County and planting his first vineyards and orchards in 1912. For many years he farmed grape and fruit ranches. In the early forties the family became interested in the idea of producing red dessert wines of top quality. They closely studied the Portuguese wine grape varieties which were being tested by the University of California under local growing conditions. The decision to establish a completely specialized vineyard complex and winery was the next step. Four of the finest Portuguese varieties were selected, Tinta Cão, Tinta Madeira, Alvarelhão, and Touriga, and the vineyards planted to them exclusively. A small but modern adobe winery was built by hand and 1948 saw the first vintage harvested.

The greatest care is taken to produce the very best wines possible. The vineyards are meticulously tended to yield a limited crop of the choicest grapes. At harvest time the grape clusters are individually cut with small hand shears and all imperfect fruit is left on the vines. The grapes are left in the vineyards in wooden boxes to cool off overnight and brought to the crusher the first thing the next morning. They are first lightly crushed in stainless steel crushers, breaking the skins and separating them from the stems. The crushed grapes are transferred to small open vats where pure yeast culture is added. As soon as fermentation starts a wooden hand plunger is used to submerge and mix the skins with the juice, extracting thereby the full color and flavor of the grapes. The free-run juice is drawn off and the skins are given a further light pressing in a basket-type press, the resulting juice being added to the free-run for further flavor. At the proper stage of fermentation the juice is transformed into port wine by the addition of pure grape brandy. The wine is clarified naturally by gradual settling and racking in small oak puncheons or barrels. It is aged in oak for three years or longer and at least a further year in the bottle. Owing to this process, the Ficklin Ports, like those from Portugal, will throw a slight sediment, a sign of maturing and of age. The wines, therefore, should be poured carefully, so as not to disturb the deposit, or be decanted before serving. If disturbed, the bottle should be placed upright until the wine has had a chance to settle.

The main variety of Port available is the so-called "Tinta Port," a blend of the four varieties grown. All wines are full Ruby Ports and are marketed under the *Ficklin Vineyards* brand.

Limited cuvées of both Tinta Madeira* Port and Tinta Cão Port have also been produced, named after the particular varieties from which they were made. It is planned also to produce vintage ports, both from blends of the four varieties and from the single varieties.

Mission Bell Wineries, Madera

Mission Bell Wineries are, like the Petri Wineries at Escalon (see there), an operating and production name for Allied Grape Growers, the co-operative winery association of some three hundred member growers which purchased both wineries from the Petri family, giving the latter the exclusive marketing rights to its total output.

The Mission Bell Winery, with its complex of beautiful buildings in the Spanish Mission style, is a monument to that colorful American of Armenian origin, K. Arakelian, who became one of the most

*It may be noted that the Tinta Madeira wine and grape, being a true Port variety, should never be confused with the Madeira wines produced in the island of that name off the coast of Africa, or with any of its imitations. Nor has the name Tinta Madeira any other than a sound affinity with that of Madera County and the town of Madera, where the Ficklin grapes are grown and the wines produced.

successful figures in the California wine industry and made his Mission Bell wines known through the country. Louis Petri acquired the winery in 1949 and operated it some two years before selling it to Allied Grape Growers.

The *Mission Bell* brand enjoys a large distribution, mainly in the Eastern part of the United States. A full line of table and aperitif and dessert wines is marketed under this brand, covering the low-priced field.

Aperitif and Dessert wines: Pale Dry Sherry, Cocktail Sherry, Sherry, and Cream Sherry; Port, Ruby Port, and Tawny Port; Muscatel, Tokay, White Port, and Angelica; Dry and Sweet Vermouth;

Sparkling wines (bulk-fermented): Champagne and Sparkling Burgundy;

Table wines: RED: Burgundy, Zinfandel, and Claret;   WHITE: Sauterne, Rhine Wine, and Chablis.

A red table wine of the "vino rosso" type is marketed under the *Mission Bell Viva* label and called Vino Rosso Amabile.

Yosemite Winery Association, Madera

A scant mile west of the city of Madera is to be found the towering building of the Yosemite Winery Association, said to be the largest unaffiliated co-operative in California and the only independent co-operative situated between the Lodi and Fresno areas.

In 1946, when the nation was still in the throes of immediate postwar shortages of men and materials, a group of determined Madera County growers met and decided to form their own winery. In spite of all obstacles the winery was built and ready to operate within seven short months. The organization is now owned by some 160 grape growers, producing wines maintaining a continuity of quality, the grapes being derived from the same San Joaquin Valley vineyards each year.

Carl W. McCollister has been the able president of the winery since its founding. Renald Mastrofini is the general manager and Thomas Oliver the wine maker and plant superintendent.

Dessert wines, as to be expected in the San Joaquin Valley, are the specialty. The higher-quality wines are marketed under the *Yosemite Grower's Select* brand and include:

Aperitif and Dessert wines: Palomino Pale Dry Sherry, Golden Sherry, and Cream Sherry; Ruby Port; Muscatel, Tokay, and White Port;

Table wines: RED: Pinot Noir, Cabernet, Burgundy, Zinfandel, and Claret; WHITE: Sauterne, Riesling, Rhine Wine, and Chablis; ROSÉ: Grenache Rosé.

The featured brand for wines of sound standard quality is *Yosemite,* with *Mariposa, Old Rose,* and *Carina* the better-known secondary brands.

Under the *Yosemite* label the following wines are marketed:

Aperitif and Dessert wines: Palomino Pale Dry Sherry, Golden Sherry, and Cream Sherry; Ruby Port; Muscatel, Tokay, and White Port; Dry and Sweet Vermouth;

Table wines: Burgundy, Zinfandel, and Claret; Sauterne and Rhine Wine.

Light Sweet wines, including Light Sweet Red and Light Sweet Muscat (white), are available under some of the secondary brands as is a Vino Rosso of the mellow red table wine type.

The Yosemite Winery Association is the first California winery since before the Second World War to engage in the *canned wine* business. The idea was prompted by a brain storm of the general manager, Renald Mastrofini. Commercial advantages are described as savings in freight, no danger of discoloration from light, no breakage, quick chilling, less required storage space, dripless containers, and ease of handling. A start was made with dessert wine types, marketed in twelve-ounce cans with a crown top furnished by the Continental Can Company.

Canned wines, marketed under the *Carina* brand with the *Kan-O-Wine* trade-mark, include: Sherry, Port, Muscatel, Tokay, and White Port.

The results of this new—or renewed—adventure in the wine industry will be awaited with interest.

FRESNO COUNTY

Alta Vineyards Company, Fresno

This corporation, also doing business as Cameo Vineyards Company, is the successor to many a famous name in the history of the California wine industry. Beverly W. Goldthwaite is president and general manager of the company, D. S. Davis vice-president, and Margaret Shahenian secretary and treasurer.

In 1949 the corporation, then newly formed, purchased the brands and listings of the old Alta Winery, formerly of Dinuba, Tulare County, where the colorful personality of Charlie Dubbs was for many years its leading light. The next year Alta bought the Cameo Winery, its present location, along with the Cameo brands and inventories. The vineyards were planted by Ed Melikian, president of the old Cameo Vineyards Company, Aram Melikian, and Ed Merzoian. Cecil Melikian, the nephew of the former Cameo president, is Alta's assistant manager.

Alta Vineyards Company is also the successor to the Mattei name and interests. It was around 1890 that Andrew Mattei, a native of Switzerland, founded his enterprise, planting vineyards near Malaga, southeast of Fresno, and building his winery nearby. For many years the Mattei name loomed large in the California wine industry and one of Alta's brands still carries his name.

A new co-operative of wine grape growers was formed in the fall of 1954, Cameo Growers, who contracted with Alta for the making and selling of wine from their grapes.

The winery's two principal brands are *Alta* and *C.V.C.* (Cameo Vineyards Company), used for a full line of dessert and table wines, while *Croix Royale* is used for the older wines. Dessert wines are the company's primary business.

Aperitif and Dessert wines:
  Alta and *C.V.C.:* Sherry, Port, Muscatel, Tokay, and White Port;
  Alta: Dry and Sweet Vermouth; *Croix Royale:* Pale Dry Sherry,
  Tawny Port, Muscatel; Dry and Sweet Vermouth.

Table wines:
  Alta and *C.V.C.:* Burgundy, Zinfandel, and Claret; Sauterne and
  Rhine.

Alta Vineyards Company also has a number of other brands, including *Cameo, Mattei, Mattevista, Scatena,* and *St. Charles,* some of which have been famous at one time or another in the history of the California wine industry.

Bisceglia Brothers Wine Company, Fresno

This enterprise was founded in 1888 by four Bisceglia brothers, Joseph, Pasquale, Bruno, and Alphonse, who came from a family of vineyardists and wine makers in their native Cosenza in the province of Calabria, Italy. The family first settled in California in the Santa Clara Valley, where they went into the wine business and also operated a large cannery. In 1939 the canning operation was discontinued and their attention fully directed to their wine enterprise.

The winery the Bisceglias are now operating was started in 1945 and completed in 1947, and is one of the most modern, with a capacity of some eight million gallons. Standard-quality table, sparkling, and aperitif and dessert wines are produced, and are distributed throughout the United States.

The last of the original founders, Alphonse F. Bisceglia, passed away in 1952 and the family members now interested in the wine business are Bruno T. Bisceglia, president, and Joseph A. Bisceglia, an officer and director of the company.

Paradise is the leading brand, while *Golden Chalice,* introduced in 1953 after five years of research, is used for marketing wines with a character all of their own, the dessert types being very sweet.

Aperitif and Dessert wines:
  Golden Chalice: Pale Dry Sherry, Cocktail Sherry, Sherry, and
    Creme Sherry; Port, Muscatel, Tokay, and White Port;

Paradise: Pale Dry Sherry, Sherry, Port, Muscatel, Tokay, White Port, and Angelica;

Table wines:
Golden Chalice: Burgundy, Sauterne, and Vin Rosé;
Paradise: Burgundy, Zinfandel, Claret, Barberone, and the featured Vino Rosso; Sauterne and Rhine Wine;

Berry wines:
Paradise: Blackberry and Loganberry.

Vermouth, both Dry and Sweet, is marketed under the *Bisceglia* label, while *La Croix* is the brand for bulk-fermented Champagne (on the sweet side) and Sparkling Burgundy.

Crest View Winery, Inc., Fresno

The winery was founded in 1935 by John B. Perenchio, who built it. A few years later Joseph Gazzara, the present owner and general manager, purchased part interest in the winery and in 1947 bought the whole of it.

Joseph Gazzara has had long experience in wine making and merchandising. He was born in Italy of a winegrowing family, one might say practically in a vineyard. He gained experience in the wine business in his native land, in France, and for many years also in this country. He was already engaged in it before Prohibition and started once more after Repeal, selling sacramental wines during the dry years, as allowed by the laws.

Dessert wines are the specialty, while some dry table wines are also available. *Crest View* is the main brand and under that label and its variations, such as *Crest,* the following sound standard-quality wines are produced and marketed:

Aperitif and Dessert wines: Sherry, Port, Muscatel, Tokay, White Port, and Angelica;

Table wines: Burgundy, Zinfandel, Claret, and Vino Rosso Gustoso; Sauterne.

B. Cribari & Sons, Fresno

The nationally known "House of Cribari" was founded in 1904 by Benjamin Cribari and his three sons Fiore, Angelo, and Anthony. In that year Benjamin Cribari, a native of Cosenza, Calabria Province, Italy, bought some forty acres of land in Paradise Valley near Morgan Hill in the foothills of southern Santa Clara County and converted them to vineyards. From this modest beginning a great enterprise was to grow.

The original holdings were gradually enlarged over the years until it became necessary to find new quarters. These were established nearby at Madrone on El Camino Real, some sixteen miles south of San Jose, and here at Madrone the Cribaris operated their winery for many years, making their products famous throughout the nation.

During Prohibition the family concentrated on the production of sacramental and medicinal wines as allowed by the dry laws. Even during the dry years it became necessary to enlarge the Madrone winery owing to the popularity of the Cribari products. Additional vineyards were planted in Santa Clara and San Benito counties; in Fresno a winery and extensive property were acquired, including the famed Las Palmas Vineyard, started in the early eighteen nineties by Benjamin R. Woodworth. The Cribari firm now was able to produce dessert wines in one of the great sweet wine centers of San Joaquin Valley and table wines in the Santa Clara Valley, always regarded as one of the finest districts for the production of dry wines. After Repeal the Madrone and Fresno wineries were further enlarged and additional vineyards planted in the rolling foothills of San Benito County.

In 1944 another move was made. The Madrone establishments were sold* and the Crimaris moved their Santa Clara County head-

*To an Eastern company which in turn sold it to Grape Gold of California. Madrone later was merged for a time with Almadén Vineyards, the merger being dissolved in 1951 and Madrone Vineyards liquidated. The main winery building became a cannery, and Richert & Sons established its winery in the front part in 1953.

quarters to the Evergreen area east of San Jose, where they pur
chased property in addition to what they had already acquired
few years before. It is at Evergreen (the winery originally built by
William Wehner before the turn of the century) that the Cribar
table wines are still produced today.

The present owners and operators of the Cribari enterprise in
clude Fiore and Anthony Cribari of the older generation, with thei
main center of activities at Evergreen. The younger generation i
established at Fresno, of whom Theodore S. (Ted) Cribari, the sor
of Fiore, is president of the concern, K. W. (Ken), and A. B. (Al)
both sons of the deceased Angelo, are respectively plant manage
and production manager-wine maker, and Robert (Bob) heads the
Cribari sales interests for the Eastern part of the country in New
York.

In 1954 the Las Palmas holdings in Fresno were sold to Gallo. The
Cribaris continue to produce a full line of table, sparkling, aperiti
and dessert, and altar wines, maintaining their headquarters in
Fresno and continuing to operate their Evergreen holdings, mainly
for the production of table wines. The dessert wines are now pro
duced at the Alta Vineyards Company winery at Fresno, while the
plans are for a gradual merger to take place between the Cribar
and Alta enterprises.

The Cribaris produce and market a large variety of sound stand
ard-quality and higher-quality wines which enjoy a national distri
bution. *Cribari Reserve* is the brand used for the higher-grade wines
with *Cribari Family, Sonnie Boy,* and *Famiglia Cribari* the more
prominent labels for wines of sound standard quality.

The following wines are available under the *Cribari Reserve*
brand:

Table wines (from Santa Clara Valley grapes mostly):
RED: Pinot Noir, Ruby Cabernet, Grignolino; Burgundy and
Claret; WHITE: Pinot Blanc, Emerald Riesling; Sauterne, Dry
Sauterne and Haut Sauterne, Chablis, and Rhine Wine; ROSÉ
Grignolino Rosé and Vin Rosé.

Sparkling wines (bulk process, from Santa Clara Valley grapes)
Extra Dry Champagne and Demi-Sec Champagne; Pink Cham

pagne, Red Champagne, and Sparkling Burgundy, Sparkling Muscat (all types except the Red Champagne also being produced under the *Saratoga* brand).

Aperitif and Dessert wines (mostly from San Joaquin Valley grapes): Palomino Pale Dry Sherry (varietally from that grape), Pale Dry Sherry, Cocktail Sherry, Golden Sherry, and Cream Sherry; Port, Ruby Port, and Tawny Port; Golden Muscatel and Muscatel.

Vermouths, Dry and Sweet, are marketed under the *Cribari* label while popular table wines of the Italian "homemade" type, called "Vino Rosso da Pranzo" and "Vino Bianco da Pranzo," are available under the *Famiglia Cribari* brand, as well as a "Mellow Zinfandel."

The standard-quality wines bottled under the *Cribari Family* and *Sonnie Boy* labels include:

Table wines:
RED: Burgundy, Claret, and Barberone; WHITE: Dry Sauterne, Sweet Sauterne, Chablis, and Rhine Wine.

The Cribaris have a long tradition in the production of sacramental wines. Cribari *altar wines* (available only to the clergy) include:

Dry wines: Claret, Burgundy, Dry Sauterne, and Haut Sauterne; *Sweet wines:* Port, Sherry, Muscatel, Tokay, Angelica, and Meloso.

Golden State Winery, Fresno

Golden State Winery is the name of the operating winery, with California Champagne Cellars, Inc.,* that of the family-owned corporation.

Wallace A. Dunton, Jr., the owner, of German-Swiss origin, has outside of his family two great interests, the Army and wine making. He has been interested in the wine business for over thirty years,

*Not to be confused with California Champagne Corporation (Schramsberg Vineyard Company) of Calistoga, Napa County.

in both Southern and Central California. His career in the Army Reserve dates back to 1917, when he served in the 75th Coast Artillery, outfitted with the rare railway artillery guns. During the Second World War he served with the 37th AAA (Anti Aircraft Artillery) Brigade and later spent nearly three and a half years in the jungles of New Guinea. He ended the war with a colonel's silver eagles and is still active in the Army Reserve.

After the war Dunton turned to his wine-making hobby and purchased from John Borello the Golden State Winery at Fresno, founded in 1908 by Frank Stefanich. The colonel is his own wine maker and specializes in sparkling wines made by the French Charmat process and in certain, often unusual, varietal table wines. He is also interested in the production of commercial brandy. The winery is small but modern, and custom bottling for others is also done. The main brands are *Golden State Winery* and *California Champagne Cellars* for sparkling wines and *Dunton* and *Borello* for table and dessert types.

Sparkling wines (bulk process): Champagne, Sparkling Burgundy, Sparkling Rosés (including Grenache), and Moscato Spumante (Sparkling Muscat);

Varietal table wines: Carignane, Mission, Grenache, Palomino, and Dry Muscat.

Other table wines, varietal and generic, are produced and include blends of San Joaquin Valley with Napa and other north coast county wines.

Aperitif and dessert wines are also available.

A. Nonini Winery, Fresno

This small family-owned and -operated winery is located some ten miles northwest of Fresno in the Rolinda district. It produces dry table wines only, made from San Joaquin Valley grapes, which are good examples of sound "country" wines of the Fresno region.

Antonio Nonini, head of the family and owner and wine maker of the enterprise, was born in Italy in the village of Cercino in the

Valtellina district, province of Sondrio in Northern Italy. He came to the United States around the turn of the century and first engaged in California in the dairy business. In 1910 he returned to his native country and brought back a bride, Angelina, and settled with her on his ranch. In 1916 he planted his ranch to vines and the family became active in the growing and shipping of grapes. The family increased over the years to five children, three boys and two girls, all born on the home ranch.

The enterprise is run by Antonio and the family, of whom Reno is in charge of sales, Gildo of the vineyards, while the girls, who both had business training at college, take care of the bookkeeping. The youngest son, Geno, on return from the service, will also take up his duties again on the ranch. A third generation of Noninis is growing up and helping their parents in the business. Angelina Nonini, the bride Antonio went to fetch in 1910, assists when necessary and is otherwise busily engaged in being a good wife and a good mother for the ever-growing family.

Nonini's Select is the prominent brand and under this label the following *table wines* are produced and marketed:

RED: Zinfandel (100 per cent varietal), Burgundy (from Barbera and other grapes), Claret (a blend of Grenache, Carignane, Mission, Alicante Bouschet, and others);

WHITE: Sauterne (dry, from 100 per cent Palomino or Golden Chasselas).

Roma Wine Company, Fresno

The largest winery in California, with a correspondingly large production. The Roma Wine Company was established when J. Battista Cella and his brother Lorenzo came to California in 1915 and acquired the small Roma Winery established at Lodi. The move to Fresno occurred in 1933, when the Roma Wine Company acquired the Santa Lucia Winery, which had been founded a few years earlier by N. D. Naman. Roma then began an expansion program which resulted in its becoming the world's largest and most modern winery of its time. In 1942 Schenley Industries, Inc., acquired Roma Wine Company and all wineries and physical assets of the company and embarked upon a further expansion and modernization program.

Colonel Albert H. Burton is in charge of over-all production of the Roma Wine Company and other Schenley wine interests. Richard Auerbach is in charge of production control, while William Shonkwiler is the chief chemist and quality-control supervisor. Sales and merchandising are handled through CVA Corporation of San Francisco under the direction of its board chairman, Harry G. Serlis.

The Roma winery at Fresno has a crushing capacity of 80,000 tons of grapes a season, while total storage capacity is over 16,700,000 gallons of wine. The Roma winery at Kingsburg has an additional capacity of 7,800,000 gallons.

Winery buildings and operating areas cover some fifty-five acres. With minor exceptions all Roma dessert wines are produced from grapes grown in the San Joaquin Valley within a radius of sixty miles of the Fresno winery. White grapes represent about 70 per cent of the total volume crushed and include chiefly Muscat of Alexandria, Feher Szagos, Palomino, Malaga, and Thompson Seedless, the last two varieties being used principally for the production of brandy and grape concentrates. The most important dark grapes used are Zinfandel, Petite Sirah, Mission, Grenache, Carignane, and Salvador.

Roma produces sound standard-quality wines which are nationally distributed and also exported to various foreign countries, including the Orient. *Roma Reserve* is the basic brand, with *Roma Estate* and *Roma Select* the two principal variations, conforming to the demand in various parts of the country.

Under the various Roma brands the following wines are available, most of which are bottled in the exclusive Roma dripless bottle, a new merchandising development:

Table wines:
   RED: Burgundy, Claret, and Zinfandel; Red Chianti and Vino di Roma (vino rosso type); WHITE: Sauterne, Chablis, and Rhine Wine; White Chianti; ROSÉ: Vin Rosé.

Sparkling wines (bulk process): Champagne, Pink Champagne, Sparkling Burgundy, and Moscato Spumante;

Aperitif and Dessert wines: Pale Dry Sherry, Cocktail Sherry, Sherry, and Cream Sherry; Port, Ruby Port, and Tawny Port; Muscatel, Tokay, and White Port; Dry and Sweet Vermouth.

Light Sweet wines: Red and White.

Berry and Fruit wines: Blackberry (of the Boysenberry variety), Currant, Loganberry, and Cherry. A Concord grape wine (from out-of-state grapes) is also produced.

A specialty is the Creme de Roma, a liqueurlike wine consisting of sherry with flavoring added and containing 18 per cent alcohol by volume.

Inexpensive Italian-type table wines are marketed under *Roma's Pride of the Vineyard* label and include Vino d'Uva (red grape wine), Vino Bianco (white grape wine), Barberone, and Chianti.

St. George Winery, Fresno

This famed old enterprise and California landmark was founded in 1879 by George H. Malter, a native of Germany who became well known in San Francisco as a mining engineer. He was a member of the Bohemian Club and the owner of the *Emerald,* a well-known yacht. He planted a large acreage of vines along Fancher Creek, some five miles west of Fresno. The winery, erected in 1884, was enlarged until it became one of the largest producers of wine and brandy of the time.

A booklet published around the turn of the century gives a fascinating picture of life at Maltermoro during the Gay Nineties. Profusely illustrated, it shows such diverse activities as rabbit drives, raisin drying, bullfights, and wine making. An eloquent catalogue, it lists and describes the wines and brandies produced at the winery as well as other spirits handled for the benefit of the customers. Such intriguing items are advertised as St. George Tonic Port, Tarragona Port of the Trousseau grape, Porto type of the Malvoisie; Sherry Bitters, Sherry from the Pedro Ximenez grape. Table wines included a Margaux-type claret from the Cabernet and St. Julien from the Grenache. Brandies were of the Cognac type, of the Muscat, of the Cooking variety and a special type for Shampoo and Sponge Baths.

The glory of Maltermoro lasted well into the twentieth century, and then gradually declined. George Malter, when he died in 1928, left only a small acreage and the manor house; Prohibition forced the winery into dormancy. After Repeal Hugo Malter, George's son, rehabilitated the winery and ran it for a while, in partnership with Frank Goldthwaite, until 1939. Beverly Goldthwaite then took over till 1942, when St. George was purchased by the well-known Eastern wine enterprise L. N. Renault & Sons, Inc., of Egg Harbor, New Jersey, the present owners. President and general manager of the winery is that genial personality with great experience in the industry, A. G. Frericks.

Dessert wines are the St. George specialty. Its table wines are supplied by another Renault-owned winery, the Montebello Wine Company of California,* with its bonded winery at St. Helena, Napa County.

The main brand of the winery is *St. George,* with *St. George Reserve Stock* limited to older wines. *Renault* (Renault Wine Company of California—Fancher Creek Cellars) is also used for marketing some California table and aperitif and dessert wines, including Vermouth. Sparkling wines, produced in the East, are not included here.

The following wines are available under the *St. George Reserve Stock* label:

Aperitif and Dessert wines: Pale Dry Sherry, Dry Sherry, Sherry, and Mellow Sherry; Ruby Port and Tawny Port; Golden Muscat (100 per cent Muscat) and Muscatel; Madeira and Grenache (one of the few if not the only Grenache sweet dessert wine of 20 per cent alcohol by volume so far produced commercially).

*The Montebello Wine Company of California, of which P. A. Bricca is the president and general manager also markets its wines under its own brands, of which *Montebello* is the most prominent.

Table wines: Burgundy and Sauterne.

The *St. George* wines include the following:

Aperitif and Dessert wines: Dry Sherry and Sherry, Port, Muscatel, Tokay, White Port, and Angelica;

Table wines: Burgundy, Zinfandel; Sauterne, Chablis, and Rhine Wine.

Cella Vineyards, Reedley

Some twenty miles east of Fresno and seven miles north of Reedley, spreading out at the foot of the hills bordering the San Joaquin Valley, lie the main vineyards and winery of the Cellas, a family famous in the wine industry for over a quarter of a century.

J. Battista Cella, who reminds one of a Roman emperor and is somewhat of a living legend, was born in Bardi, in the province of Parma, Italy. He came to this country as a youngster soon after the Spanish-American War and one of his earliest recollections in his newly adopted land was Admiral George Dewey's victory parade in New York City, which he witnessed in 1899.

Young Cella first went into the restaurant business in Jamaica, Long Island, and then became a partner in the wholesale wine and liquor firm of Cella and Broglio in midtown New York. When Broglio went to Cleveland to open a restaurant on his own, J. Battista Cella's brother Lorenzo (Lori) took his place. The brothers later decided to go to California and came West in 1915. They have been in the wine business together ever since.

In California the Cellas first made wine from purchased grapes and during Prohibition shipped grapes East. In 1922 J. Battista bought the old Roma Winery at Lodi from the Scatena brothers and after Repeal, established in 1935, with growing ambition, the Santa Lucia Winery at Fresno, which became the Roma Wine Company. It was then that the Cellas made their wines and name famous throughout the nation, with J. Battista the presiding genius at Fresno and Lori in charge of the company's Eastern markets in New York

City. Roma was built up and expanded by J. Battista Cella until it became one of the largest wineries in the world and a small empire unto itself.

In 1942 the Cellas sold Roma to the Schenley interests for a record figure, J. Battista staying on in an advisory capacity for a few years. In 1944 they purchased the famed old Wahtoke Winery, with its old Indian name, at Reedley, founded in the eighteen nineties by Louis Rusconi, a native of Switzerland. Since then the headquarters of the Cella enterprise have remained at Reedley, the Wahtoke Winery and vineyards being considerably enlarged. The Cellas also own a winery and vineyards at Manteca in San Joaquin County and, for the production of north coast counties dry wines, the Napa Wine Company of Oakville, Napa County, purchased in 1947. In all the Cella family owns some 4,000 acres of vineyards and besides their wine-production activities have one of the finest grape-juice plants in the country.

J. Battista Cella is president of Cella Vineyards, while Lori Cella is executive vice-president with offices in New York and in charge of all sales. Of the younger generation J. (Johnnie) B. Cella II is vice-president and secretary, while B. B. Turner, J. Battista's son-in-law, has been with him for over twenty years, helping to build the name of Roma and later of Cella Vineyards. Alma Cella, the popular lyric soprano who was discovered by the famed tenor, Beniamino Gigli, is J. Battista Cella's daughter.

Cella Vineyards produce both sound standard-quality and higher-quality wines. Mostly derived from northern coastal grapes are the wines marketed under the *Napa Wine Company* label and these include:

Table wines: Burgundy, Charbono, and Zinfandel; Sauterne, Riesling, and Rhine; Grenache Vin Rosé;

Aperitif and Dessert wines: Palomino Pale Sherry, Cream Sherry, and Tawny Port.

Wines marketed in the original and familiar barrel-shaped bottles under the *Wine Barrel* brand number the following:

Table wines: Burgundy, Claret, and Zinfandel; Sauterne and Rhine; Grenache Vin Rosé; and wines of the "homemade" Italian type, the popular Vino Rosso (red) and Vino Bianco (white);

Aperitif and Dessert wines: Sherry, Port, Ruby Port, and Tawny Port; Golden Muscatel and Muscatel; Tokay and White Port, and the high-grade Pale Dry Sherry, Palomino Cocktail Sherry, and Cream Sherry.

Cella Vineyards Private Stock and *Parma Private Stock* (named in honor of Cella's native province) are other major brands for both *table wines* and *aperitif and dessert wines,* the former being older wines and including such rare varietals as the Mission, Mondeuse, and Valdepeñas table types.

Vermouth, both Dry and Sweet, is marketed under the *Parma* brand. Cella's sparkling wines (bulk-fermented), produced and marketed both under the *Cella Vineyards* and *Parma* labels, include Champagne, Grenache Pink Champagne, and Sparkling Burgundy.

An interesting specialty is Cella Vineyards' *Betsy Ross Wine,* an American Malaga of 13 per cent alcohol by volume, dark red, rich, and sweet, produced from a variety of grapes selected for their natural sweetness, including Concord grapes grown in Cella's San Joaquin Valley vineyards. The wine, marketed in distinctive decanter bottles, is suitable as a dessert wine or one between meals or as a flavoring wine over desserts. It is a kosher wine, suitable also for sacramental purposes of the Hebrew faith.

Other specialties include Moscato Secco (Dry Muscat), Light Sweet types, such as Sweet Red and Muscat Grape wines, and Loganberry wine, all marketed under the *Parma di California* brand.

Nicholas G. Verry, Inc., Parlier

This winery, located at Parlier, some eighteen miles southeast of Fresno, near Reedley, is mainly devoted to the production of "Retsina," the resin-flavored wine which is especially popular with those of Greek descent or origin. It is the only winery producing this type of wine in California on a commercial basis.

The Verry family are of Greek origin. The founder and president of the company, Nicholas Verry, was born in Sparta, Greece, in 1896. He came to this country in 1906, but has often returned to Europe on visits and business trips. He learned the art of wine making from his brother-in-law, George Solomos, a well-known enologist and chemist of Sparta. He is assisted in the family enterprise by Mrs. Verry, who bears the noble name of Athena and is secretary-treasurer, and by their son John N. Verry, vice-president.

The Verry family first established themselves in the wine business in California in 1933 with a winery in Glendale, moving to their present location in 1942. Besides Retsina the winery also markets a wine called Philery (said to mean "Quick Love"), a light wine, produced in the same manner as Retsina but without the resin flavoring. It is somewhat similar to a rhine wine, but with its own distinctive bouquet and flavor.

TULARE COUNTY
California Growers Wineries, Cutler

This is a co-operative winery whose presiding genius is the well-known Arpaxat Setrakian, better known by his nickname of "Sox." A native of Armenia who once peddled produce through the streets of San Francisco, Arpaxat Setrakian rose to an important position in the California wine and grape industry by his dynamic energy and personality. Now in his early seventies, he has always been an ardent champion of the grape grower, whose interests are sometimes neglected and whose economic position is often insecure. The farming interests of the grower, so important a part of the California and national agricultural picture, should be harmoniously balanced with those of the producer and the merchandiser of California wines, to the detriment of none. Such is Setrakian's and the California Growers Wineries' principal philosophy.

It was in 1936 that "Sox" Setrakian, now president and sales manager of the concern, founded California Growers Wineries together with Charles F. Clapp, now vice-president, and with H. B. "Dutch" Leonard, the big-league ball player and famous pitcher of his time, best remembered perhaps when he played with the Boston Red Sox of the American League.* Other officers of the company include Souren Setrakian, a nephew of Arpaxat, secretary, Leonard P. LeBlanc, treasurer, and Earle M. Cobb, manager. Nino Muzio is the wine maker and chemist.

As is to be expected in the hot climate of the lower San Joaquin Valley, the main accent at California Growers Wineries is on the production of sweet dessert wines.

The featured brand is *Growers Old Reserve* and includes the following sound standard-quality wines:

Aperitif and Dessert wines: Pale Dry Sherry and Sherry, Port, Muscatel, Tokay, and White Port;

Table wines: Burgundy, Claret, and Zinfandel; Sauterne and Chablis; Grignolino Rosé, a recent specialty.

Light Sweet wines: Red and White.

Growers is the top brand, used for quality vintage and aged *aperitif and dessert* wines, including:
Cocktail Sherry and Amber Sherry (medium sweet), Tawny Port, and Golden Muscatel.

Golden Bear and *Calgro Select* are the more important secondary brands used for *aperitif and dessert wines* as follows:
Pale Dry Sherry and Sherry, Port, Muscatel, Tokay, and White Port.

KERN COUNTY

Kern County deserves special mention. It is one of the largest dessert wine producers of California and with its vast vineyard acreage one of the most productive vineyard areas anywhere in the world. It so happens that the county's number of wineries is small and that none of these produces directly for the public under its own brands.

*Dutch Leonard was one of the pioneers in the modernization of the table-grape shipping industry and developed the "Ribier" grape, the principal black table-grape variety of California.

At the same time Kern County's wineries, few as they are, loom large in importance and size. In the Delano area in the northern part of the county there is the Delano Growers Cooperative Winery, founded in 1940, and A. Perelli-Minetti & Sons, established in 1934, both producing for the California Wine Association of San Francisco.

Southeast of Bakersfield, in the heart of Kern County, the Di Giorgio Wine Company is to be found near Arvin at Di Giorgio. The winery was founded in 1945 by the fabulous Joseph Di Giorgio, who rose from lemon packer on his father's little fruit farm at Cefalù in Sicily to be the boss of the multimillion-dollar Di Giorgio Fruit Corporation. This company has nationwide interests, ranging from Florida to California, including the vast vineyard and orchard acreage known as Di Giorgio Farms, with its ultra-modern winery having a capacity of nearly ten million gallons. Robert Di Giorgio, nephew of the founder, is now president of the concern.

Another large winery, the Giumarra Vineyards Corporation, is located in the area east of Bakersfield, at Edison. This family-owned enterprise was founded in 1946. Joe Giumarra is the president and George Giumarra the second-in-command. Like the Di Giorgio Wine Company, Giumarra Vineyards Corporation is a bulk wine producer.

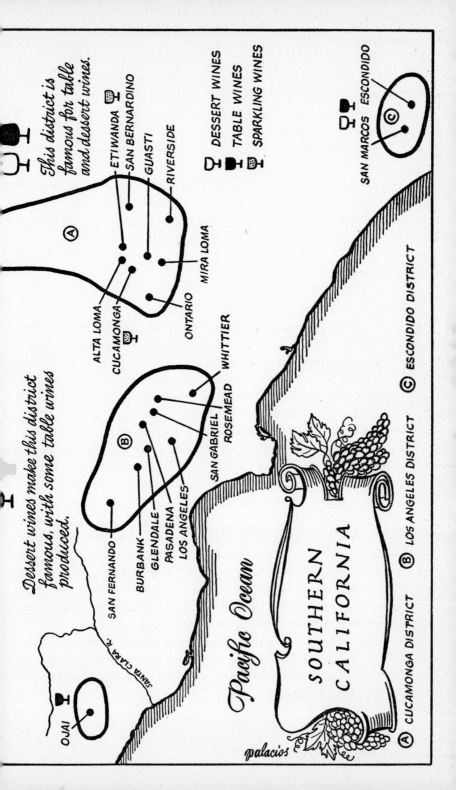

SOUTHERN CALIFORNIA

Pacific Ocean

Dessert wines make this district famous, with some table wines produced.

This district is famous for table and dessert wines.

OJAI

SANTA CLARA R.

SAN FERNANDO
BURBANK
GLENDALE
PASADENA
LOS ANGELES
SAN GABRIEL
ROSEMEAD
WHITTIER

ALTA LOMA
CUCAMONGA
ONTARIO
MIRA LOMA
ETIWANDA
SAN BERNARDINO
GUASTI
RIVERSIDE

Ⓐ

Ⓑ

SAN MARCOS   ESCONDIDO

Ⓒ

☐ DESSERT WINES
█ TABLE WINES
▦ SPARKLING WINES

Ⓐ CUCAMONGA DISTRICT   Ⓑ LOS ANGELES DISTRICT   Ⓒ ESCONDIDO DISTRICT

palacios

XI

SOUTHERN CALIFORNIA REGION

*T*HIS, THE THIRD of the great wine-producing regions of California, covers the southern part of the state, from Los Angeles and San Bernardino counties down south to the Mexican border. Its over-all climate is warm, though less hot than that of the San Joaquin Valley in the great inland valley region. It is especially noted for its dessert wines, while good table wines, notably of the red varieties, and champagnes of quality are also produced.

Southern California consists of a number of separate wine-producing districts of which the Cucamonga district in the southwestern tip of San Bernardino County is by far the best known. It is followed by the Los Angeles district in Los Angeles County with some well-known wineries. Ventura County has a single winery in the Ojai Valley.

There are two further districts in the region, the Riverside district in the northwest section of Riverside County adjoining Cucamonga and the Escondido district centering around the city of that name in San Diego County. No wineries of more than local importance are located in the last two districts, although some very good dessert wines are produced there, notably muscatels in the Escondido district, where the Muscat of Alexandria grape attains its highest quality. It was in San Diego County that the Franciscan missionary Padre Junipero Serra planted, according to tradition, the first Mission vines in 1769.

It may be noted here that one of the best-known Mexican wineries is located at Santo Tomás, south of Ensenada in the state of Baja California del Norte, Mexico.

A. *LOS ANGELES DISTRICT*

The Los Angeles wine-producing district spreads out from the city of Los Angeles northwards to San Fernando in the San Fernando Valley and takes in to the east of Los Angeles the section of the county covering San Gabriel and Rosemead on south to Whittier.

Los Angeles County and City

Santa Fe Vintage Company, Los Angeles

The largest and by far the most important winery in the Los Angeles district and located in downtown Los Angeles. It is owned and operated by the Guerrieri family, well-known winegrowers and wine makers for many years. Lewis Guerrieri is the general manager of the company as well as president of the Guerrieri-owned Santa Fe Winery at Kerman in Fresno County.

The Guerrieris were in the wine and grape business in Perugia, Italy, for generations before Giuseppe Guerrieri came to the United States in 1903. Giuseppe Guerrieri first worked for Italian Swiss Colony in San Francisco and in 1905 moved to Guasti in Southern California, where he became wine maker and superintendent for the Italian Vineyard Company. In 1915 he went into business for himself in Los Angeles, operating the Ramona Wine and Liquor Company. A few years later he purchased the Old Mission Winery located in Los Angeles right by the Los Angeles River and in 1919 he bought the old Santa Fe Winery at Santa Fe Springs, California.

In 1935 Giuseppe Guerrieri founded the Santa Fe Vintage Company in its present location. Late that same year his son, Lewis Guerrieri, who had already had personal winery experience and around 1927 had operated the California Mission Vintage Company, became associated with his father. Together they operated the Los Angeles winery and gradually developed the enterprise, acquiring vineyards in the Cucamonga district in San Bernardino County and in Riverside County. In June 1953 the family purchased the large Morello Winery at Kerman, west of Fresno, since renamed the Santa Fe Winery, to take care of the increasing demand for their wines.

Since Guiseppe Guerrieri passed away the entire family business, including the vineyards and wineries, has been owned and operated by Lewis Guerrieri, assisted by his two sisters. Henry Hutter is the wine maker at the Los Angeles winery and Ted Yamada resident manager and wine maker at the Kerman plant.

While the Santa Fe Vintage Company does some business outside of California, it is mainly interested in the Southern California market. *Dessert wines* of sound standard quality are the main products and these, as well as some table wines, are featured under the popularly priced *Santa Fe Three Crown* brand, enjoying a wide distribution in Southern California and adjoining districts. A few higher-priced dessert and table wines are marketed under the *Santa Fe "Supreme"* brand.

The following wines are produced under the *Santa Fe Three Crown* label:

Aperitif and Dessert wines: Pale Dry Sherry, Dry Sherry, Cocktail Sherry, Sherry, and Cream Sherry; Port, Ruby Port, and Tawny Port; Muscatel, Tokay, and White Port;

Table wines: Burgundy, Zinfandel, and Claret; Sauterne.

Wines available in limited quantity under the *Santa Fe "Supreme"* label include:

Aperitif and Dessert wines: Pale Dry Sherry and Sherry; Port and Tawny Port; Muscatel and Tokay.

Table wines: Burgundy and Sauterne.

A number of *Santa Fe Berry Wines* are available as follows: Blackberry, Boysenberry, Loganberry, Red Currant, and Raspberry. A Concord Grape wine is also marketed.

San Gabriel Vineyard Company, San Gabriel

This famous old winery is located near the historic San Gabriel Mission, some ten miles northeast of the heart of downtown Los Angeles.

Giovanni Demateis, the founder, was descended from a family long engaged in winegrowing in their native Asti in Piedmont, Italy. He chose Southern California as an ideal location to produce wines, comparable to those of his homeland. He planted his first vineyards in the Cucamonga area in 1888, founding thereby the family wine enterprise. He spared no trouble in obtaining the best, and oak casks for wine aging were purchased which had come around Cape Horn from the Black Forest in Germany. These casks are still in use and stand also as a tribute to the winery's founder.

After Giovanni Demateis passed on in 1929, the family concern was run for many years by his widow, Margherita, and their son Charles John Demateis. After Mrs. Demateis died in 1952, operation of the enterprise devolved on Charles John and his brother Robert A. Demateis, who continue the tradition of fine wine production set by their parents.

In following a change of policy it was decided to produce only aperitif and dessert wines, specializing, as before, in aged sherry and port wines, for which the winery had become especially well known.

Old San Gabriel is the featured brand, as of old, and under this label the following wines are available:

Aperitif and Dessert wines: Pale Dry Sherry and Sherry (medium); Port; Muscatel, Tokay, and White Port.

B. *CUCAMONGA DISTRICT*

Cucamonga, one of the few places in California to retain its old Indian name, is said to be derived from "Cucamongabit," meaning "Land of Many Springs." Cucamonga Indians were living in the district when the Spaniards came and built their El Camino Real. In 1839 Don Tiburcio Tapia, who became president of the Ayuntamiento, or City Council, of Los Angeles and the city's first *alcalde,* obtained the Cucamonga grant from the Mexican Government. It is known that Don Tapia also planted grape vines on the ranch.

Cucamonga was the scene of many turbulent events in its early days and its history makes fascinating reading. Gradually it passed from the violent and romantic Wild West stages to an equally romantic but more peaceful era of agriculture and industry. Magnificently situated in the San Bernardino Valley in the extreme southwestern corner of the county of that name, it lies at the foot of the grandiose range of the San Gabriel Mountains with Cucamonga Peak dominating the scene from an altitude of some 8000 feet.

The Cucamonga winegrowing district has become increasingly famous over the years. It centers around the town of Cucamonga, straddling Highways 66 and 99 and spreading north to Etiwanda and Alta Loma and south to Ontario, Guasti, and the Riverside County line. San Bernardino County, thanks to its Cucamonga district, with its thirty-nine active bonded wineries, rates second in that respect, exceeded only by Sonoma.

The Cucamonga district is noted for its red table wines, especially grignolino (often bottled as Grignolino Rosé, for the wine is naturally light in color), zinfandel, and chianti. These should be consumed young, as they mature early, owing to the warm climate in which the grapes are grown. Cucamonga is also well known for its quality champagnes and aperitif and dessert wines, including ports, sherries, and vermouths.

SAN BERNARDINO COUNTY

Cucamonga Winery, Cucamonga

This winery claims to be the original one of the district containing the Cucamonga name, and has contributed a great deal to making the Cucamonga name famous for its table wines, not only in California, but also in the Eastern part of the country. It is mainly owned and operated by the Accomazzo family.

Alfred (Fred) Accomazzo and his brother Eduardo, natives of San Desiderio in the Asti region of Piedmont, Italy, came to California as youngsters in 1902. They engaged in various trades in San Francisco and in the Los Angeles neighborhood, including running a winery in Glendale. During Prohibition they turned to the real estate business and with Repeal the Accomazzos became permanently identified with the wine industry.

The Cucamonga Winery was founded in 1933, when Alfred Accomazzo joined forces with several partners to operate a winery in the heart of Cucamonga. Vineyards were acquired and gradually extended. In 1935 Louis Gotto, one of the partners, sold out his interest to Joseph Ettor, the man who became mainly responsible for developing the winery's business in the East and who contributed greatly to making the Cucamonga name famous as synonymous with high-quality wines from that district.

The Accomazzo family owns half the Cucamonga Winery enterprise, the other being shared by the Joseph Ettor estate and by an Eastern interest. Fred Accomazzo is president and general manager of the company and Sam Kurland vice-president. Arthur Accomazzo, Fred's son, is secretary and sales manager, and his cousin Edmund E. (Ed), a son of Eduardo Accomazzo, who acquired an interest in the winery in 1948 but who died four years later, is vineyard superintendent and treasurer. Mauro Accomazzo, another son of Eduardo, has a retail outlet in Los Angeles and takes care of the winery's distribution in that city and surrounding area.

It is interesting to note that some of the Cucamonga Winery's vineyards are irrigated and some are not. While the north coast counties vineyards are non-irrigated and those in the great inland valley region mostly are, those in Southern California are often mixed. The *Guide* has refrained from indicating whether particular vineyards are irrigated or not in areas where either might be the case, because, as the Accomazzos also point out, the idea that non-irrigated vineyards produce better grapes in warm climates is not always correct. In extremely dry years or in a succession of dry years non-irrigated vineyards will produce crops with grapes lacking the necessary juices to make good wines. On the other hand irrigated vineyards should never be overirrigated. The answer is the _proper_ amount of water, whether vineyards are irrigated or not, and that is the responsibility of a good vineyardist or winegrower.

The Cucamonga Winery produces only _table wines,_ one of the few in the district to do so. All wines are of high quality, the reds being more typical of the district. They are mainly distributed in the East and Midwest. The regular brand is _Original Cucamonga Winery_ and under this label the following wines are available:

> RED: Zinfandel, Chianti, Burgundy, Claret, Barberone, and Vino Nativo (vino rosso type); WHITE: Sauterne, Chablis, and Rhine Wine; Dry Muscat; ROSÉ: Vin Rosé.

A few older table wines are marketed under the _Original Cucamonga Winery "Special Selection"_ label, first introduced in 1953. These include:

> RED: Zinfandel, Barbera, and Burgundy; WHITE: Dry Sauterne, Chablis, and Rhine Wine; ROSÉ: Grignolino Rosé.

Padre Vineyard Company, Cucamonga

The Padre Vineyard Company has contributed much to the general fame of Cucamonga for its wines. The owners of this celebrated winery have been prominently identified with the wine industry of Southern California since the turn of the century. James L. (Jimmy) Vai, president of the company, and his brother Giovanni Vai, the vice-president, own and operate the family enterprise, with its winery located on the outskirts of Cucamonga and with the company's main offices in Los Angeles. Louis Valperga is executive vice-president, R. Bruce Meeker the secretary-treasurer, and Frank Pilone the wine maker.

The winery is modern in every department, the buildings covering several acres, including a great fermenting room, storage cellars, laboratory, refrigeration system, distillery for brandy, bonded warehouse, fortifying rooms, champagne cellars, and machine shops. The cooperage is oak and redwood and in addition to the high tonnage yielded by their own vineyards a considerable supply is purchased from neighboring independent growers. Among the great specialties are the *champagnes,* the finest of which are produced by fermentation in the bottle, while the winery has, at the same time, pioneered in the Charmat process of bulk fermentation, importing much equipment for the purpose from France. Distribution is on a national basis.

The original winery at Cucamonga, founded in 1870, was rebuilt by the Vai family in 1909. Quality wines are produced, including table wines, the famed sparkling wines, and aperitif and dessert wines, of which the *vermouths* are especially popular.

The Padre Vineyard Company winery enjoys the distinction of being listed as California Bonded Winery No. 1. Table, sparkling, and aperitif and dessert wines are produced, with *Padre Reserve, Padre,* and *Vai Bros.* the featured brands. Under the *Padre Reserve* label the following wines are available:

Aperitif and Dessert wines: Sherry, Port, Muscatel, Tokay, White Port, and Angelica;

Table wines: Burgundy, Zinfandel, and Claret; Sauterne and Rhine Wine.

The *Padre* label is used for a special Pale Dry Sherry and for a Vino Rosso of the mellow Italian table wine type. A high-quality Cocktail Sherry is marketed under the *Padre Fine Reserve* brand, and Vermouth, Dry and Sweet, under the *Vai Bros.* label.

The great specialties of the house, the sparkling wines, are produced according to both bottle- and bulk-fermented processes and are marketed under the *Padre* and the *Vai Bros.* labelings.

Sparkling wines (bottle-fermented): Padre Brut Champagne, American, vintaged, and Padre Sec Champagne, American, vintaged;

Sparkling wines (bulk process): Padre Sec Champagne, Padre Crystal Sweet Champagne, Gran Spumante (Sparkling Muscat), and Padre Sparkling Burgundy, all vintaged.

Vai Bros. Sparkling Moselle, vintaged; Vai Bros. Extra Dry Champagne and Sparkling Burgundy, both non-vintaged.

Ellena Brothers, Etiwanda

It was soon after the turn of the century that Claudio Ellena came to the United States from Australia, seeking the right location and climate to establish his vineyards. He chose the Cucamonga district on the warm and sunny slopes of the foothills of the San Gabriel Mountains. Here he felt that wine could be produced comparable to the finer ones of Southern Europe, where the Ellenas originated and had been winegrowers for many generations. He founded his winery at Etiwanda, a few miles northeast of the town of Cucamonga, where his sons John B. and Frank Ellena carry on the family tradition, producing some of the finest wines of Southern California.

John B. Ellena, the president of the company, and Frank Ellena, the vice-president, own the family enterprise. Two other brothers are active in the winery, Arnold Ellena, the wine maker, chemist, and secretary of the concern, and Louis Ellena, the master distiller.

The featured brand is *Regina* Cucamonga Wine with *Ellena Brothers* a secondary label. Table wines, sparkling wines, and aperitif and dessert wines of fine quality are produced, available mainly in the Western states. They are marketed in distinctive and original squat or long-necked bottles, trade-marks of the house.

Wines available under the *Regina* brand include the following:

Table wines:
> RED: Chianti, Barbera, Grignolino, Zinfandel, Burgundy, Claret, and Vino Buon Gusto, a mellow wine of the vino rosso type; WHITE: Sauterne, Chablis, and Rhine Wine; ROSÉ: Vin Rosé (made 100 per cent from Grignolino grapes);

Light Sweet wines: Natural Muscat, Red Grape Wine, and White Grape Wine;

Aperitif and Dessert wines: Pale Dry Sherry and Sherry, Port, Muscatel, Tokay, White Port, and Angelica; Dry and Sweet Vermouth;

Sparkling wines (bulk process): Regina Champagne and Sparkling
  Burgundy and Wedding Party Pink Champagne.

Brookside Vineyard Company, Ontario

This family enterprise, established in its present location since
1952, has a history which goes back to the eighteen eighties in
Southern California and way back further in Northern California
and Europe. The owners are members of the Biane family, well-
known winegrowers and wine makers in the district for four generations. Marius Biane, Sr., the senior partner of the enterprise, has
made wine in the region continuously for the past fifty-two years
with the sole exception of the year 1917.

Philo Biane, the son of Marius, is the general manager. He
worked for the California Wine Association in various capacities,
including chemist, production manager, and sales manager, leaving
in 1951 to establish the revived Brookside Vineyard Company at
Ontario. His brother François (Frank) Biane is the wine maker and
was the manager of the Cucamonga Growers Cooperative Winery
of Ontario which has been incorporated as the Brookside Winery,
Inc., and is also affiliated with the California Wine Association of
San Francisco.

The Brookside enterprise was originally founded by the Vaché
family, who hailed from the island of Oléron off the Atlantic coast
of France at the mouth of the Charente River, where they were
engaged in the production of wines and brandy.

The first of the Vaché family to come to California was Théophile Vaché the elder (great-grand uncle of Philo Biane), who
landed in Monterey, then still under the Mexican flag, in 1830. This
Théophile Vaché must be considerd as one of the great pioneers
of the modern California wine industry. In 1849, or even earlier,
he planted the first vines south of Hollister in what was to become
known as the "Vineyard District" of San Benito County and grew
into the Valliant Vineyards enterprise (see there).

Three nephews of Théophile Vaché the elder came to California
to join their uncle. Emile came first, then Théophile the younger,

and finally Adolphe, in 1855. A fourth brother, Alfred, remained in France operating the winery and distillery there. Emile later returned to his native country to join Alfred, while Théophile the younger and Adolphe remained in California, eventually coming down south on account of the extensive vineyard plantings that were taking place around Los Angeles during the eighteen sixties. They first founded a wholesale importing business of fine wines and spirits in the heart of downtown Los Angeles and in 1882 established themselves as "Wholesale Dealers and Rectifiers and Manufacturers of Native Wines, Brandies, Wine Vinegar, Syrups Etc.," at Old San Bernardino, the winery being situated "on Dr. Barton's place." The brothers did business as "Vaché Frères" and in 1883 moved to Redlands Junction, hardly a town at that time, some ten miles southeast of San Bernardino, where they built and founded the Brookside Winery. Théophile Vaché the elder, incidentally, had returned to France and his family in 1865.

A Gascon youngster by the name of Marius Biane arrived in Redlands in 1892 from his native department of Gers in the ancient province of Gascony in Southern France, north of the Pyrenees. After attending school for a year he went to work for the Vaché brothers at Brookside. He fell in love with Marcelline, the daughter of Adolphe Vaché, and married her. In due course the Biane family carried on the Vaché tradition of wine making in Redlands, Marius also acquiring vineyards in the Cucamonga district. In 1916 the winery was sold and the Biane sons, Philo and François, went to work for Garrett & Company and later for Fruit Industries, as the California Wine Association was known at one time. It was not till 1952 that the Bianes revived their own enterprise by re-establishing the Brookside Vineyard Company at Ontario, some seven miles south of Cucamonga.

Fine table wines are the specialty of the enterprise, while finequality dessert wines, notably sherries and ports, are also produced, as is to be expected in the district. Angelica is the most popular of the altar wine group.

Brookside is the featured brand for quality wines and under this label the following are available:

Table wines:

RED: Burgundy, Zinfandel, Claret, and Vino Rosso; WHITE: Sauterne, Haut Sauterne, Chablis, and Rhine Wine;

Aperitif and Dessert wines: Sherry, Port, Muscatel, and Tokay.

A full line of standard wines is marketed under the *E. Vaché* and *Pico* brands, while under the *Pancho* label a Light Sweet Wine is merchandised, similar to the Vino Rosso.

Altar wines, available only to the clergy, are produced under the *Guasti* brand, under a special arrangement with the California Wine Association. These include:

Dry wines: Burgundy, Zinfandel, and Claret; Sauterne, Haut Sauterne, Chablis, and Rhine Wine;

Sweet wines: Angelica, Sherry, Port, Muscatel, Tokay, St. Benedict, and Guasti Special.

Garrett & Company, Inc., Guasti

Two great stories of American wine enterprise are merged here, the one of the Garrett family, famed in the wine industry for well over a century, and the other that of Secundo Guasti, who founded the Italian Vineyard Company including the town in the Cucamonga district to which he gave his name and the vineyards which were to become known as the largest in the world.

Garrett & Company had its beginning in 1835 in the heart of the vineyard country of the South. There, at Medoc, North Carolina, named after the Médoc district near Bordeaux in France, the Garrett brothers established their first vineyards and winery. It was there that they produced, from native Eastern grapes of the *Vitis rotundifolia* variety, the wine first called "Garrett's Scuppernong," which was later to become so popular under the name of Virginia Dare,* said to be the first child of English parentage born on the American shores.

As the nation expanded, so did Garrett's. The Southern vineyards

*Virginia Dare white wine has a basis of Scuppernong, the red Virginia Dare wine of Muscadine grapes, also of the *Vitis rotundifolia* species.

were enlarged and company branches were opened in the Midwest. In 1911 the growth of Garrett's reached the Pacific when they acquired vineyards and a winery at Cucamonga. Two years later another expansion took place when vineyards and wineries were purchased in the Finger Lake district in upper New York State. Two further expansions occurred in the nineteen forties when holdings were acquired in Ukiah, Mendocino County, for the production of dry table wines, in 1944, and a year later the entire property of the famed Italian Vineyard Company was purchased in Guasti, just south of Cucamonga. Today Garrett & Company owns and operates some 7000 acres of vineyards and three wineries in California besides further acreage and wineries in New York State and North Carolina. The main offices of the company are located in Brooklyn, New York.

Secundo Guasti was a native of Piedmont who came to California by way of Mexico. In or about 1883 he planted his first vineyards in the Cucamonga area, the foundation of an enterprise which he gradually built into the huge Italian Vineyard Company with its 5000 acres of vines. It took some ten years after its beginning for Guasti's company to gain impetus and size and he built his first winery just prior to the turn of the century. From then it grew and expanded rapidly. Secundo Guasti established a small town for his workers, including homes, a store, a firehouse, a school, a church, and an inn. The church is a well-known landmark and has been painted by many artists and amateurs because of its Italian style and atmosphere, with its bells and art objects imported from Italy.

The Italian Vineyard Company flourished until after the death of the founder's son, Secundo Guasti the second, in 1932. During Prohibition the company merged its resources with several other large wineries to form Fruit Industries, Ltd. (now California Wine Association), but withdrew from that organization with the advent of Repeal to operate independently under the management of Nicola Giulii, the first Secundo Guasti's son-in-law, until its acquisition in 1945 by Garrett & Company, Inc.

In spite of its size Garrett & Company has always been a family-owned and operated concern. The company was actually founded by Dr. Frank Garrett, but remained quite small during his lifetime. It was Paul Garrett, his nephew, who built the enterprise into prominence and was its president for many decades before his death in 1940. Affectionately known as Captain Garrett, he became a dominating figure in the whole of the American wine industry and was known as the dean of American wine growers.

The third generation of the Garrett family now runs the concern. H. C. Paulsen, chairman of the board, D. B. Weed, president of the company, and Llewellyn J. Barden, vice-president and Pacific-coast manager with headquarters at Guasti, all married daughters of Paul Garrett. C. B. Cole and J. Campbell Moore are vice-presidents with offices in Brooklyn, New York. Herbert Minor is the wine maker at the Guasti winery, Samuel Elder the wine maker and plant manager at the Cucamonga winery, and F. Bricarelli has the same positions at the Ukiah, Mendocino County, winery.

Garrett & Company produces and markets wines of sound standard and higher quality which enjoy a national distribution. The principal featured brand is *Garrett's* for the medium-priced wines, while *Paul Garrett* and *I.V.C.* (continued from the days of the Italian Vineyard Company) are the labels for wines in the higher-priced categories. The table wines and aperitif and dessert wines are produced in California; the Virginia Dare wines, sparkling wines (bottle-fermented), and berry wines are produced in the East and therefore not included in this text.

The following California wines are available under the various brands:

Table wines:
   Paul Garrett (Signature Label): Grignolino; Burgundy; Sauterne and Rhine Wine;
   Garrett's: Burgundy, Zinfandel, and Claret; Sauterne and Rhine Wine;
   I.V.C.: Grignolino (one of the best known of all Southern California wines and one for which the Italian Vineyard Company was famed), Grey Riesling, and Vin Rosé.

Aperitif and Dessert wines:

   Paul Garrett (Signature Label) : Pale Dry Sherry and Sherry, Port
   and Muscatel;

   Garrett's: Pale Dry Sherry and Sherry, Port, Muscatel, Tokay, and
   White Port; Dry and Sweet Vermouth.

XII

OTHER CALIFORNIA WINERIES

*T*HIS *Guide* has not aimed at being an encyclopedia or a directory of California wineries. Nor has it ambitioned to appraise every winery discussed and every wine produced. The latter would be a superhuman, endless, and intensely thankless task. The *Guide* does contain, however, many general indications of the quality of the wines available, from the least expensive to the very finest produced.

The *Guide* has limited itself to presenting and discussing what it considered to be the more notable wineries of the state, producers of wines under brands which are available to the public. There are many enterprises, however, large and small, which produce only, or mostly, for other wineries, selling their output in bulk. A number of such wineries, affiliated with large co-operative merchandising organizations, have been named individually in the text. There are others, both family-owned and co-operative wineries, which should be mentioned, even if their names cannot be as familiar to the public as those bottling under their own labels and brands.

Among these are the following (proceeding from north to south, conforming to the main text):

Seghesio Winery, with wineries at Cloverdale and Healdsburg, Sonoma County. A famous old family enterprise, founded in 1902 and owned and operated by Frank, Arthur, and Eugene Seghesio. Producers of table wines only (*Seghesio Winery* brand).

Larkmead Cooperative Winery of St. Helena, Napa County, founded in 1947. A well-known concern, producing Napa Valley table wines for Italian Swiss Colony. B. H. Skillings is the president of the co-operative and P. L. Halpern the general manager and wine maker of the winery.

Sanger Winery Association of Sanger, Fresno County. An independent co-operative winery with some ninety grower members, producers of dessert wines. Jake Rheingans is the co-operative president, Art Tempel the general manager, and Louis Szakal the wine maker and chemist. Founded in 1939.

Selma Winery, Inc., of Selma, Fresno County. Founded in 1947, producers of dessert wines and brandy. Kenneth Knapp is the president and general manager, J. L. Buchman the vice-president, and Henry A. Bishop the superintendent and wine maker (*Selma* and *Ark Royal* brands).

Muscat Cooperative Winery Association of Kingsburg, Fresno County. One of California's oldest co-operative wineries with some 125 grower members. Producers of table and dessert wines and brandy. Founded in 1935. E. L. Barr is the president, W. E. Staley the general manager, and W. J. Sorenson the wine maker (*San Ramon* brand).

Argun Wine Company of Tulare, Tulare County. Producers of table and dessert wines. The enterprise belongs to the estate of Eddie Arakelian and Vas Gunner, partners. Eddie Gunner is the plant manager.

California Grape Products Corporation in Tulare County, right across the Kern County line from Delano and with offices in San Francisco. Producers of table and dessert wines. Harry Baccigaluppi, a well-known figure in the California wine industry, is the president and general manager. Tony Marusick is the wine maker (*Calgrape, Caligrapo,* and other brands).

Lack of space is the reason why many of the smaller wineries have not been discussed in the text. The northern inland counties of Butte, Yolo, Placer, and Amador have one or more wineries, all devoted to the production of table wines. Yolo County, of course, is famous for the Viticultural Department of the University of California and its experimental station located at Davis.

Other counties only casually mentioned are San Mateo, with one winery producing both table and dessert wines very close to the San Francisco County line at Daly City; Kings County, with a single winery at Hanford; and Ventura County, with its table wine enterprise at Ojai. Monterey County has, besides F. W. Silvear's vineyards discussed under that area, an operating winery at Soledad.

The Riverside County winegrowing section, with a number of wineries producing both table and dessert types centering mostly around Mira Loma, is actually an extension of the Cucamonga district. If space permitted, more enterprises would have been discussed in San Bernardino County, so rich in its Cucamonga wineries. *Thomas Vineyards* at Cucamonga, with its retail outlet, is a popular place for tourists and others. It lays claim to being the oldest California winery and markets, besides the usual types of wines such specialties as Aleatico, Madeira, and Malvasia. The brand *Old Rancho* is named after the old Cucamonga Ranch, of which it forms a part.

San Diego County boasts some eight wineries, most of them in or near Escondido, famed for its muscatels of high quality. The most prominent wine enterprise in the district is the *Borra Winery* at Escondido. Founded in 1933, it produces both table and dessert wines, with *Escondido* the featured label. George Borra is the owner. The oldest winery in the area is the *Mighetto Winery,* also at Escondido, which traces its origin back to 1881. Joe B. Mighetto is the owner, who labels his table and dessert wines under the *Don Pio* and other brands.

This chapter, the final one dedicated to the presentation of California wineries, finds a fitting end with a salute to Baja California, south of the border. It was there that the California wine industry received its original impetus, thanks to the enterprise of the Franciscan Fathers. From there it moved north to Alta California and along El Camino Real.

In 1767 the Padres founded the Mission of Santo Tomás some thirty kilometers south of Ensenada in what is now the state of Baja California del Norte. The romantic winery called Bodegas de Santo Tomás produces well-known Mexican table and other wines from its three large vineyards in the Santo Tomás Valley, named so expressively Rancho de Cantarramas (Ranch of the Singing Frogs), site of the old mission, Rancho de los Dolores, and Rancho de la Cañada Verde (Ranch of the Green Valley). Owner is the well-known General Abelardo Rodriguez, former governor of the state of Sinaloa.

Part Three

XIII

CALIFORNIA BRANDY

THE SPIRIT called and labeled "California Brandy" is always pure grape brandy, distilled from wine. Brandies distilled from fruit other than grapes are required by law to be labeled with the designation of the particular fruit from which they are derived, such as "Apple Brandy." Federal regulations define brandy as a distillate obtained solely from the fermented juice or wine of the fruit, distilled at less than 190 proof and bottled at not less than 80 proof. Only beverage brandies are discussed here, those which are available to the public. Much high-proof brandy is also made, used in the production of aperitif and dessert wines.

Proof is an ancient term for the alcoholic strength of spirits or liquors. In the United States proof spirit or 100° proof spirit contains 50 per cent alcohol by volume, absolute alcohol being 200° proof spirit. Whereas wines are always labeled with the percentage of alcohol they contain by volume, brandies, like other spirits, indicate their proof. Most California brandies are about 84 proof (42 per cent alcohol by volume), the bottled-in-bond brandies being 100 proof (50 per cent alcohol by volume), like all bonded liquors.

Nearly all the (grape) brandies produced in the United States are distilled in California and derived from California wines, although some of them are blended or bottled elsewhere. The two most popular kinds of brandy produced in the United States are brandy (as grape brandy is always referred to) and apple brandy, distilled from the fermented juice of apples, and also known as apple jack. Apple brandy is made in various parts of the country, including California.

Experiments with other types of fruit brandy have, so far, not been generally successful in this country. Some California producers during and immediately after the Second World War made considerable quantities of fruit brandies, particularly plum and apricot. Difficulties were encountered, however, principally because of the fact that a high content of methyl alcohol resulted which brought on complications. The flavor was not very desirable, anyway, and the sugar content of stone fruit is so low compared to grapes and apples that the production of brandy from them proved commercially unprofitable. Further experiments are being made and it is entirely possible that eventually fruit brandies which find a ready acceptance in Europe, such as apricot brandy (barack palinka), blackberry brandy, cherry brandy (kirsch), plum brandy (slivovitz, mirabelle, and quetsch), raspberry brandy (eau-de-vie de framboises), and strawberry brandy (eau-de-vie de fraises) will also be produced in this country on a large scale. Some fine kirsch (cherry brandy) is produced in the West at Hood River, Oregon.

Such true fruit brandies must, of course, not be confused with the sweet liqueurs or cordials, such as apricot liqueur, which is called apricot brandy in Europe owing to differences in regulations. Nor must they be mistaken for what is known in the United States as "fruit-flavored brandies," which are also liqueurs or cordials, with a brandy base, and of a higher proof and usually less sweet than the regular liqueurs.

True brandies such as California brandy and apple brandy or apple jack in this country and foreign brandies like Cognac, Armagnac, Marc, Pisco, Calvados, Kirsch, Slivovitz, and many others are typically dry in character, although some may have a little sweetening added.

CALIFORNIA BRANDY OR GRAPE BRANDY

California brandies should be judged on their own merits and not be compared with cognac, the most famous brandy of all, produced in the Charente region of Southern France, of which the town of Cognac is the world-renowned center. A fine cognac, especially when produced from either of the two Champagne districts of the Charente region, is probably the noblest beverage produced anywhere under the sun. California brandy, a totally different product, can be very good indeed, and some have achieved a very high standard.

California brandy and cognac are produced from different kinds of grapes, grown on different types of soil and in varying climates. They are produced and aged differently.

Brandy in California is derived from a variety of grapes, depending on the location of the distillery and the producer. In the Lodi area the Flame Tokay is important and in the Fresno area Thompson Seedless. Others include Burger, Green Hungarian, French Colombard, Malaga, Muscat of Alexandria (for muscat brandy). Even red grapes are used for California brandy, such as the historic Mission, from which the first brandy in the state was made, and the popular Grenache, considered by some producers to yield a fine wine for brandy distillation. Cognac is distilled from wine made from the Saint Emilion (also known as Trebbiano, Cadillac, and Ugni blanc), which is gradually ousting in favor the traditional Folle blanche. In California there is, as yet, no defined brandy district as in the Charente region. The soil in Cognac is chalky and calcareous; that in California varies according to the place where the grapes for brandy production are grown. Practically all California brandy is distilled in continuous column stills, while for cognac pot stills are used.

On the other hand the laws in the United States for brandy production and marketing are stricter. California brandy is a sound product, with its own characteristics and flavor, and has its own place in the sun. Its history is as old as that of the California wine industry. The Padres made brandy as well as wine and some of their *aguardiente* achieved a certain renown.

Most California brandies are distilled from white wines, like other grape brandies. They are usually distilled right after fermentation, allowing the lees or wine sediment to impart its flavoring to the final product. Brandy must be aged for a number of years in oak to become smooth and mellow and to acquire the typical amber color. Once bottled, brandy, like any other spirit, and unlike some good wines, does not improve with age. A brandy bottled twenty years ago will be no better than the same kind of brandy, bottled yesterday. It may, however, have lost some of its contents through evaporation. At the same time it will never spoil, retaining its character unchanged in the bottle.

The best-known and most popular type of California brandy is that which is simply called Brandy or Grape Brandy. It can either be straight or blended (rectified). Muscat brandy, distilled from wine made from muscat grapes, had a certain vogue at one time, but its production now is very limited. Grappa Brandy, distilled from the grape pomace and white in color, is produced in small quantities. Lees brandy, distilled from the lees of wine, and which also was quite popular at one time, is only very rarely seen today.

Nearly all the California brandies available on the market are of the first type, either straight or blended. They should be light to medium amber in color, are from 80 to 100 proof (40 to 50 per cent alcohol by volume) and should possess the typical aroma, flavor, and character associated with fine brandy, owing to proper distillation from clean, sound wines and to sufficient aging in oak. They should be mellow and smooth, clean and satisfying to the palate and taste.

If the brandy is straight, it is dry, no sweetening, smoothing, or flavoring substances having been added. If bottled in bond, it must be 100 proof and at least four years old. Many California brandies are a great deal older.

Numerous California brandies are of the blended type, to which it is permissible, by law, to add sweetening, coloring, and flavoring substances. These should, however, never mask the typical character of the brandy, nor should they exceed 2½ per cent alcohol by volume. Experience has indicated that such agents should usually constitute less than 1 per cent.

There is no general preference between straight and blended California brandies. Some prefer the drier straight varieties and others the blends.

Muscat brandy is a grape brandy derived from muscat wine, for which the Muscat of Alexandria has usually been used. This kind of California brandy has been replaced in popular favor by the regular brandies distilled from wines made from other grapes. Muscat brandy should have the typical muscat aroma and flavor, while sweetening is not required, as the muscat character itself is already quite sweet.

Grappa, produced from the pomace or pulp of the grapes after crushing, is called after the Italian brandy of that name. The reason, presumably, is that the winegrowers and distillers who have produced that type of brandy in California have been of Italian descent. It could equally well have been called Marc (Mar) as that is what it is called in France, where it is quite popular, some of the best being produced in Burgundy (Marc de Bourgogne) and in Champagne (Marc de Champagne). Marc and Grappa are not to everyone's liking, as they all have a rather sharp, distinctive character and woody flavor, owing to the fact that the pips, skins, and stems contained in the grape pomace impart to the product its typical taste. There are *aficionados* who prefer this type of brandy to any other.

Lees brandy, distilled from the sediment or lees of the wine in the casks, has its own characteristic aroma and flavor. It is much milder to the taste than grappa and, unlike the latter, amber in color.

A List of the Better-known California (Grape) Brandies

Almadén Vineyards, Los Gatos, Santa Clara County.
This winery introduced a few years ago its *Almadén Centennial* brandy, so named in commemoration of the fact that the winery was founded in 1852. It is a straight, 84 proof brandy of high quality, four years old.

Beringer Bros., Inc., St. Helena, Napa County.

The featured brandy and a very popular one is the straight *Beringer Brandy,* 84 proof, varying in age from 11 to 14 years old. All brandies marketed are produced at the Beringer wineries, including a straight, 84 proof, 7 years old, and a bottled-in-bond, 100 proof, 7-year and older brandy. The last two products are not always available.

California Growers Wineries, Cutler, Tulare County.

Two fine brandies are produced by this concern, a straight, 5- to 6-year-old brandy and a blended type, both 84 proof and marketed under the *California Growers* brand.

California Wine Association, San Francisco.

This famous company produces its well-known brandies at Lodi, San Joaquin County. Under the *A. R. Morrow* brand, named in honor of the man who was the guiding spirit of the concern for many years and a dominating figure in the California wine industry, a bonded, 100 proof brandy is marketed, 6 to 7 years old, an outstanding product, and one of the finest straight brandies produced in the state.

Equally fine in the blended class is the company's 84 proof brandy, marketed under both the *A. R. Morrow* and *Aristocrat* brands.

The Christian Brothers (Mont La Salle Vineyards), Napa, Napa County.

Headquarters for the production of the Mont La Salle Vineyards brandy production by The Christian Brothers is conducted at Reedley, Fresno County. The *Christian Brothers* brandy, probably the most familiar one in the country, is of the blended type, 84 proof, and very fine indeed at its best.

Cucamonga Valley Wine Company, Ontario, San Bernardino County.

Giovanni Vai, who founded this enterprise with the advent of Repeal in 1933, produces a straight 6-year-old brandy, 84 proof, under the *G. V. Grape Brandy* label.

East-Side Winery, Lodi, San Joaquin County.

Two outstanding brandies are produced by this well-known concern and are marketed under the *Royal Host* brand. The one is a 6-year-old straight brandy and the other a blend, both 84 proof. They rate among the very finest in their respective classes.

Ellena Brothers, Etiwanda, San Bernardino County.

A fine Cucamonga brandy is featured at this winery. It is a straight brandy, 5 to 6 years old, 84 proof, marketed under the *Regina Pure Cucamonga Grape Brandy* label.

An 8-year-old straight, 84 proof Cucamonga brandy has also been produced under the *Ellena* brand.

Glen Ellen Winery and Distillery, Inc., Glen Ellen, Sonoma County.

This winery produces Sonoma County brandies which are well worthy of mention. They are straight brandies, 84 and 90 proof, marketed under the *Glen Hills* brand.

Italian Swiss Colony, Asti, Sonoma County.

This famous old company, now owned by the Petri interests, purchased the Hartley and Lejon brands from National Distillers in 1954. The brandies marketed under those labels are produced for the greater part at the Shewan-Jones plant at Clovis, Fresno County.

The *Hartley* brand is used for the straight brandy, which is a very fine quality. It is 84 proof and from 5 to 6 years old. A bonded, 100 proof brandy has also been produced under that label.

Lejon brandy is a blended type, 84 proof, and also rates high. It is called after that famous figure in the wine industry, Lee Jones, who founded the Shewan-Jones enterprise shortly after Repeal.

Paul Masson Vineyards, Saratoga, Santa Clara County.

This winery markets a brandy of high quality under the *Masson* brand. It is a light-bodied blend of straight brandies, 84 proof.

Napa and Sonoma Wine Company (Castler Cellars), Sonoma, Sonoma County.

Paul Rossigneux markets a delicate brandy of great distinction under his *Oro Fino* (Fine Gold) brand. It is a blended type, 84 proof.

Padre Vineyards Company, Cucamonga, San Bernardino County.

Two well-known Cucamonga brandies are produced and marketed by this winery. A straight brandy, 4 and 5 years old, carries the *Vai Bros. Old Reserve* label and a blended type is available under the *Padre 3 Star* brand. Both are 84 proof.

Petri Wineries, Escalon, San Joaquin County.

Two brandies are produced by Petri Wineries, operating name of the Allied Grape Growers co-operative. They are marketed by the Petri Wine Company of San Francisco.

The *Petri Brandy* is a blended type of fine quality, 84 proof. A grape pomace brandy is also produced, the only one of its type made commercially in California as far as the *Guide* is aware. *Petri Grappa Brandy* is white in color, 4 years old, and 100 proof.

Schenley Industries, Inc. (Roma Wine Company), Fresno, Fresno County.

A number of California brandies are produced by this large concern, all distilled at the Roma Wine Company plant in Fresno, although some of them are bottled in other states. They are merchandised by Brandy Distillers, a division of Associated Brands, a Schenley subsidiary.

The best known of the Schenley brandies is *Coronet V.S.Q.* (Very Special Quality), a blended brandy of high quality, 84 proof. Other brands marketed, similar or identical to Coronet, are *J. Bavet, Old Monastery Brand,* and *Louis* brandies, all blended types and 84 proof.

A bottled in bond brandy, 100 proof, is produced and marketed under the *Jean Robert* label, while a low-proof blended type, called *Director's Choice* (Roma Wine Company), has been merchandised at 80.6 proof.

L'Chayim Kosher California Grape Brandy, suitable also for sacramental purposes of the Hebrew faith, is a blended brandy, 84 proof. The word "L'Chayim" has a profound meaning, being the traditional toast to life by which friends wish one another well.

Wine Growers Guild, Lodi, San Joaquin County.

This great co-operative produces two well-known straight brandies, 84 proof, under the *Ceremony* brand, the 5-year-old "White Label" and the 8-year-old "Black Label." They are both delicate and dry in character and the 8-year-old is considered by many to be the finest brandy produced in California.

A fine blended brandy, 84 proof, is also produced and merchandised under the *Guild* label. The *Guild Special Export* brandy, also a blend and 84 proof, is no longer produced.

George Zaninovich, Inc., Orange Cove, Fresno County.

Some thirty miles southeast of Fresno at Orange Cove on the Tulare County line is to be found the distillery of George Zaninovich, who produces only brandy. He is the owner, president, and general manager of the enterprise, which he founded in 1937, setting up his distillery in that year in the district where he had been growing grapes since 1915.

Most of the distillery's business is in bulk sales, but some bottling is done under the *Zanbro* brand, the name being a contraction of Zaninovich Bros., the firm through which the company markets fresh grapes and citrus fruits.

Zanbro brandy is of the straight type, light and delicate, and is bottled at 84 or 86 proof. Best known in the Midwest under that label, this brandy deserves wider recognition.

Note: The famous Korbel & Bros. concern of Guerneville, Sonoma County, used to market a fine 8-year-old, 84 proof, straight brandy under the *Korbel* brand. It may still be found occasionally, but has not been produced for some years.

It will be seen that most of the better-known California brandies are distilled in the great inland valley region, notably in the Lodi and Fresno districts. Others are produced in Sonoma and Napa counties in the northern coastal region and in the Cucamonga district of San Bernardino County.

While most of the brandies listed above have won enviable awards at the California State and Los Angeles County Fairs in recent years, not all distillers send their brandies to the Fairs for competitive judgment, nor do those who send them necessarily do so every year. Awards given to California brandies are listed together with the wine awards and those who are further interested can apply for copies of the yearly awards to any office of the Wine Institute or to the Fairs themselves.

For the convenience of the readers the better-known California brandies having a national or near national distribution are listed here alphabetically, grouped according to whether they are straight or of the blended type. These then are the great names in the California brandy picture:

California straight brandies (ages will vary according to current production and are not always indicated on the labeling; nor does older age necessarily mean superior quality, as between the various straight brandies or between the straights and those of the blended type):

Almadén (4 years), *Beringer* (12 years), *Ceremony* (5 and 8 years), *Hartley* (5 to 6 years), *A. R. Morrow* (bonded), *Regina* (5 to 6 years), *Royal Host* (6 years), *Vai Bros. Old Reserve* (4 and 5 years);

California blended brandies:

Aristocrat or *A. R. Morrow, Christian Brothers, Coronet V.S.Q., Guild, Lejon, Masson, Oro Fino, Padre 3 Star, Petri, Royal Host.*

There are numerous other brands of California brandy, many of them merchandised by bottling concerns or sold by firms throughout the country under their own labels.

Use and Service of California Brandy—As a straight brandy after dinner; in brandy old-fashioneds or in brandy on the rocks; in cocktails such as the popular sidecar, and many others; in brandy bucks, cobblers, collinses, coolers, crustas, daisies, eggnogs, fixes, fizzes, flips, highballs, hots, juleps, punches, rickeys, sangarees, scaffas, shrubs, slings, smashes, and sours; as a base for wine punches, in Tom and Jerries and in hot toddies for getting warm or to help lick a cold; in cooking and flavoring fruit salads, plum puddings, and other desserts; in Café Brulot, Café Diablo, and in hot black coffee or hot tea. Brandy is also helpful when feeling faint or suffering from shock. No household should be without a flask or bottle of good brandy.

When served after dinner any brandy worthy of the name calls for a balloon-shaped glass of the snifter type, the larger the bowl the better, in order to release the full aroma and bouquet of the brandy and to increase enjoyment of its rich and warming flavor, aptly described as the essence of wine.

CALIFORNIA APPLE BRANDY (APPLE JACK)

Considering that fruit wines and (grape) brandy have been discussed in the *Guide,* it is only logical to include a short notice on the production of California fruit brandy.

The only fruit brandy currently produced in the state for the public is, to the *Guide's* best knowledge, the apple brandy distilled and marketed by the *Speas Company.* This well-known concern, founded in 1888, maintains its head office in Kansas City, Missouri, with its winery and distillery located at Sebastopol, Sonoma County. V. E. Speas is chairman of the board, C. N. Kemper is president, and F. M. Butler is vice-president and manager of the company.

Its popular and high-quality apple brandy is marketed under the *Speas Apple Brandy* apple jack label. The brandy, distilled from late varieties of apples in the Sebastopol area, including Red Delicious, Rome Beauties, Jonathans, and sometimes Newton Pippins, is 4 years old and 86.5 proof.

Use and Service of Apple Brandy—Apple brandy or apple jack is used in many cocktails, notably the Jack Rose and Pink Lady and in short and long drinks instead of whiskey. It makes an excellent old-fashioned and is also served on the rocks. It can be served straight or with ice mixed with one of the soft-drink sparkling beverages. Apple brandy is also popular in collinses, coolers, flips, freezes, highballs, rickeys, slings, sours, and toddies.

*A*ppendix

A LIST OF OUTSTANDING
CALIFORNIA WINES

THE LIST is arranged according to wine type and alphabetically within the district where the wine is produced. Preference has been given to the varietal wines as being more typically Californian both in character and in name. An asterisk (*) denotes especial excellence. Vintage wines are indicated with (V).

A. RED TABLE WINES

California Clarets

Cabernet Sauvignon (the premier claret of California)
NAPA VALLEY
    Beaulieu Georges de Latour Special Reserve (V)*
    Beaulieu Cabernet Sauvignon (V)
    Inglenook Cabernet Sauvignon (V)*
    Louis Martini Cabernet Sauvignon (V)*
      (available in special years as Special Reserve)
    Signature Tasters' Selection Cabernet Sauvignon
SANTA CLARA VALLEY
    Almadén Cabernet Sauvignon
    Paul Masson Cabernet Sauvignon
    Martin Ray Cabernet Sauvignon (V)*
    Martin Ray La Montana Woodside Cabernet

SANTA CRUZ COUNTY
    Hallcrest Cabernet Sauvignon (V)

Zinfandel (characteristic California red table wine of better-than-average
  quality, fruity and zestful)
SONOMA COUNTY, Sonoma Valley
    Buena Vista Zinfandel
    Italian Swiss Colony Zinfandel
NAPA VALLEY
    Louis Martini Mountain Zinfandel (V)
    Souverain Mountain Zinfandel
SOLANO COUNTY
    Cadenasso Zinfandel
CONTRA COSTA COUNTY
    Digardi Zinfandel
LIVERMORE VALLEY
    Concannon Zinfandel
SAN LUIS OBISPO COUNTY
    York Mountain Zinfandel
CUCAMONGA DISTRICT
    Cucamonga Winery Zinfandel

California Red Burgundies

Pinot Noir (the great red burgundy of California; limited production)
NAPA VALLEY
    Beaulieu's Beaumont Pinot Noir (V)*
    Inglenook Pinot Noir (V)*
    Louis Martini Mountain Pinot Noir (V)*
      (also available in magnums)
SANTA CLARA VALLEY
    Almadén Pinot Noir
    Paul Masson Pinot Noir
    Martin Ray Pinot Noir (V)*

Gamay and *Gamay Beaujolais* (light-bodied red burgundy wines from
  Napa Valley Gamay or from Gamay Beaujolais grapes)
NAPA VALLEY
    Inglenook Gamay (V)

Charles Krug Gamay (V)
Signature Tasters' Selection Gamay
CONTRA COSTA COUNTY
Digardi Mountain Gamay
SANTA CLARA VALLEY
Paul Masson Gamay Beaujolais

California Red Wines of Italian Type

Barbera (robust and full-flavored)
NAPA VALLEY
Louis Martini Mountain Barbera (V)
LIVERMORE VALLEY
Ruby Hill Barbera

Grignolino, sometimes bottled as *Grignolino Rosé* on account of its light red color
NAPA VALLEY
Brendel's "Only One" Grignolino
SOLANO COUNTY
Cadenasso Grignolino
CUCAMONGA DISTRICT
Cucamonga Winery Grignolino Rosé
Ellena's Regina Grignolino and Rosé
I.V.C. Grignolino

B. WHITE TABLE WINES

California Sauternes

Semillon (the finest of the California sauternes)
LIVERMORE VALLEY
Concannon Dry Semillon (V)
Ruby Hill Semillon
Wente Dry Semillon (V)*
Wente Sweet Semillon*
NAPA VALLEY
Charles Krug Semillon
Louis Martini Mountain Dry Semillon (V)

SANTA CLARA VALLEY
  Almadén Dry Semillon
  Paul Masson Dry Semillon
  Chateau Masson (Sweet Semillon)
  Mirassou Semillon
  Novitiate of Los Gatos Dry Semillon

Sauvignon Blanc (a great white table wine on its own account)
LIVERMORE VALLEY
  Concannon Sauvignon Blanc (V)*
  Wente Sauvignon Blanc (V)*
SANTA CLARA VALLEY
  Novitiate of Los Gatos Sauvignon Blanc

Chateau Sauternes (from Semillon and Sauvignon blanc grapes)
LIVERMORE VALLEY
  Chateau Concannon
  Chateau Wente*
NAPA VALLEY
  Chateau Beaulieu*
SANTA CLARA VALLEY
  Chateau Novitiate

California White Burgundies

Chardonnay, also known as *Pinot Chardonnay* (the great white burgundy of California; very limited production)
LIVERMORE VALLEY
  Wente Pinot Chardonnay (V)*
SOUTHERN ALAMEDA COUNTY
  Weibel Pinot Chardonnay (V)
NAPA VALLEY
  Beaulieu Pinot Chardonnay (V)*
  Inglenook Pinot Chardonnay (V)*
  Mayacamas Chardonnay (V)
SANTA CLARA VALLEY
  Almadén Pinot Chardonnay
  Paul Masson Pinot Chardonnay
  Martin Ray Chardonnay (V)*

Pinot Blanc, also known as *Pinot Blanc Vrai* (from Pinot blanc grapes)
    LIVERMORE VALLEY
        Wente Pinot Blanc (V)*
    SANTA CLARA VALLEY
        Almadén Pinot Blanc
        Paul Masson Pinot Blanc Vrai*
        Mirassou Pinot Blanc
        Novitiate of Los Gatos Pinot Blanc*

White Pinot (from Chenin blanc or Pineau de la Loire grapes)
    NAPA VALLEY
        Inglenook White Pinot (V)
        Charles Krug White Pinot (V)
        Louis Martini White Pinot (V)
        Signature Tasters' Selection White Pinot
        Mayacamas White Pinot (V)

Folle Blanche (a fresh and light luncheon wine)
    NAPA VALLEY
        Louis Martini Mountain Folle Blanche (V)

California Rhine Wines*

White Riesling, also known as *Johannisberg* or *Johannisberger Riesling*
    (the premier California rhine wine)
    SONOMA COUNTY, Sonoma Valley
        Buena Vista Johannisberger Riesling
    NAPA VALLEY
        Beaulieu's Beauclair Johannisberger Riesling (V)*
        Louis Martini Mountain Johannisberg Riesling (V)*
        Souverain Johannisberger Riesling
    SANTA CLARA VALLEY
        Almadén Johannisberg Riesling
        Mirassou White Riesling
    SANTA CRUZ COUNTY
        Hallcrest White Riesling

*California Rieslings are not included in this listing as they are produced from various Riesling grapes and are not true varietal wines.

Traminer and *Gewurztraminer* (spicy California white wines of the
  Alsatian type from Traminer grapes)
  SONOMA COUNTY, Sonoma Valley
    Buena Vista Traminer*
  NAPA VALLEY
    Inglenook Traminer (V)
    Charles Krug Traminer*
    Louis Martini Mountain Gewurztraminer (V)*
  SANTA CLARA VALLEY
    Almadén Traminer

Sylvaner (California white wine of the Alsatian type from Franken
  Riesling grapes)
  SONOMA COUNTY, Sonoma Valley
    Buena Vista Sylvaner*
  NAPA VALLEY
    Louis Martini Mountain Sylvaner (V)
    Souverain Sylvaner
  SANTA CLARA VALLEY
    Almadén Sylvaner
    Mirassou Sylvaner

Grey Riesling (from Chauché gris or grey Riesling grapes)
  LIVERMORE VALLEY
    Wente Grey Riesling (V)*
  NAPA VALLEY
    Charles Krug Grey Riesling
    Signature Tasters' Selection Grey Riesling

C. ROSÉ TABLE WINES

Grenache Rosé
  SANTA CLARA VALLEY
    Almadén Grenache Rosé*
    Bertero Grenache Rosé
  NAPA VALLEY
    Souverain Grenache Rosé
  STANISLAUS COUNTY
    Gallo Grenache Rosé

Gamay Rosé (from Napa Valley Gamay grapes)
    NAPA VALLEY
        Inglenook Navalle Rosé (V)
        Charles Krug Vin Rosé
        Louis Martini Napa Gamay Rosé

Pinot Noir Rosé
    SANTA CLARA VALLEY
        Martin Ray Pinot Noir Rosé (V)*

Grignolino Rosé, see Grignolino red table wine

Other Rosés
    SONOMA COUNTY, Sonoma Valley
        Buena Vista Rosebrook
    LIVERMORE VALLEY
        Concannon Cardinal Rosé
        Wente Valle de Oro Rosé
    NAPA VALLEY
        Beaulieu's Beaurosé* (from Cabernet Sauvignon grapes mainly)

D. SPARKLING WINES†

California Champagnes

SONOMA COUNTY, Russian River Valley
        Korbel Brut Champagne*
        Korbel Sec Champagne
SANTA CLARA VALLEY
        Almadén Brut Champagne* (available also in magnums)
        Almadén Extra Dry Champagne
        Paul Masson Brut Champagne*
        Paul Masson Extra Dry Champagne
        Martin Ray Madame Pinot Champagne (V)* (Blanc de noir,
    from Pinot noir grapes only)
LIVERMORE VALLEY
        Cresta Blanca Brut Champagne
        Cresta Blanca Champagne (available also in magnums)

†Bottle-fermented according to the champagne process.

Southern Alameda County
Weibel Grand Cru Champagne Brut (from Pinot Chardonnay grapes)

California Pink (Rosé) Champagnes

Sonoma County, Russian River Valley
Korbel Sparkling Rosé Champagne
Santa Clara Valley
Almadén Pink Champagne
Paul Masson Pink Champagne (Oeil de Perdrix)
Martin Ray Sang de Pinot Champagne (V)* (Rosé de noir, from first light pressing of Pinot noir grapes)
Southern Alameda County
Weibel Grand Cru Pink Champagne

California Red Champagnes and Sparkling Burgundies

Sonoma County, Russian River Valley
Korbel Rouge
Santa Clara Valley
Almadén Sparkling Burgundy
Paul Masson Red Champagne (Triple Red)
Paul Masson Sparkling Burgundy (Cuvée Rouge)
Southern Alameda County
Weibel Grand Cru Champagne Rouge

E. APERITIF AND DESSERT WINES

California Sherries, Dry

Santa Clara Valley
Almadén Solera Cocktail Sherry*
Napa Valley
Louis Martini Pale Dry Sherry*
Livermore Valley
Cresta Blanca Dry Watch Sherry
Southern Alameda County
Los Amigos Sherry Sack*
Weibel Solera Cocktail *flor* Sherry

San Joaquin County
    Guild's Ceremony Palomino Pale Dry Sherry

California Sherries, Sweet

Santa Clara Valley
    Almadén Solera Cream Sherry*
    Masson Rare Cream Sherry
Napa Valley
    Beaulieu Cream Sherry
Livermore Valley
    Cresta Blanca Triple Cream Sherry*
San Joaquin County
    Guild's Ceremony Palomino Cream Sherry

Note: In the selection of California sherries for this list preference has
generally been given to those made from Palomino grapes and produced
by the *flor* and Solera methods, as these yield the finest of the California
sherry wines.

California Ports

Madera County
    Ficklin Tinta Port*
    Ficklin Tinta Madeira Port*
San Joaquin County
    Signature Tasters' Selection Royal Velvet Port
    Guild's Ceremony Tawny Port
Santa Clara Valley
    Almadén Solera Tawny Port
    Almadén Solera Ruby Port
    Masson Rare Tawny Port
Napa Valley
    Louis Martini Tawny Port
Sonoma County, Sonoma Valley
    Buena Vista Vintage Port

California Muscat Wines

Muscat de Frontignan
Napa Valley
    Beaulieu Muscat de Frontignan

LIVERMORE VALLEY
    Concannon Muscat de Frontignan
SANTA CLARA VALLEY
    Novitiate of Los Gatos Muscat Frontignan

Black Muscat
SANTA CLARA VALLEY
    Novitiate of Los Gatos Black Muscat
SOUTHERN ALAMEDA COUNTY
    Weibel Black Muscatel or Cream of Black Muscat

BIBLIOGRAPHY

AMERINE, M. A., AND JOSLYN, M. A., "Commercial Production of Dessert Wines," Bulletin 651, University of California, Sept. 1941.

———., "Commercial Production of Brandies," Bulletin 652, University of California, September 1941.

———., *Table Wines, The Technology of Their Production in California.* University of California Press. 1951.

AMERINE, M. A., AND WINKLER, A. J., "Grape Varieties for Wine Production," Circular 356, University of California. 1943.

———., *Hilgardia, A Journal of Agricultural Science,* Vol. 15, No. 6. University of California, February 1944.

BALZER, ROBERT LAWRENCE, *California's Best Wines,* Ward Ritchie Press. 1948.

CAROSSO, VINCENT P., *The California Wine Industry, a Study of the Formative Years* (1830–1895). University of California Press. 1951.

HEDRICK, U. P., *Grapes and Wines from Home Vineyards.* Oxford University Press. 1945.

JACOB, H. E. (revised by Winkler, A. J.), Grape Growing in California, Circular 116, revised edition, University of California, November 1950.

JONES, IDWAL, *Vines in the Sun, a Journey through the California Vineyards.* Morrow. 1949.

LUCIA, SALVATORE P., *Wine as Food and Medicine.* Blakiston. 1954.

MABON, MARY FROST, *ABC of America's Wines.* Knopf. 1942.

McKee, Irving, Various historical articles appearing in *California Magazine of the Pacific* and *Wine Review*.

Olmo, H. P., "Ruby Cabernet and Emerald Riesling," Bulletin 704, University of California, May 1948.

Schoonmaker, Frank, *Dictionary of Wines*. Edited by Tom Marvel. Hastings House. 1951.

Schoonmaker, Frank, and Marvel, Tom, *American Wines*. Duell, Sloan & Pearce. 1941.

Street, Julian, *Wines, Their Selection, Care, and Service*. Revised and edited by A.I.M.S. Street. Knopf. 1948.

Wagner, Philip M., *A Wine-Grower's Guide*. Knopf. 1945.

Wine Awards, California State Fairs 1949–54, incl.

Wine Awards, Los Angeles County Fairs 1949–54, incl.

Wine Institute, "California Wine Type Specifications." Revised December 1953.

Wine Institute, Wine Handbook Series No. 1. "The Wine Industry."

Wine Institute, Wine Handbook Series No. 2. "Wine Growing and Wine Types."

Miscellaneous articles and information published in "Wines and Vines," San Francisco.

INDEX

Index entries in italics represent brand names. Numbers in italics designate pages on which companies producing the listed wines are given.